# An Eye for an Eye:

## In Defense of the Death Penalty

By

# William T. Harper

Published by: CreateSpace, an Amazon.com subsidiary

Copyright © by the Author, 2012

All rights reserved. No part of this book may be reproduced, stored in a retrieval system, or transmitted in any form or by any means – electronic, mechanical, recording or otherwise – without prior written consent of the Author, except that brief passages may be quoted for reviews.

ISBN-13: 978-1479264988
ISBN-10: 1479264989

Harper, William T.,
    *Eleven Days in Hell: The 1974 Carrasco Prison Siege at Huntsville, Texas*, University of North Texas Press, 2004
    *We Three: Fred, the Ferry Boat, and Me*, Amazon Kindle, 2009; CreateSpace-a subsidiary of Amazon.com, 2012
    *The Rivers of Life – and Death*, M.E.T. Publishing, 2010
    *Second Thoughts: Presidential Regrets with their Supreme Court Nominations*, CreateSpace-a subsidiary of Amazon.com, 2011
    *An Eye for An Eye: In Defense of the Death Penalty*, Kindle, Amazon, 2007; CreateSpace-a subsidiary of Amazon.com, 2012

Keywords:
1. Prejean, Sister Helen
2. Life Without Parole
3. Deterrence
4. Damned Lies
5. Legal Mischief

# An Eye for an Eye
*William T. Harper*

## Dedication

*This book is dedicated to Bill, Bob, Barb, Beverley, Beth and their Mother who know only too well the absence of* An Eye for an Eye *justice following the murder of their brother and son, Brian Patrick. May God love him and you.*

# An Eye for an Eye
*William T. Harper*

# An Eye for an Eye
*William T. Harper*

## Table of Contents

|  |  |  |
|---|---|---|
|  | Dedication | 3 |
|  | Introduction | 7 |
| Chapter 1 | And Now…for the Rest of the Story | 11 |
| Chapter 2 | Do the Abolitionist Say Anything…We Can Believe? | 37 |
| Chapter 3 | If They're Interred…They're Deterred | 69 |
| Chapter 4 | Life-Without-Parole is a Joke…But it isn't Funny | 89 |
| Chapter 5 | It Isn't the Law…It's the Lawyers | 133 |
| Chapter 6 | Pity the Killers…Forget the Victims | 169 |
| Chapter 7 | Wrongly Sentenced Doesn't Mean…Wrongly Convicted | 221 |
| Chapter 8 | There Are Statistics and Then…There Are Damned Lies | 239 |
| Chapter 9 | In Football…Interference Gets Penalized | 267 |
| Chapter 10 | The Bible, the Baby and…What If? | 291 |
|  | Epilogue | 317 |
|  | Post Script | 321 |
|  | Index | 323 |
|  | Notes | 347 |

# An Eye for an Eye
*William T. Harper*

# An Eye for an Eye

*William T. Harper*

> "The world is a dangerous place to live;
> not because of the people who are evil,
> but because of the people who don't do
> anything about it."
> – Albert Einstein

# Introduction

There is a distinct and vitally active move afoot in this country to do away with the death penalty – a movement generally headed up by social liberals in search of a "cause." And, as most polls show, they are winning. Support for the death penalty is diminishing. The United States State Department, a source that might not have an axe to grind in the death penalty debate, reported that as of 2002, "public support [for the death penalty] has dropped from 80 percent to 63 percent since 1994."[1] A more recent Gallup Poll study shows the in-favor figure dropping to 61 percent in 2011.[2] The death penalty opponents are winning because most of America's vast "silent majority" is conceding the argument through inaction and default, and through ignorance and apathy, through "I don't know and I don't care".

Furthermore, there is even an attempt to end the use of the death penalty in the Lone Star State of Texas – wherein is located Harris County, called by death penalty opponents "the death house capitol of the Nation." To paraphrase an old political chant, "If Texas goes, so goes the Nation."

*An Eye for an Eye: In Defense of the Death Penalty* is an attempt to overcome that ignorance and apathy – especially in light of a June 2007 newspaper report. It notes that which "gets little notice, however, is a series of academic studies over the last half-dozen years that claim to settle a once hotly debated argument – whether the death penalty acts as a

# An Eye for an Eye
*William T. Harper*

deterrent to murder. The analyses say yes. They count between *three and 18 lives* that would be saved by the execution of each convicted killer (emphasis added)."[3]

*An Eye for an Eye* is a response to, among other things, Sister Helen Prejean's books, *Dead Man Walking* (1993) and *The Death of Innocents* (2005). Others who have taken similar anti-death penalty stances are also met head-on by *An Eye for an Eye* as it strives to preserve, protect, and defend the concept:

> For a crime there must be a punishment; the punishment must fit the crime – and for the ultimate crime there must be the ultimate punishment.

Via a series of chapter-opening vignettes illustrating the ghastly, brutal, monstrous murders committed by some of those the death penalty dissenters would spare, the book goes on to prove the so-called "panacea" – Life-Without-Parole – is a joke that isn't funny.

*An Eye for an Eye* also covers some religious aspects of the death penalty, offers an undeniable stance for the validity of deterrence, examines foreign and social influences, and exposes the extensive stretch of credulity by capital punishment opponents. The book shows undeniably that as executions go up, murders go down. It concludes with a "What If" segment addressing the horrible possibility of an innocent person's execution.

Many death penalty abolitionists invariably quote Mohandas K. Gandhi, political and spiritual leader of the Indian national independence movement who said, "If everyone took an eye for an eye, the whole world would be blind." That pithy comment misses the point entirely. Not every convicted murderer needs such retribution. It's only those who truly deserve it – "the worst of the worst." There is justice in applying the death penalty – just as there is justice

# An Eye for an Eye
*William T. Harper*

in pulling the trigger on your gun when someone else is pointing his gun at you.

In April of 2005, then-Governor Mitt Romney introduced a bill to reinstate capital punishment in Massachusetts. In discussing the bill, Romney said, "…there are some crimes that deserve the ultimate penalty and just as science can free the innocent, it can also identify the guilty."[4]

*An Eye for an Eye* refutes the arguments of those abolitionists who would do away with capital punishment. *An Eye for an Eye* presents an undeniable case for preserving the death penalty and for its rational but expedited *use*.

\* \* \*

# An Eye for an Eye
*William T. Harper*

# An Eye for an Eye
*William T. Harper*

## Chapter One

### And Now...for the Rest of the Story –
*Paul Harvey, radio commentator*

The death penalty dissenters, as personified by Sister Helen Prejean, C. S. J., via her two books – *Dead Man Walking* and *The Death of Innocents* – tell us that nobody, absolutely nobody deserves to die for crimes they commit, no matter how heinous. Let's talk about that.

**Jessica Lunsford**
(AP/Citrus County Sheriff's Dept)

*Jessica Lunsford, a nine-year-old little girl, was kidnapped from her home in Homosassa, Florida on February 24, 2005. She was raped over and over for several days, and then she was buried alive by a forty-six-year-old convicted and registered sex offender named John Evander Couey who later confessed to the brutal killing.*

John Evander Couey is one of those odious killers whose life the death penalty objectors would want to spare and merely sentence him to prison for the rest of his existence. On August 24, 2007, Couey was sentenced to death for his heinous crime. Think about the "sentence" Jessica's loved ones are serving. Can you imagine how they are waking up in the middle of so many nights with nightmares about how Couey spent days and nights committing vile sex acts on

# An Eye for an Eye
*William T. Harper*

their sobbing baby girl? Can you imagine the dashed hope and the grinding hurt her family must feel every day as they try to wake from their nightmare wishing desperately to find little Jessica coming through their front door and their bad dream is all over? And then she doesn't walk through the door – and the nightmare never ends.

Can you imagine Jessica's struggle for life as she lay trapped in that shallow grave under a foot of dirt, encased in two plastic bags knotted around her head and her feet and clutching her stuffed dolphin while each breath became more labored – until finally she could breath no more? Can the death penalty objectors hear her screams? Can they hear her crying? In sentencing Couey to death for the brutal murder of Jessica Lunsford, Judge Ric Howard said, "Jessica futilely poked two fingers out in the inner bag indicating that she was trying to dig her way out of what would become her grave. Her last thoughts," concluded the judge "cannot be fathomed."

This is the criminal record of the animal that hovered over Jessica Lunsford during some of her last helpless, pleading moments:

Passing Bad Checks
Disorderly Conduct
Drunk and Disorderly
Driving While Intoxicated
Fraud
Unlawful Possession of a Firearm (carrying a concealed weapon)
Indecent Exposure
Larceny
Burglary 1978
Lewd Act upon a Child Kissimmee, FL (1991)
Drug Possession: Marijuana 2004
Polygraphed
Registered As Sex Offender
Violating Probation: Failure to register change of

# An Eye for an Eye
*William T. Harper*

address as required of sex offenders (19-Mar-2005)
Burglary Charged 21-Mar-2005
Sexual Battery Charged 21-Mar-2005
Kidnapping Charged 21-Mar-2005
Murder Charged 21-Mar-2005[5]

(The last four charges are related to Couey's kidnapping, rape, and murder of Jessica Lunsford.)

Can you imagine how Jessica's devastated parents and grand-parents and other family members are going to feel every single time Jessica's birthday rolls around; each Christmas, each Thanksgiving, each and every February 24, the anniversary of their daughter's abduction? Can you imagine how many appeals and perhaps re-trials those people might have had to suffer through while defense attorneys beg for the mercy Couey never showed Jessica and prosecutors again try to bring justice to John Evander Couey.

At least Couey finally did something good in his worthless life. He died of colon cancer in a Jacksonville, Florida prison on September 30, 2009. Even with that act of God (perhaps), he denied society its legitimate claim for final justice.

How many times were Jessica's mother and father going to have to cover their eyes when prosecutors have to show the coroner's pictures of their baby's body mutilated by John Evander Couey?

If the law of averages held up, it will be something like ten years before Couey's death sentence would have been carried out, assuming some hot-shot lawyer didn't get it overturned. With an average of more than 16,000 murders committed every year in the U. S., that means 160,000 innocent people would have been killed before John Evander Couey gave up his eye-for-an-eye. By the time justice would have been administered to John Evander Couey, the equivalent of the entire population of the Missouri's capitol city, Springfield, would have been murdered. Where is the outrage about that from the death penalty opponents?

# An Eye for an Eye
*William T. Harper*

Is there no compassion, abolitionists, in your bleeding hearts for Jessica? For her family? Are you so wrapped up in your self-righteous zeal for her killer, for his "dignity," for his "humanity," that you can't feel Jessica's pain? Are you so concerned that death row occupants like John Evander Couey might cough and gasp and may be somewhat uncomfortable (IF they are!) for the few minutes it might take for lethal injection chemicals to course through Couey's body in this case – finally bringing some form of Jessica's justice?

It undoubtedly took a lot more than only a few minutes for frightened little Jessica to die a horrible, painful, suffocating death buried in that makeshift grave, in something not nearly as sanitary as a gurney in a Florida prison death house. Wrapped in a plastic sack, Jessica didn't have the comfort of loved ones standing by as she died as killers like John Evander Couey do when they pay the price. Can't you feel her pain? How can you say savage killers such as John Evander Couey don't deserve retribution? Is this an animal whose life you want to spare?

**John Evander Couey**

No, executing John Evander Couey would not have brought back Jessica Lunsford. Neither would Life-Without-Parole. Nothing will. But, considering all the possibilities that Couey could have been back out on the street again – as have others of his ilk via bleeding-heart judges and parole boards, changing sentencing guidelines, escaping convicted killers,

# An Eye for an Eye

*William T. Harper*

Hollywood's glitterati, the international interference, and poor-mouthing of people of the cloth — the death penalty exacted upon John Evander Couey would have done what colon cancer did: Make sure he will never again victimize another Jessica Lunsford.

Can you hear her screams? Can you feel her panic? Can you suffer her last breath? If there's a God in Heaven, how can you death penalty opponents plead for life sentences for the likes of John Evander Couey after he so brutally and cowardly took the life of Jessica Lunsford, for whom the newly enacted "Jessica's Law" was named?

\* \* \*

On Thursday, December 2, 2004, at Sam Houston State University in Huntsville, Texas, Sister Helen Prejean (PRAY-jon), author of the best-selling book, *Dead Man Walking* (which became an Academy Award-winning movie for actress Susan Sarandon), spent 45 minutes in an impassioned (and sometimes amusing) speech advocating the death penalty's elimination with:

- accusations about racial imbalance in death sentences among races (80 percent she said, were assessed against blacks)
- castigation of "cruel and unusual punishment" of prisoners — such as that "inflicted on prisoners in Iraq's Abu Ghraib prison" by the U. S. military. (She did not compare those "humiliations" with beheadings of enemies by Al Qaeda), and
- assorted and sundry similar comments on what would usually be called socially liberal causes.

"While the O. J.'s walk out the door," said the nun at Sam Houston State University's forum, "the No-J's get the death penalty." If she's right, then her campaign should be

# An Eye for an Eye
*William T. Harper*

directed at that inequity in the system. Absent traditional black garb that used to make Sisters of the Church look like "angels" and dressed, she said, like "normal people," she joked with her audience: "Capital punishment means them without the capital get the punishment."

The thing that is most repelling about the Huntsville presentation for those who have lost a loved one to a vicious killer in a heinous crime (dictionary-defined as a shockingly brutal, monstrous, cruel, atrocious act), was that the evening's program planners offered not a single iota of counter-balance to the nun's exhortations, despite the fact that most in the audience were impressionable college students. It was like teaching them the history of the War Between the States from Ulysses S. Grant's viewpoint without mentioning Robert E. Lee's. Sam Houston State University was not alone in that omission. *An Eye for an Eye* is an attempt to offer that counter-balance. It is a defense of the validity of the death penalty.

This work you are reading will most assuredly be attacked by death penalty abolitionists who will proclaim *An Eye for an Eye* is an all-out attack on a Sister of the Church, Helen Prejean, C.S.J. It is not. While we respect dissenters' defense of their position in this matter and commend their zeal, ours is no less passionate – and we don't have any hidden agenda. Since Sister Prejean and her two books now appear to be the gospel and a hymnal for anti-death penalty choirs, it is right and proper that this pro-death penalty stand be directed in large part at its opponents' arguments as preached from Sister Prejean's bully pulpit.

\* \* \*

There are many who believe in the death penalty; who truly believe in *An Eye for an Eye*. Some even contend there is a need to "take on" death penalty opponents (a phrase Sister Prejean used during a brief encounter with U. S. Supreme Court Associate Justice Antonin Scalia, and about which, he

# An Eye for an Eye

*William T. Harper*

recalls, she "milks our chance meeting in the New Orleans airport for all the sales value it's worth – and distorts it significantly)."[6]

The lack of balance, of alternative viewpoints in the nun's performances gets even worse. Officials at Presentation High School in Willow Glen, California felt privileged to have Sister Prejean in their midst on January 19, 2000. "In our ethics class, we discuss whether capital punishment is just and right. [What are your guesses as to the outcome of those discussions?] So, to have the guru on capital punishment come was perfect," gushed *high school* Vice Principal Dina Garrett.[7]

Even while admitting to the aforementioned Huntsville student body she had never been tested by personal loss in having a loved-one murdered, she proclaimed she was sure she would feel remorse for the perpetrator should such a horror happen in her family. "No one has shot my loved ones in the back of the head," she confessed.[8] It isn't hard to believe something like that could change a person's mind. There's an old saying about "walking in another Indian's moccasins."

She claims families of victims should reject their natural feelings of revenge, their "eye-for-an-eye" biblical teachings, and *embrace* killers of their loved ones. She seemed to be saying, in the vernacular, families should "just get over it." She wishes the parents of one victim whose killer she spiritually advised would "move on" with their grief.[9] This is the advice given to the parents of another 18-year-old daughter who was repeatedly raped and stabbed to death by two other savage killers.

She contends, while presenting what some would call bogus and contrived case histories which she claims back her point, innocent people have received capital punishment – a penalty from which there is no pardon; from which there is no reprieve. The fact of the matter is, however, as of the summer of 2012, no one – repeat, NO one – who has been executed since the death penalty was reinstituted by the

# An Eye for an Eye
*William T. Harper*

United States Supreme Court in 1976, has been proved definitively innocent.[10]

Support for that statement comes from Joshua K. Marquis, with the National District Attorneys Association and a district attorney in Clatsop County, Oregon. He said, "The well-organized and even better-funded abolitionists cannot point to a single case of a demonstrably innocent person executed in the modern era of American capital punishment."[11]

If necessary, further support for the "no one" statement comes from the United States Supreme Court. "It should be noted," writes Justice Scalia, "...that the dissent [in this case before the Court] does not discuss a single case – not one – in which it is clear that a person was executed for a crime he did not commit. If such an event had occurred in recent years, we would not have to hunt for it; the innocent's name would be shouted from the rooftops by the abolition lobby."[12]

Meanwhile, the "abolition lobby," regarding what it calls unjustified criminal executions, blatantly claims "that we do it all the time."[13] Still, the anti-death penalty cabal's propaganda machine has been highly effective in getting out its message. For instance, in a poll conducted by the University of Houston's Center for Public Policy Survey Research Institute in November-December 2005 and published in the *Houston Chronicle* shortly thereafter, the study showed 55.3 percent of those surveyed in Texas believed the state has executed an innocent person.

One of the reasons 55.3 percent of those surveyed in Texas believes the state has executed an innocent person is due to the inflammatory collusion of some parts of the media as shown many times below.

The above comments and their citations are made despite what Sister Prejean writes on pages 218-220 of *Dead Man Walking*: "A two-year study of capital punishment in the U.S. by Hugo A. Bedau of Tufts University and Michael L. Radelet of the University of Florida [in 1987] documents that

# An Eye for an Eye
*William T. Harper*

in this century 417 people were wrongly convicted of capital offenses and 23 were actually executed. In recent years cases have surfaced of people sent to death row in error and later released."

The nun then goes on to list five detailed examples of those sent to death row and later released (though not necessarily from prison, as implied). "In 1974," Sister Prejean writes, "[James] Adams, a black man, was convicted of first-degree murder and sentenced to death."[14] If indeed the Bedau-Radelet study can prove 223 "wrongly convicted [inmates]"…were actually executed, why are not each and every one of them spelled out in detail in *Dead Man Walking*? Why is only one cited? (And that "one" is covered in greater detail herein.)

Maybe it's because the infamous Bedau-Radelet study, acclaimed so many times by the abolitionist lobby, is flat-out bogus! At least it is in the eyes of Supreme Court Justice Scalia, who called the study "unverified" to say the least – as shall also be shown herein later.[15]

There is no end to the opponents' eternal drumbeat and their incessant pounding of false information. "Some of us, [they write in a reference to the American public in general being coarsened by the death penalty] say that even if *innocent* people are sometimes executed along with the guilty, we support the death penalty anyway."[16] Even if the *innocent* are *sometimes* executed? Let it be said again: "The fact of the matter is, however, that as of the summer of 2012, no one – repeat, NO one – who has been executed since the death penalty was reinstituted in 1976 has been proved definitively innocent."

Yet again, we read that "Honorable people have disagreed about the justice of executing the guilty, but can anyone argue about the justice of executing the innocent? And," it continues, "can anyone doubt, after the revelations of the past five years, that *we do it all the time*?" [emphasis again added].[17] Sister Prejean is absolutely right. No one can "argue about the justice of executing the innocent." But, let it be said

# An Eye for an Eye
*William T. Harper*

again – and again. "As of the summer of 2007, no one – repeat, NO one – who has been executed since 1976, has been proved definitively innocent."

That hardly sounds like "we do it all the time."

\* \* \*

But sometimes, Sister Prejean, et al., some innocent people do die – as 168 of them did at the hands of mass-murderer Timothy McVeigh in Oklahoma City, Oklahoma on the morning of April 19, 1995 – just after some parents dropped off 18 of their babies at a nursery school in the Murrah Federal Building. (McVeigh called those kids "collateral damage".) In whatever means satisfy your inner being, yes, we should pray for those innocent victims. But, are we to grieve as much for their killer as we do for those 168 men, women, and children McVeigh blew to bits?

And what of the 42 passengers and crew that died a hero's death while reciting the 23$^{rd}$ Psalm aboard hijacked United Airlines flight #93 as it plummeted into a vacant Schenksville, Pennsylvania field on September 11, 2001? Are we to weep for Ziad Jarrah and his three hijacking cohorts on that plane the same as we weep for Todd Beamer and the other 39 gallant passengers and crew members who went to their flaming death while possibly saving the United States Capitol Building and all its inhabitants that day from Dante's Inferno? "Let's roll!"

Think of the almost 3,000 of our fellow citizens who died horrible deaths in the crumbling and enflamed Twin Towers in New York City on that same morning. Remember the falling bodies and the agony of those who had to decide whether the lingering horror of incineration or a leap of 800 feet or so to their death was the better way to meet their Maker. It takes about seven to eight seconds for a human body to fall 80 stories. How many thoughts can pass through the human brain in those horrific seconds?

# An Eye for an Eye

*William T. Harper*

One-thousand and one,
One-thousand and two,
One-thousand and three,
One-thousand and four,
One-thousand and five,
One-thousand and six,
One-thousand and seven....

Think of the heroic New York firefighters and police officers who raced into that inferno trying to save those people, only to die along with them – one even cradling a pregnant woman in his arms as all three were callously murdered by those terrorists. And abolitionists tell us vile mass-murderers like these deserve "dignity"?

The next time family members of those 9/11 victims gather at Ground Zero to toll the bell and speak their names in remembrance and prayer, should they also pray for Mohammed Atta, who crashed American Airlines Flight #11 into the North Tower of the World Trade Center on that fateful day? Had Atta and the rest of his killer clan survived to be tried, convicted, and sentenced to death for slaughtering more than 3,000 human beings, would the demonstrators be lined up at the court house door wailing because those murderers had been abused as youths? Would they be marching with placards outside prison walls on execution day screaming lethal injection is "cruel and unusual" punishment? Would they say, "Let's just sentence Atta and friends to Life-Without-Parole?" How long do you think it would take those fanatics to get out, with or without help, and inflict "9-11 – The Sequel" on the world?

\* \* \*

In *Dead Man Walking* and in her follow-up tome, *The Death of Innocents*, Sister Prejean goes to great lengths to cite what she calls failures in our judicial system for irreversible executions. She excoriates some (most?) prosecutors and judges for what she claims is their win-at-all-costs attitude – even if, as she contends, one of those costs is lethal injection for an

# An Eye for an Eye
*William T. Harper*

innocent man. She and other death penalty opponents rail against "inept" defense attorneys who lose the cases for killers such as those she spiritually advises.

Many of those who would do away with the death penalty continually cite the case of "the sleeping lawyer" as if it were a daily occurrence inflicted only upon low-paid, court-appointed defense attorneys. As far as can be documented and as is shown below herein, that "sleeping lawyer" example was hardly more than a one-time, unfortunate misunderstanding in our legal system. It was not, as shall be seen later in this tome and as anti-death penalty bloc would have us believe, a happening as often and as regular as an ice cream truck cruising through a kid-filled summertime neighborhood.

The anti-death penalty coalition's primary contention is the death penalty must be abolished – no matter how heinous the crime; no matter how heinous the criminal, no matter how many are slaughtered, no matter how brutal the murder for the victims and the never-ending suffering of their families. According to abolitionists if they had their way, had Adolph Hitler been captured by victorious Allied armies in 1945, he would have spent the rest of his years in a Life-Without-Parole sentence writing *Mein Kampf II* in Germany's Spandau Prison.

That would have been the extent of the penalty inflicted by death penalty opponents for the Nazi butcher's implementation of the Holocaust, genocide, and other war crimes against humanity. Do we hear Auschwitz? Buchenwald? Dachau? Do we hear the screams of six million Jews in gas chambers? Adolph Hitler serving Life-Without-Parole? Imagine the deleterious effects that would have had on "skin-head" apparitions that have since cropped up in Germany and elsewhere around the globe.

In the cell next to Hitler would be Joseph Stalin – if death penalty opponents were deciding his fate for the Russians he had murdered in the Gulags of the Soviet Union. Can we hear the dying cries of 20,000,000 of Uncle Joe's own

# An Eye for an Eye
*William T. Harper*

people? Of the peoples of Poland? Of Finland? Of Hungary? The Baltics?

If abolitionists sat in judgment at the trial of Saddam Hussein, he would have had no fear of the death penalty. He could have planned to write his memoirs about his mass graves, his gassing of his Kurdish countrymen, his rape and torture camps. Such a book would have been an instant bestseller in Hollywood; another Academy Award-winning flick, no doubt. Pol Pot and his Khmer Rouge party with their "killing fields" for millions in the 1970s might be ensconced in a neighboring cell providing Saddam with adjectives for butchery – if abolitionists had their way.

No crime, **no crime whatsoever**, would merit the death penalty, according to the views of those in the death penalty abolition march. How can anyone say Hitler wouldn't deserve the death penalty? How can anyone – in their right mind – say Stalin wouldn't deserve the death penalty? Saddam Hussein? Pol Pot? People who believe that have taken a position that is extreme to the point of incredulity; to a point that invalidates any other argument they may have.

**No crime whatsoever?** None. Nil. Nadda. Zip. Not even the "Boston Strangler" (Albert De Salvo), the "Son of Sam" (David Berkowitz), Jeffrey Dahmer, Ted Bundy, John Wayne Gacy, Richard Speck, and Charles Manson? Almost one-hundred people have verifiably been murdered by these serial killers. Richard "The Iceman" Kuklinski alone surpassed that crowd with somewhere between 100 and 200 killings, many of them as a mob "hit man." Not even "Jack the Ripper" and others on this list that will live in the infamy of horror would get the death sentence they so justly deserve if abolitionists win in the court of public opinion.

\* \* \*

*An Eye for an Eye.*

One can only hope enough of our fellow Americans will share these views, make them known to their neighbors

# An Eye for an Eye
*William T. Harper*

and co-workers, their elected representatives, their clergy, and to the media so abolitionists will be stopped in their knee-deep tracks of innuendo and deceit. Those who believe in the need for the death penalty also know there are many gradations for those labeled as "the worst-of-the-worst," or the "consensus killers," as Ben M. Crouch, professor of sociology at Texas A&M University and noted authority on criminal behavior, called them.[18] The abolitionists, when talking about the U. S. Supreme Court's attempt to find a worst-of-the-worst standard, mock and compare it to the Court's attempt to define pornography: "You know it when you see it."

They go further. They offer U. S. Supreme Court Associate Justice John Marshall Harlan's citation that "any attempt to formulate 'guiding standards' for weighing degrees of guilt was 'beyond present human capacity'." They call the Justice's comment "a stunning understatement."[19] That may well have been the case when that jurist said it – 35 years ago, back in technology's dinosaur age. That was before Bill Gates, Microsoft, DVDs, cell phones, Facebook, Twitter, *et al.* Now, in the 21$^{st}$ Century, a true measure of a "scale of evil" – those "guiding standards" – is at hand.

Forensic psychiatrist and professor of psychiatry at Columbia University, Dr. Michael Stone, has examined, researched and interviewed hundreds of killers to develop a hierarchy of "people who commit breathtaking acts."[20] Listing 22 categories of evil, they range from those who kill in self-defense (Category No. 1), to jealous psychopathic lovers (Category No. 9), to serial torturers and killers (Category No. 22) – the most evil on Dr. Stone's scale.

Another researcher in the depravity-rating field, Dr. Michael Welner, a forensic psychiatrist and professor at New York University, said: "We are finding widespread agreement about what is evil."[21] Those who are or would be at the upper reaches of Dr. Stone's "Scale of Evil" or Dr. Welner's scientific definition of "aggravating" factors in crimes are those we're talking about in this text. They are those who,

# An Eye for an Eye

*William T. Harper*

without a doubt, deserve the ultimate penalty for their ultimate crimes; those in the area of Dr. Stone's Category 22: serial killers, child killers, cop killers, terrorists, multiple murderers, torturers, etc. Another category that fits in here – one that has been around for a long time but has recently fallen into disuse – is "premeditated."

Those who believe in the death penalty are not naïve enough to believe its application is infallible. Sometimes, the wheels of criminal justice do fall off, innocent people are convicted. There is now no doubt that the Houston (Texas) Crime Lab fouled up monumentally as investigators and forensics scientists severely criticized the forensic analysis performed by the DNA/Serology Section of the Crime Lab in a number of specific cases.[22]

The recent rash of sentences overturned by new techniques in DNA testing has proven that similar mistakes have been made nationwide. Those circumstances are indeed regrettable but they are mitigated by, as we shall see here later, the fact that no definitively proven innocent person has been executed in the United States since the death penalty was reinstituted in 1976. The new procedures have also proven the system does, in fact, work. Advocates for the use of capital punishment are the first to say that that penalty should not be enacted unless the offender is convicted "beyond a shadow of a doubt."

Most law enforcement officers interviewed by this author are at least ambivalent when it comes to the death penalty. Jim Willett is typical. He served 30 years in the Texas Department of Criminal Justice (nee, Texas Department of Corrections) – three of them as warden of "The Walls" Unit in Huntsville, Texas. Inside the Walls Unit is what some death penalty opponents like to refer to as "the killing chamber." In that chamber, Warden Willett officiated at over 89 executions (more than anyone else at the time of his retirement in 2001). Five of them he described in his 2005 book aptly titled, *Warden*. In talking with this writer, Willett

# An Eye for an Eye
*William T. Harper*

used exactly that word, ambivalent, to describe his feelings about the death penalty.

Like many others in his profession, however, he agrees there are some convicted killers who most assuredly do deserve "the full extent of the law." As Willett put in his book, all ambivalence he had about the death penalty evaporated when he presided at Kenneth Allen McDuff's execution (and you'll learn why later in this book when you read about McDuff). "Tonight," Willett wrote, "no matter what the opponents of capital punishment might say, I know that we ridded the world of a man that it will be better off without."[23]

But all agree there are cases where someone commits a murder when, for instance, they are high on drugs, are deranged parents who murder their children, or are someone in a state of perceived offense who kills the offender in a fit of uncontrollable rage. These are the cases that result in ambiguity. A guideline, a standard, a "Scale of Evil" would be an antidote for judges, juries and prison officials such as Warden Jim Willett.

In the state of Arizona in an effort to overcome such ambiguity, "cruel, heinous or depraved" is pretty well spelled out in *State of Arizona v. Willie Lee Richmond*, 1983. The Court ruled: "'Cruel' has been defined as 'disposed to inflict pain especially in a wanton, insensate or vindictive manner: sadistic'.... 'Heinous' has been defined as 'hatefully or shockingly evil; grossly bad,' and 'depraved' is marked by debasement, corruption, perversion or deterioration'."[24] In reviewing murders discussed herein, it would be hard to find even one that did not fit at least one part of the above "cruel, heinous or depraved" definition.

The essence of these definitions is re-stated as recently as May 17, 2012 in *The State of Arizona v. James Darrell Johnson* (No. 2 CA–CR 2010–0380).

There are many in the anti-death penalty camp who willy-nilly cite names of "legions" who are "opposed to the death penalty." However, those abolitionists do not bother

# An Eye for an Eye
*William T. Harper*

to go beyond that simple, flat statement of opposition. Yet, some of those who say they are against the death penalty are not against it *per se*, but rather for various reasons. For instance, noted penologist and former Director of the Texas Department of Corrections with 40 years of experience in the criminal justice system, G. J. "Walking George" Beto, said although he was "firmly in agreement with the concept of the death penalty, he *opposed it in practice* [author's emphasis] because it was not equally administered."[25] Those last six words and other similar equivocating sentiments are often overlooked (to say the least) by abolitionist zealots.

\* \* \*

However, those who believe in the righteousness of the death penalty are a long way behind in this race for its preservation. Go, if you will, to Google or just about any other Internet search engine and enter the name of any murderer you can think of who is facing or has faced the death penalty. What you'll no doubt find are dozens if not hundreds of websites defending the killer vs. those supporting the sentence, the concept and the victim(s).

Every *pro-death* penalty website such as Justice for All (http://jfa.net/) is heavily outweighed by others, such as the American Civil Liberties Union's (ACLU's) www.aclu.org/capital/index.html and Amnesty International's www.amnestyusa.org, *ad infinitum*. The following is just an abbreviated list of some organizations linked to the death penalty's abolition from Sister Prejean's *The Death of Innocents* and her "Moratorium Campaign" website:[26]

> Prison Talk
> Students Against The Death Penalty
> Alaskans Against The Death Penalty
> Campaign To End The Death Penalty

# An Eye for an Eye
*William T. Harper*

Coalition Of Arizonians To Abolish The Death Penalty
Coloradans Against The Death Penalty
Connecticut Network To Abolish The Death Penalty
Death Penalty Focus Of California
Floridians For Alternatives To The Death Penalty
Illinois Coalition Against The Death Penalty
Iowans Against The Death Penalty
Kentucky Coalition To Abolish The Death Penalty
Massachusetts Citizens Against The Death Penalty
New Mexico Coalition To Repeal The Death Penalty
Ohioans To Stop Executions
Pennsylvania Abolitionists United Against
    The Death Penalty
South Florida Committee Against The Death Penalty
Tennessee Coalition To Abolish The Death Penalty
Texas Moratorium Network
New Yorkers Against The Death Penalty
Washington Coalition To Abolish The Death Penalty
International Youth For A Moratorium
Moratorium 2000 Community Of St. Egidio

    Against this formidable coalition, one is very hard-pressed to find organizations supporting the counter view – that for the safety and good of society in this country, the death penalty must be retained and implemented for those in the top rungs of the "scale of evil," consensus killers, if you will. Such a list promoting an opposite view runs rather short and includes lonely voices like the aforementioned Justice for All, and

    www.murdervictims.com,
    www.prodeathppenalty.com

# An Eye for an Eye
*William T. Harper*

Throw Away the Key
www.wesleylowe.com/cp.htm
and
Criminal Justice Legal Foundation

— all dedicated to innocent victims of murder.

According to people at the website www.prodeathpenalty.com, "If you search the internet via search engines for 'death penalty,' you are likely to find thousands, if not tens of thousands of 'hits' to web sites related to the topic. With very few exceptions, these sites are anti-death penalty. Is this because the majority of people are against the death penalty? Not according to recent Gallup Poll surveys showing 61 percent of the people in this country still support the death penalty. Alarmingly, that figure is down from 80 percent in 1995.[27]

The drop is simply because people who are adamantly opposed to the death penalty tend to take an activist stance and become involved in working to stop the death penalty. For the most part, people who support the death penalty do so quietly, in their own minds, and feel no need to do so in any public fashion. It is the law and they expect it to be carried out." It is, however, a Great Expectation that isn't being realized.

But even with such strong adherents of the death penalty as Justice for All, the Death Penalty Web Page, et al., one has to be wary. There apparently are wolves in sheep's clothing lurking. Some victims' rights organizations with members and families that have suffered terrible tragedies at the hands of heinous killers have now, according to the *Houston Press*, turned the other cheek and are engaged primarily in joining death penalty abolitionists. Even some non-victims are said to be carrying personal agendas. The newspaper reported Diane Clements, president of Justice for All, charged the Murder Victim's Families for Reconciliation

# An Eye for an Eye
*William T. Harper*

was "really a bunch of abolitionists who just happened to have family members killed."[28]

\* \* \*

Sister Helen Prejean is equally direct. She puts her position right on the line — and not quietly. "I have no doubt," she avows, "that we will one day abolish the death penalty in America. It will come sooner if people like me who know the truth about executions do our work well and educate the public."[29] The abolitionists — who seem to "know the truth about executions" but precious little about the horrors suffered by victims and their families — leave no stone unturned in their zeal to eliminate the death penalty.

The world premiere of the opera *Dead Man Walking* was performed in San Francisco in October, 2000. "The Boss," Bruce Springsteen, won an Academy Award for the *song* he composed and played in the movie of the same name. The movie based on the book *Dead Man Walking* has now even been converted into a *stage play* being offered to high schools all across the country. It claims to "provide an opportunity to broaden discussion about the death penalty and involve schools and their local communities in an inter-disciplinary dialogue about this major social issue."[30] To some, "inter-disciplinary" means both sides of the street. In this case, one has no doubt this is a one-way street. Joseph Goebbels, Adolph Hitler's master of propaganda before and during World War II, could not have put together a better justification campaign.

One of the problems anti-abolitionists have is they don't have the exposure for their point of view via the world of the social elitists, the liberal mainstream media, the glitterati and the literati and celebrities in klieg lights. People like Susan Sarandon, Sean Penn, Tim Robbins, Bianca Jagger, Mike Farrell, Jesse Jackson, author Norman Mailer, rapper Snoop Dogg, South Africa's former first lady, Winnie Mandela, et al. When you read newspapers, you almost never

# An Eye for an Eye
*William T. Harper*

see columnists defending the death penalty. And when was the last time you saw a page one story in the *New York Times* or *Washington Post* defending the death penalty? Letters to the Editor writers almost never are pro-death penalty. Unfortunately, those who support the death penalty are remnants from the past millennium's much maligned and seldom heard "Silent Majority."

Websites are now the Waldorf-Astoria Hotel for abolitionists as they check in and invite the world to share their suites and their anti-death penalty views, such as:

www.policestudies.eku.edu/kpotter/speech3.htm

> Juvenile Death Penalty Speech, delivered by Karen Potter, November 18, 1999, commemorating the 10th Anniversary of the United Nations Convention on the Rights of the Child....

www.geocities.com/savepenry/

> Lost Souls: Stop Killing Mentally Retarded And Mentally Ill....

www.coadp.org/thepublications/pub-2002-5-ExecuteRetarded.html

> The mission of Coloradans Against the Death Penalty is to abolish the death penalty in Colorado through religious, educational, political, and victims rights efforts....

www.amnestyusa.org/abolish/index.do

> The death penalty is the ultimate, irreversible denial of human rights. By working towards the abolition of the death penalty worldwide, Amnesty International USA's Program to Abolish the Death Penalty looks to end the cycle of violence created by a system riddled with economic and racial bias and tainted by human error. Please join us in taking action against the death penalty....

http://bmj.bmjjournals.com/cgi/content/full/312/7045/1548

# An Eye for an Eye

*William T. Harper*

> The death penalty industry in the United States is possibly the most heavily medicalised in the world.... The American Medical Association (AMA) has prohibited virtually all involvement by doctors in executions....

As the late Jimmy Durante used to so amusingly say, "Everybody wants to get into the act!" Only this time, as Mollie Magee used to say to her husband Fibber back in the days of radio comedy shows, "It ain't funny, Magee." Abolitionists have even set up Internet blogs for convicted murderers so they (the murderers) can engage the public in Q&A sessions – and guess how "fair and balanced" the killers' answers to the questions are going to be. By the way, some of those same blogs have become sales outlets for "murderabilia" – such as hair-clippings and finger nails – mementoes from killers of their heinous acts.

\* \* \*

If death penalty preservationists don't wake up now and make their call for justice heard, abolitionists among us will open the doors of every prison death house in the nation and send some of the most brutal killers the world has ever known back to their cellblocks or worse yet, back to the streets. No matter what the conditions are in penitentiaries today (and how much more favorable they are most likely to become in the future), life there is infinitely better than were the last moments of their slain victims' lives.

And it is in those prisons that many of those killers – who, via the propaganda of the abolitionists, have been and are being transformed into "victims" – will sit and wait for bleeding-heart legislators, lawyers, judges, parole boards, etc., to find a way to reduce even the so-called Life-Without-Parole sentencing abolitionists see as their excuse for denying victims and their families of the retribution they so justly deserve.

# An Eye for an Eye
*William T. Harper*

Incidentally, "Retribution is a term that means balancing a wrong through punishment. While revenge is personal and not necessarily balanced, retribution is impersonal and balanced."[31] This point needs to be emphasized again and again. "Retribution" is an impersonal approach to the philosophy of punishment. Revenge is a personal action – almost a one-on-one. This is the inflammatory rhetoric used by abolitionists as they often imply those who want to retain the death penalty just want revenge. <u>Retribution is the will of the people</u>.

The growing clamor for Life-Without-Parole could very well be transformed into Life-Without-Parole – for maybe 30, 20, 10 years, somewhere down the legislative road. Unfortunately and tragically, we don't have to look even one day "down the legislative road." It has already happened!

Megan Liebengood, an 18-year old newlywed married only three months, was returning home in Lexington, Kentucky shortly after 10:45 pm on September 15, 2004. Suddenly, three teenage thugs approached her and demanded her purse. After realizing she had no money, they eventually shot her four times in the back of the head and left her to die in the parking lot.

Patrick Cook, 17, Michael Shepherd, 16, and Robert Miller, 16 were later arrested and charged with murder. Cook pled guilty and testified at trial. Only two hours passed before the jury returned guilty verdicts for Michael Shepherd and Robert Miller. The jury recommended a sentence of Life-Without-Parole **for 25 years** for the shooter, Shepherd. Miller was sentenced to 40 years in prison.[32]

Incidentally, it is a fact that most prison term sentences come with a little realized caveat. It's called a "Good Time" reward. For every two days served without negative incidents, the inmate gets one day removed from his sentence. (In some prison systems, it's a one-for-one break.) That means if Robert Miller behaves himself, his 40 sentence for the murder of Megan Liebengood comes 30 years. Miller would only be 46 years old. He could still start a family.

# An Eye for an Eye
*William T. Harper*

Wonder what kind of a family Megan Liebengood would have had?

And while you're at it, think of this: Michael Shepherd, the shooter of Megan Liebengood, via his Life-Without-Parole **for 25 years** sentence, will be out of jail long before Miller does his 30 years!

Life-Without-Parole — for whatever length it turns in to — merely means blatant killers can even rain total Hell on their confines and their confiners. Prison employees (and yes, even other prisoners) have been and no doubt are still being attacked and killed without fear of reprisal (what do their killers have to lose?). The Life-Without-Parolees can only be given more time added to their sentence; more years to plan an escape, to kill once more within the walls, or to get a totally ill-advised parole. Or, they can simply wait for future abolitionists to demand and get even softer-sentencing.

Sure. Ease your conscience, ladies and gentlemen of the jury. Give these killers Life-Without-Parole. That, in effect, is what they gave Henry Brisbon Jr., convicted of three monstrous "I-57 murders" in 1973. Brisbon escaped the death penalty because of the U. S. Supreme Court's 1972 ruling in the *Furman v. Georgia* case made the death penalty unconstitutional for four years. So the judge sentenced him to a term of 1,000 to 3,000 years in prison. To be eligible for parole, he'd have to serve at least 500 years. That ought to take care of multi-murderer Henry Brisbon, right? Lock him up and throw away the key. That way, we can all sleep easy at night, right?

Wrong. On October 19, 1978 — with less than one year of those 500 served — Brisbon murdered fellow Stateville prison inmate Richard "Hippie" Morgan with a shank, a sharpened handle of a soup ladle. At the trial for this murder, Will County (Illinois) State's Attorney Edward Petka described Brisbon as "a walking testimonial for the death penalty." The jury agreed.

Even so, Brisbon beat the rap again when Illinois Governor George Ryan issued his infamous blanket

# An Eye for an Eye
*William T. Harper*

commutation of all death penalty sentences in the Land of Lincoln on January 12, 2003. During his years confined in Stateville, Brisbon was involved in 15 attacks on inmates and guards, instigated at least one prison riot, trashed a courtroom during a trial and hit a warden with a broom handle. Yes, abolitionists, Life-Without-Parole is the answer!!

Pity the poor victims and their families? Don't waste your time. The real "victims," according to those who would make the death penalty disappear, are those like Elmo Patrick Sonnier, Robert Lee Willie, Joseph O'Dell, and Dobie Gillis Williams — all of whom Sister Prejean spiritually-advised on death row. Add their names to the entire roster of heinous, heartless, brutal, savage murderers abolitionists would have us weep for.

"Weep no more, my ladies…." and gentlemen. Read on, as commentator Paul Harvey would say, to get "the rest of the story" — the one you'll never hear if all you do is listen to unfair, one-sided, narrow viewpoints of bleeding hearts who "would feel nothing but remorse for the perpetrators."

\* \* \*

# An Eye for an Eye

*William T. Harper*

# An Eye for an Eye
*William T. Harper*

# Chapter Two

## Do the Abolitionist Say Anything... We Can Believe?

*"On the evening of November 4, 1977, David LeBlanc, age sixteen, and Loretta Ann Bourque, age eighteen, attended a high school football game. Later that evening, the couple parked in a remote area of St. Martin Parish, about one-hundred miles due west of New Orleans. At approximately one o'clock A.M., defendant* [Elmo Patrick Sonnier] *and his brother, Eddie James Sonnier, who were rabbit hunting together, came across the couple's car. Using a badge one of the brothers had obtained while working as a security guard and armed with 22-caliber rifles, the two posed as police officers and approached and entered the car. The victims were informed they were trespassing and they would have to be brought to the landowner to determine if the landowner desired to press charges. At this time the driver's licenses of both victims were confiscated. The two victims were then handcuffed and placed in the back seat of their (the victims') car. Leaving their own car behind, the defendant and his brother drove the couple twenty-one miles to a remote oilfield located in Iberia Parish, an area known to the defendant.*

*"Once at the oilfield, both victims were removed from the car. David LeBlanc was taken into the woods and handcuffed to a tree. Loretta Bourque was taken a short distance away and raped by the defendant, Elmo Patrick Sonnier. She then agreed to have intercourse with Eddie Sonnier in exchange for the couple's safe release. Upon completion of the rapes, the two youngsters were un-handcuffed and brought back toward the road where the car was parked.*

*At that point, Elmo Patrick Sonnier told his brother they could not let the couple go because if the youngsters talked, it would mean he (Elmo) would have to go back to Angola [Prison]. David LeBlanc and Loretta Bourque were then forced to lie side by side, face down, and*

# An Eye for an Eye
*William T. Harper*

*were each shot three times at close range in the back of the head. Eddie Sonnier testified that he held a flashlight while the defendant shot the youngsters with a 22-caliber rifle. He further related that Bourque began to cry when the defendant fired a first shot at her which missed. The defendant then fired a second shot which succeeded in striking Bourque in the back of the head. The third shot likewise struck LeBlanc in the back of the head. Each victim was then shot two additional times."*[33]

And the abolitionists say predatory animals such as Elmo Patrick Sonnier deserve to "die with dignity."

\* \* \*

There is no doubt that on the evening of November 4, 1977, either one or both of the Sonnier brothers brutally and with malice aforethought murdered David LeBlanc, 16, and Loretta Ann Bourque, 18. Both brothers separately admitted to the killings. Both brothers also recanted and blamed the other. Both deserved the ultimate penalty (which only Elmo Patrick Sonnier paid). Yet, the abolitionists say execution is too high a price to pay for such savagery as was inflicted on the teenagers (especially Ms. Bourque). They say it's too high for any killer, no matter how heinous, brutal, savage, and multiple the senseless slaughters may be. They weep for John Wayne Gacy, for Ted Bundy, for Kenneth Allen McDuff, for the BTK killer, the "Son of Sam," the "night stalker," Joseph O'Dell, Dobie Gillis Williams, Robert Lee Willie, and other killers we'll read about herein who have torn the life out of their victims – and their victims' families.

When a pit bull dog attacks a human being, that animal is often shot dead on the scene or otherwise "put down" by animal control authorities. One can argue (perhaps not too strongly here and in some other cases) the Sonnier brothers – having similar animal instincts – did have more powers of reason than would a pit bull dog. But, the brothers Elmo Patrick and Eddie James Sonnier and the litany listed above also deserve to be "put down" like the mad dogs they are for their attacks on human beings.

# An Eye for an Eye
*William T. Harper*

\* \* \*

'Way back in 1951 a television pilot aired and soon evolved in a permanent slot on NBC's Thursday night lineup. They called it, "Dragnet." Remember? The lead character, Detective Sergeant Joe Friday (actor Jack Webb) had a catch-line that became part of the national jargon: "Just gimme the facts," he growled at his fictional perpetrators. Evidently, many of today's anti-death penalty activists never saw that TV show nor do they respond well when someone asks them to "just gimme the facts."

Facts to them are, all too often, misstatements or embellishments, errors of omission at best or, errors of commission at worst, flat-out lies and other distortions of the truth. The litany of some of the more egregious misstatements brought forth by death penalty apologists begins with the following tale that soon rises pretty close to the top of the all-time list of exaggerations and alabaster wishful-thinking.

By way of background, 55-year-old Joseph Roger O'Dell, accompanied by his spiritual advisor Sister Helen Prejean, was sent to his death by the State of Virginia on July 27, 1997 for "the murder, rape, and sodomy" of 44-year-old Helen Schartner who was "bludgeoned and strangled to death" on the night of February 5, 1985 in Virginia Beach, Virginia.[34] Buoyed by international appeals from Pope John Paul II, Mother Teresa and thousands of Italian citizens, after twelve years, O'Dell still lost his final appeal to the U. S. Supreme Court. It agreed with Virginia Governor George Allen who said O'Dell's guilt had been firmly established.[35]

Even after he was convicted and while his case was on appeal, "O'Dell and his [appeals] lawyers, who seem to believe anything goes in trying to keep a murderer from being executed, contacted witnesses who testified against him at trial urging them to recant their testimony and threatening legal action against them if they [did] not. (To date, no

# An Eye for an Eye
*William T. Harper*

witness has recanted.)"[36]

Still, for 112 pages in *The Death of Innocents* (54-166), Sister Prejean tries fruitlessly to prove O'Dell was innocent. The result of her effort was the same as was O'Dell's in the courtroom. "The jury convicted O'Dell of capital murder and rape; and because of a long history of convictions for crimes of violence, the jury recommended that O'Dell be sentenced to death. Joseph O'Dell," according to Virginia Commonwealth Attorney Robert J. Humphreys, "is a rapist and a murderer. This was the conclusion of the jury and it is amply supported by the trial record and O'Dell's own DNA report. He has killed before; and in my judgment, if he is ever released, he will kill again. The death penalty is reserved for the worst of the worst. This was such a case and Joseph O'Dell is such a person."[37]

These are the answers to Joseph O'Dell's guilt or innocence when you ask Mr. Humphreys to "just gimme the facts." In asking Sister Helen Prejean to "just gimme the facts" about murderer Joseph O'Dell, you get preposterous statements such as these:

"Joseph O'Dell's life and death resembles that of Jesus," she quotes an anonymous priest at O'Dell's funeral. The priest goes on to say, "both were innocent and executed by the state. Both endured humiliation, agony, and cruel suffering. But now we believe that Joseph O'Dell has joined Jesus in glory; life eternal has conquered earthly death."[38] As if canonization by the church isn't enough, we're told "the mayor of Palermo, Italy, has made Joe an honorary citizen."[39] The mayor of Palermo, Italy has made O'Dell an honorary citizen – even though he's a convicted murderer? If that is the case, what honors does the city of Palermo have for Benito Mussolini?

In this never-ending Theater of the Absurd, Sister Prejean compares lethal injection to how Algerians would handle enemies of the government. They "would gag and tie these persons hand and foot and fly them over the sea in a helicopter, split open their abdomens with a machete, and

# An Eye for an Eye
*William T. Harper*

push them into the sea."[40] Apparently the good nun forgot all about her sarcastic comment earlier regarding the antiseptic nature of today's American prison death houses where "the attendant will even swab the 'patient's' arm with alcohol before inserting the needle – *to prevent infection.*"[41] Swabbing the patient's arm with alcohol hardly compares with splitting open one's abdomen with a machete.

Sister Prejean goes on to tell us, "Surely, the reasoning goes, lethal injection is a far more 'humane' method of execution than methods practiced in times past (and not-so-past – the last four methods on the following list are current): poisoning, stoning, beheading, crucifying, burning, casting from heights onto rocks, pouring molten lead on the body, starving, sawing into pieces, burying alive, impaling, drowning, drawing and quartering, crushing with heavy weights, boiling, throwing into a pit with reptiles, giving to wild animals to be eaten alive, disemboweling, garroting (strangulation), beating to death, breaking on the wheel, stretching on the rack, flaying, hanging,* electrocuting, shooting, gassing. *The states of Washington, New Hampshire still allow hanging."[42] And the Algerians thought they had it tough.

\* \* \*

In the world of make-believe, where the abolitionists live, can be found some of the most ridiculous arguments imaginable when it comes to the death penalty. Like this one: In speaking with Faith Hathaway's parents after her brutal death at the hands of Robert Lee Willie and Joe Vaccaro (more on this case to come), the slain girl's step-father, Vernon Harvey, tells Sister Prejean "'the only way to be sure that we get rid of someone like Willie is to kill him.' Elizabeth [his wife] agrees. 'That's the only way we can be sure that he'll never kill again,' she says. 'In prison he could kill a guard or another inmate. Someone like Willie can escape from prison.'" The nun's response? "I disagree with these arguments…."[43]

# An Eye for an Eye
*William T. Harper*

How in the world can anyone this side of NeverNerverLand not agree that inmates can escape from any prison in the world – from a local one-man jail in Tucumcari, Arizona to Alcatraz, "The Rock" in San Francisco Bay? How can anyone be so blinded by their "cause" that they can't, or won't, see the obvious? The Harveys were right. Inmates kill other inmates – and sometimes prison personnel, too – on an all too frequent basis. Going back just one decade to 2002, homicide rates in local jails and state prisons average about 3.5 per 100,000. There were 2,033,022 total federal, state and local inmates in custody for that year.[44] Those figures extrapolate to approximately 70 murders per year inside the nation's prison walls, excluding federal penitentiaries where some of the most violent convicts are housed. Yet, Sister Prejean begs to disagree.

Furthermore, according to Bureau of Justice Statistics, in the reporting year (2004), 4,375 inmates have escaped or otherwise gone AWOL from state prisons and they're not all petty thieves. Witness March 12, 2005. Brian Nichols, a rapist with a rap-sheet a mile long, murdered a county judge, a court stenographer, a police officer and badly wounded another police officer in a court room in Atlanta, Georgia. Serial-killer Theodore (Ted) Bundy is somewhere in BOJ stats from years back. Three times Richard Lee McNair escaped from jail (see page 91). With more than 4,000 inmates (out of an annual inmate population that averages close to 1.5 million) a year going "over the wall," there would be at least 20,000 prisoners back on the streets in just the past five years – even though the vast majority of them are returned to incarceration. Still, Sister Prejean begs to disagree.

\* \* \*

Now that lethal injection is the dominant and most humane method of death penalty executions, abolitionists still like to hark back to the days of old with horror story after horror

# An Eye for an Eye

*William T. Harper*

story about death in the electric chair. The abolitionists are, naturally, quick to quote experts supporting their cause, such as Dr. Harold Hillman, a founding member of Amnesty International and director of the Unity Laboratory in Applied Neurology, University of Surrey, England. He "concluded that such executions are 'intensely painful' because prisoner may for some time retain consciousness."[45] What we aren't told by such tellers of tales is "the rest of the story."

Does the electric chair constitute cruel and unusual punishment? The answer depends as often as not on political motivations and legal maneuverings. However, an authoritative opinion is offered by Dr. Harold W. Kipp, who as chief medical officer at Sing Sing prison in New York state attended more than 200 executions. He observed, "The effect of electricity is instantaneous brain death. What observers see are muscle contractions, not agony."[46]

To carry on the charade of misinformation and distortion of fact abolitionists use to make their point, consider the following from *The Death of Innocents*: "A district attorney's manual surfaced in Dallas that cautioned prosecutors, 'Do not take Jews, Negroes, Dagos, Mexicans or a member of any minority race on a jury, no matter how rich or well educated.' Although dated, such blatant documentation indicates the climate of racism that existed and still persists in some places."[47]

"Upon further review," as they say in National Football League replays about a questionable decision, the district attorney's training manual quoted herein is indeed "dated," as the author concedes. The referenced manual was written in 1963. It has been revised and updated to current moral standards a number of times in the 40-plus years since the author cited it as a point of concern in the O'Dell murder trial. With that kind of convoluted logic, it could have been argued O'Dell suffered "cruel and unusual punishment" as he worried about being burned at the stake. Is there no end to the twisting of fact and distortions – if not flat-out lies – abolitionists will go to and try to make their point? Obviously not.

# An Eye for an Eye
*William T. Harper*

* * *

Our national history is replete with battle cries. "Remember the Alamo!" "Remember the Maine!" "Remember Pearl Harbor!" "54-40 or Fight!" "Tippecanoe and Tyler Too!" Though not nearly as punchy nor as brief as these historical reminders, death penalty abolitionists have their rallying cry, too. It goes like this: "From this day forward I no longer shall tinker with the machinery of death." So said Supreme Court Justice Harry A. Blackmun in his abolitionist-made-famous 1994 *Callins v. Collins* dissent.

Blackmun started out as a firm believer in capital punishment. But toward the end of his 24-year term on the highest court in the land, he wrote a dissenting opinion, saying the death penalty could no longer be constitutionally imposed.[48] Just like G. J. "Walking George" Beto, cited in the previous chapter as being firmly in agreement with the concept of the death penalty, he opposed it in practice because it was not equally administered. Blackmun's written objection was not to the death penalty in itself but to its constitutional application. Still, any extensive reading of the anti-death penalty advocates' position will almost invariably bring up Justice Blackmun's "machinery of death" quote.

What abolitionists again do not mention in *Callins v. Collins* (February 22, 1994) is the murder case upon which the justice chose to opt out. It was, according to one of Blackmun's associates, fellow Supreme Court Justice Antonin Scalia, "the murder of a man ripped by a bullet…and left to bleed to death on a tavern floor…." Continuing, Scalia rightly noted, "Justice Blackmun did not select as the vehicle for his announcement…the case of the 11-year-old girl raped by four men and then killed by stuffing her panties down her throat. How enviable a quiet death by lethal injection compared to that," Scalia concluded.[49]

In *The Death of Innocents*, Sister Prejean doesn't miss a

# An Eye for an Eye
*William T. Harper*

chance to raise the "machinery of death" banner as she almost gleefully makes note of the Justice Blackman's defection to her cause. She goes on to cite another case that led to his decision: *Coleman v. Thompson*, fully believing therein she had found the Holy Grail of death penalty abolition.

Roger Keith Coleman, the nun wrote, had "substantial evidence of innocence" and his case dragged on for years as his advocates demanded more DNA testing because "new evidence suggested the possibility that Coleman may not have been the murderer."[50] He was the cover boy for *Time* magazine in 1992 where its editors shrieked: "This Man Might be Innocent. This Man is Due to Die." He was interviewed from death row on "Larry King Live," the "Today" show, "Primetime Live," "Good Morning America," and "the Phil Donahue Show."[51]

After Coleman's defense team had "proved" him innocent and had even identified "the real killer" (with whom they eventually settled a defamation suit[52]), the abolitionists finally got what they demanded. Be careful what you ask for. Virginia Governor Mark Warner ordered a new round of DNA tests. Unfortunately for the abolitionists, the most modern DNA testing available "confirmed instead that Roger Keith Coleman was guilty when he went to the electric chair in 1992."[53] No matter how many ways the abolitionists tried to spin it in the Coleman case, the juries, the prosecutors, the courts, and even one of his most out-spoken backers were convinced beyond a reasonable doubt that Roger Keith Coleman was a sham and a scam artist and was guilty of the gruesome rape and murder of his sister-in-law as charged.

Evan so, Peter Neufeld, co-director of the New York-based anti-death penalty Innocence Project, said of the Coleman test, "Today we got just one answer, and one man cannot speak for the correctness of the verdicts in a thousand other capital cases."[54] Had the Coleman case gone the other way, you can bet your bottom dollar Mr. Neufeld and all the other death penalty opponents would have been screaming

# An Eye for an Eye

*William T. Harper*

that "one man *can* speak for the correctness of the verdicts…."

Roger Keith Coleman's story of innocence, as later admitted by his disappointed, demoralized, and staunchest allies, was as fraudulent as was Joseph Roger O'Dell's. Coleman was, his friends confirmed, an Oscar Award-deserving "actor." O'Dell may have been his understudy. The abolitionists were duped by both.

Score: Integrity, 1 – Blackmun, Coleman, O'Dell and the abolitionists, 0.

\* \* \*

It is absolutely amazing – and dismaying – to note the number of corners the death penalty abolitionists will cut, the deceptions they will resort to, the half-truths they will tell, the innuendoes they will present to try to justify their position against the death penalty. And the honest injustice of their position is they really don't care a hoot about those on death row for whom they argue. Those lives are merely pawns on their chess table. As Kevin Scudder, an Ohio death-row inmate convicted of murdering a 14-year-old girl, put it regarding the anti-death-penalty advocates, "They don't give a shit about me personally."

All they really care about is the abolition of the death penalty. It's a banner. It's a cause. It's Jean Valjean astride the barricades in Paris in *Les Miserable*. (Or maybe it's simply Sister Prejean marching forth proclaiming, "I cannot stand by silently as my government executes its citizens," which is a bit over-the-top one might say). It's Joan of Arc burning at the stake. It's terrorists in the Middle East blowing themselves up along with countless mothers with babies in their arms so they can be with 70-some virgins in the great beyond. It's Mohammed Atta crashing American Airlines Flight #11 into the North Tower of the World Trade Center on 9/11. It's that kind of fanaticism.

# An Eye for an Eye
*William T. Harper*

Another area of doubt comes from Sabine County (Michigan) District Attorney Don Burkett, who prosecuted Dobie Gillis Williams, another murderer whose cause Sister Prejean also advocates. The DA believes *The Death of Innocents*

> "'belongs on the fiction shelf of bookstores because of the many inaccuracies he says it contains.... I don't know whether she is deliberately trying to mislead the public or if she's being misled by others. But she's wrong,' Burkett said [and]...court records dispute many of Prejean's claims, specifically her assertion Williams was mentally handicapped and had a low IQ of 65. Further, Burkett bristles at Prejean's suggestion that an innocent man was executed. 'In this case, the right thing was done and the right man was convicted'." [55]

Millard Farmer, at Sister Prejean's behest, represented convicted killer Elmo Patrick Sonnier in his petitions to the Fifth Circuit Court of Appeals, the United States Supreme Court, and his clemency appeal. But Farmer too had later reservations about the nun's work. In criticizing the film *Dead Man Walking*, he said, "If I'd known that redemption was the goal, this case would've been a lot easier and I wouldn't have suffered as much – I thought we were trying to save a man's life." [56] Not surprisingly, the family of at least one victim of convicted killer Sonnier who Sister Prejean spiritually advised also has its doubts about that movie. Lloyd LeBlanc, whose son David was murdered by Sonnier (or his brother Eddie or both), watched the film three times and said, "There's very little truth in it." [57]

Also as shall be seen, so much of what is "said" by abolitionist activists – is "heard" only by the tale-tellers and many, many times there is absolutely no verification. All too often, the only thing given is the writer's interpretation of what someone *could* have said or *would* have said. Then too, there are often evasive claims that "several studies show" but

# An Eye for an Eye
*William T. Harper*

no follow up information on those studies. Unsubstantiated statements, designed solely to inflame abolitionists' passions, enroll new recruits, and humanize demons make almost any reader wish for corroboration.

For instance, convicted killer Elmo Patrick Sonnier is quoted in *Dead Man Walking* as saying, "I will go to my grave feeling bad about those kids [Loretta Bourque and David LeBlanc whom he and his brother shot to death after raping Loretta – rape being a common indignity practiced by those killers]. Every night when they dim the lights on the [prison] tier I kneel by my bunk and pray for those kids and their parents."[58] Based on some of the killer's other so-called quotes that show no such pleasant command of the English language (i.e., "…what me and Eddie done, but Eddie done it…."[59]), the reader has no way of knowing if these are the killer's real sentiments regarding "those kids" he and his brother murdered or if they are the writer's wishful thinking.

In another case in *The Death of Innocents*, the nun writes,

> "We're all sitting around a table with Dobie [Williams, one of those to whom she offered spiritual counseling] in the death house visiting room: Jean Walker, Dobie's childhood sweetheart; his mama; his aunt Royce; his brother Patrick; his four-year-old nephew, Antonio; two lawyer friends, Carol Kolinchak and Paula Montonye; and me. Dobie's mama has her Bible open and puts her hand on it, saying, 'No, not this time, either, they're not going to kill you, Dobie, because in Jesus' name I've claimed the victory, oh yes, in faith I claim the victory because God's in charge, not man, God is the lord of life and death, and in Him is the victory, and you must believe, Dobie, you must trust, as the psalm says, Oh, God, you are my rock. Do you believe, Dobie, are you trusting God to bring you through this? Do you have faith'?"

# An Eye for an Eye
*William T. Harper*

A reader has to wonder: did she take notes so she could quote this speech verbatim? Even some of the best court stenographers might miss some of that.

* * *

To illustrate again the old bromide that "figures don't lie but liars figure," the following extract from an October 20, 2000 broadcast on National Public Radio's "Morning Edition" program is presented:

> Under the title, *A Broken System*, the study looked at more than 4,500 death penalty cases from 1973 to 1995, the most exhaustive survey ever. The primary author is Columbia law professor Sir James Liebman, a nationally-known *habeas corpus* scholar who has defended at least 10 death penalty cases himself. The study looked at state and federal court records and found serious, reversible error, which required re-trials in 68% of death penalty cases. The mistakes included faulty jury instructions, prosecutors hiding evidence, and incompetent defense lawyers.

Do the abolitionists say anything...we can believe?

Barry Latzer, a professor of criminal justice at the renowned John Jay College of Criminal Justice in New York, counters. "Liebman failed to take into account the difference between reversing a conviction of murder and reversing a death sentence," said Latzer. "And this is a very serious shortcoming because if an appeals courts were to reverse a death sentence alone and leave the underlying murder conviction intact, that would mean, of course, that the defendant is still culpable, he's still guilty of murder."[60]

Another disputing Liebman's study was the Office of the Attorney General of the State of Nevada. In a Response

# An Eye for an Eye
*William T. Harper*

to Professor Liebman, then Nevada Attorney General Frankie Sue Del Papa charged among other things that Liebman – at least as far as his study regarded the Silver State – "picked and chose his cases, tailoring the study to get certain results." Furthermore, in her "Response to Prof. Liebman," the AG charged, "Liebman creates the impression that the reversals are due to innocence, but most are attorney or judge procedural errors. Some are cases where juries followed the existing law, but later the Supreme Court changed it, and constitutional changes are applied retroactively on death cases, to give the defendant every benefit."[61]

The attorney general's scathing rebuttal revealed that "Liebman took only a 2-year 'snapshot' of federal *habeas*, found that four Nevada cases were reviewed and two of those were reversed. From that, Liebman concluded that Nevada has a 50% overall error rate for all years. We researched all reported Nevada federal *habeas* cases for the whole period. We found 17 federal decisions with four reversals. That is only a 23% error rate. Again, Liebman failed to report that two of those four defendants received new death sentences upon re-sentencing.

"The ACLU's claims," Del Papa continued, "of 'gross patterns of [racial] discrimination in death penalty administration,' aren't true for Nevada either. They said death was disproportionately given to non-white killers of white victims, and men instead of women. However, of the 50 men executed here since 1905, 42 were white; four were native American; two were black; and two were Asian...."[62]

Florida's then-deputy general counsel to the state's governor also takes issue with the Liebman report. More than that, Reg Brown emphatically disputes it. "We found," he said on the "Morning Edition" radio program, "that in 64 of the 64 Florida post-conviction cases that he cites in the study, the convicted individual was never exonerated in a single one of those cases." Again, the Liebman study appears to be another of those Big Lies where death penalty abolitionists

# An Eye for an Eye
*William T. Harper*

falsely imply inmates "released" from death row have been "exonerated."[63]

When capital punishment was declared "cruel and unusual punishment" by the U.S. Supreme Court on June 29, 1972, there were 45 men on death row in Texas and seven in county jails with a death sentence. All of the sentences were commuted to life sentences by the Governor of Texas, Preston Smith, and death row was clear by March 1973. Death penalty abolitionists would contend that these 52 convicted killers were exonerated because their death sentences were commuted.[64]

What is really sad about these "studies" is how quickly they find themselves in the main stream of public – and more sadly – political-legislative thinking and action. On June 20, 2000 in a capital punishment hearing before the United States House of Representatives subcommittee of the Judiciary Committee chaired by 20-year (1983-2003) Representative George W. Gekas (R-PA), the discredited Liebman report was presented – just eight days after its initial release – by Representative Robert C. Scott (D-VA) again as "the gospel" and without question and, one would imagine, not too much thoughtful analysis.[65] It doesn't take a lot of imagination to guess how that erroneous study found its way into Congressman Scott's prepared remarks.

And finally, a refutation of the Liebman study comes via a draft of a 2007 study commissioned by the U. S. Department of Justice that definitively shows "death-sentence appeals take too long, traumatize victims' families and burden states with millions in extra costs for housing convicted killers. The study also found death penalty cases are not hopelessly flawed by errors, as opponents of capital punishment have charged."[66]

The study, by above-noted Professor Latzer and his John Jay College of Criminal Justice colleague, Associate Professor James Cauthen, reviewed state death sentences issued in the 1990s and it challenges death penalty foe Liebman's above 2000 report that concluded the capital

# An Eye for an Eye
*William T. Harper*

punishment system is "broken" because 68% of all death penalty cases from 1973 to 1995 were eventually overturned. Liebman's report, said the Latzer/Cauthan study, "provided a false picture of the death penalty because it included many cases from the 1970s and 1980s, when the U.S. Supreme Court rewrote death penalty rules and caused many sentences to be reversed." The Latzer/Cauthen report tracked 1,676 death sentences issued in 14 "representative" states from 1992 through 2002.

The report further found that on direct appeal (the first stage in the three-part capital appeals process) the reversal rate was 26.3%. Liebman found a rate of 41.2% in the same stage. That is a major difference, and it significantly undercuts Liebman's overall (all three stages) finding of a 68% reversal rate.[67]

Yet another debunker of the Liebman report was Paul G. Cassell, then a law professor at the University of Utah. He wrote:

> "The 68% factoid, however, is quite deceptive. For starters, it has nothing to do with 'wrong man' mistakes -- that is, cases in which an innocent person is convicted for a murder he did not commit. Indeed, missing from the media coverage was the most critical statistic: After reviewing 23 years of capital sentences, the study's authors (like other researchers) were unable to find a single case in which an innocent person was executed. Thus, the most important error rate -- the rate of mistaken executions -- is zero.
>
> "What, then," Professor Cassell questioned, "does the 68% 'error rate' mean? It turns out to include any reversal of a capital sentence at any stage by appellate courts -- even if those courts ultimately uphold the capital sentence. If an appellate court asks for additional findings from the trial court, the trial court complies, and the appellate court then

# An Eye for an Eye

*William T. Harper*

affirms the capital sentence, the report finds not extraordinary due process but a mistake. Under such curious scorekeeping, the report can list 64 Florida post conviction cases as involving 'serious errors,' even though more than one-third of these cases ultimately resulted in a re-imposed death sentence, and in not one of the Florida cases did a court ultimately overturn the murder conviction."[68]

\* \* \*

One might think after this barrage of rebuttals, Sir James Liebman would have "put up or shut up." He did neither. And the ever-obliging Public Broadcasting System was right there promoting his flimsy claims in another "PBS Reports" segment aired on March 24, 2012.[69] The teller of tall tales lures in the audience by proclaiming – with all the attendant drama – this in its on-screen headline:

The "Carlos DeLuna Case [is] the Fight to Prove an Innocent Man Was Executed."

Opening himself wide to another round of judicial ridicule, the Columbia Law School professor James Liebman, was interviewed and attempted to make the case for Carlos DeLuna. Liebman insists DeLuna was innocent of the murder of a gasoline station clerk, 24-year-old mother Wanda Lopez, in Corpus Christi, Texas on February 4, 1983. Within 40 minutes of her fatal screams and her begging for her life heard during her frantic 9-1-1 call, local police picked up DeLuna and he was charged with Ms. Lopez' murder – based on multiple eye-witness accounts of the onslaught at or near the crime scene.

DeLuna claimed his innocence until the day he died by lethal injection on December 7, 1989. And the good Columbia professor wraps his <u>entire defense</u> of DeLuna in the PBS interview around the fact that no blood from the gory scene was ever found on DeLuna or his clothing. Is it not possible that DeLuna, knowing that if he was picked up

# An Eye for an Eye
*William T. Harper*

and because of his previous criminal record – attempted rape, auto theft, burglary – he was a dead duck and that he might have raced home, showered off any blood residue and that he just might have disposed of any clothing that would incriminate him?

Liebman goes on to support Carlos DeLuna's claim that another neighborhood Carlos (Hernandez) was later boasting throughout the ghetto that he committed the crime. Taking that charge for gospel, did Liebman and his team of university law students never hear of the multiple cases where the "macho man" gets satisfaction by telling tall tales about crimes he's adopted from others to make himself look tough?

Even worse than the PBS blaring headline about "the Fight to Prove an Innocent Man was Executed," another of the media's "screamin' Meemies," the paragon of objectivity in reporting – the *Huffington Post* – even went so far in a May 16, 2012 article to falsely proclaim, "Liebman and his team of students *have proven* [emphasis added] Texas gave a lethal injection to the wrong man."[70]

The *Huffington Post* and Professor Liebman go on and on with their nebulous theses, despite the blistering disclaimers of his veracity in the professor's work by – to name a few:

> Barry Latzer, Professor of criminal justice, John Jay College of Criminal Justice in New York,
> James Cauthen, Associate Professor, John Jay College of Criminal Justice,
> Frankie Sue Del Papa, Nevada Attorney General,
> Reg Brown, Florida deputy general counsel to the governor,
> Paul G. Cassell, law professor, University of Utah.
> and the United States House of Representatives subcommittee of the Judiciary Committee,
> plus the U. S. Department of Justice,

\* \* \*

# An Eye for an Eye

*William T. Harper*

Death penalty supporters say the study shows delays are part of a strategy to undermine a sentence most Americans support. "Opponents of the death penalty can't get an outright repeal anywhere, but are working to impede the process by slowing it down to a crawl," says John McAdams, political science professor at Marquette University in Milwaukee.[71]

There is, apparently, no level too low for abolitionists to stoop to as they try fraudulently to make their case. For instance, *The Death of Innocents* makes the following statement replete with its false implications:

> "Not surprisingly, Dobie [Williams] and Joseph [O'Dell] were indigent. It's also no surprise their defenses at trial were abysmal. In fact, Joseph O'Dell defended himself."[72]

The implication here is because he was indigent, therefore his defense was abysmal, ergo O'Dell had to defend himself. The fact of the matter is O'Dell "adamantly resisted the attorney appointed to defend him by the court and insisted on providing his own defense at trial...."[73] With a cascade of further editorial tears, a reader is further led to believe the poor, unfortunate "O'Dell wouldn't know how to raise a formal objection or cross-examine a witness or put forward a properly phrased motion."[74]

These latest sympathy-inducing assertions were adamantly refuted in O'Dell's appeal before the Fifth Circuit Court Coourt of Appeals, which wrote:

> "If there was any problem in the attorney-client relationship, it was likely caused by O'Dell. As the federal *habeas* court concluded, 'O'Dell's distrust of [his court-appointed attorney] was not based on objective facts; it was based on pure speculation.' And, an independent and thorough examination of

# An Eye for an Eye
*William T. Harper*

the record reveals O'Dell, who was 'very intelligent,' had a college equivalency education, and 'exhibit[ed] tremendous [courtroom] skills,' defended himself far more ably than many practicing attorneys could have done."[75]

Do the abolitionists say anything we can believe?

\* \* \*

Speaking of court rooms, abolitionists constantly decry findings of the Fourth Circuit Court of Appeals for the United States (responsible for Maryland, Virginia, West Virginia, North and South Carolina) and the Fifth Circuit Courts of Appeals for the United States (responsible for Texas, Louisiana, and Mississippi). We are bombarded with vitriolic comments such as:

> "The courts of America are corrupt."
> "...the prosecution has the highest federal appeals court in its back pocket."
> "This court always sides with the prosecution...."
> "I [should not] expect fairness from the Fourth Circuit Court of Appeals or any such court in the southern death penalty belt."

Naturally of course, death penalty abolitionists fail to tell us "the rest of the story." You probably will not, for instance, find any mention anywhere as they make their damning, blanket accusations about unfair courts, of the notorious California Supreme Court under Chief Justice Rose Bird. During the years 1979 to 1986, it reversed 64 out of 68 death penalty cases on appeal.[76] It is beyond credulity that death penalty cases can be reversed in 94 percent of such cases based on merit alone. At least that is what many California voters felt when they voted Bird and two of her

# An Eye for an Eye

*William T. Harper*

like-minded justices out of office in 1986. The Golden State voters obviously agreed with a comment made by U.S. Supreme Court Justice Antonin Scalia when he said judges take "an oath to apply [the] laws, and [have] been given no power to supplant them with rules of [their] own.[77]

In another case of judicial implementation versus judicial application, the New York Court of Appeals blocked the death penalty by striking down a small part of the statute – the part dealing with instructions to the jury – and then declaring that entire statute was unenforceable until amended.[78] The dissenters called the majority position "astonishing," and said:

> "The majority's holding contradicts the view of the United States Supreme Court, and is supported by no precedent in this or any other jurisdiction. We perceive no basis for it except the majority's refusal to countenance any procedure in a capital case other than the procedure thought least likely to produce a death sentence."[79]

\* \* \*

There apparently is no end to the deceptions death penalty opponents foist upon the public in their undisguised zeal to save their "projects" from the penalties they deserve. Again, take the case of Joseph Roger O'Dell. In *The Death of Innocents*, Sister Prejean goes to extreme lengths full of maybes, what-ifs, perhapses and other nebulous arguments to present O'Dell as a poor, misguided youth, an innocent babe in the woods who ran afoul of the law due to pressures of poverty and physical and sexual abuse during his formative years.

As noted herein, Joseph Roger O'Dell III was tried, convicted and sentenced to death for the February 5, 1985 murder of Helen Schartner. A trial jury heard his case – in which O'Dell determined he was best qualified to act as his own defense attorney – and convicted him. An appeals court

# An Eye for an Eye
*William T. Harper*

heard his case and denied his appeal. Federal District Court Judge James R. Spencer did move it on to the Virginia Supreme Court which "refused to review" O'Dell's claims. The United States Court of Appeals for the Fourth Circuit heard O'Dell's petition to overrule and denied it. The United States Supreme Court listened to his arguments and its "decision not to hear O'Dell's case was unanimous."[80] That's six separate and distinct trials and hearings – all with the same opinion: O'Dell was guilty as charged.

But all these good men and women were, in the abolitionists' view, simply wrong. Of course, Sister Prejean had a spiritual interest in O'Dell. Lori Urs, who brought O'Dell's case to the nun's attention while she was "separated from her husband [who] had built her a million-dollar home [which] wasn't enough and she was tired of her social life," had a romantic interest in O'Dell.[81] Barry Scheck, DNA expert of the O. J. Simpson trial fame, joined O'Dell's team. Their one unifying interest was not, it seems, Joseph Roger O'Dell's guilt or innocence. Apparently, it was then and still is plain, pure and simply: the abolition of the death penalty for even those proved guilty of terrible crimes.

The abolitionists knew "surely any court with integrity" and "surely any court that was fair" [what, one may ask, does this say about any of those previous courts that heard the evidence?] would agree with their enumeration of their spurious claims of O'Dell's innocence, such as:

1. the witnesses who proved the victim's body had been put into the field later than 1:00 a.m.,

2. the witnesses who could verify that the victim had a room in the Executive Inn,

3. the witnesses who had seen the victim arguing with her boyfriend,

# An Eye for an Eye
*William T. Harper*

4. that finding blood that was "consistent with" did not mean a "match,"

5. a jailhouse informer's [Steven Watson's] testimony was untrustworthy, and

6. that O'Dell was no match for impassioned state prosecutors like [Albert] Alberi and [Stephen G.] Test.[82]

The United States Court Of Appeals for the Fourth Circuit – surely "a court with integrity" and "surely [one] that was fair" – heard all these claims on December 5, 1995. After due deliberation, on September 10, 1996, the Court ruled:

"The judgment of the district court [i.e., Judge Spencer – see above] granting the petitioner's writ of *habeas corpus* is reversed, and the case is remanded with instructions to reinstate the death penalty."[83]

At the December 5, 1995 hearing for this case, the court listened not to the indigent O'Dell who so "cogently and clearly" wrote about his original case; this time it heard from a defendants' advocacy organization and high-powered suits and skirts from big-time law firms, such as:

Robert S. Smith and Jeffrey M. Eilender (of Paul, Weiss, Rifkind, Wharton & Garrison, New York, New York) Patricia M. Schwarzschild (of Hunton & Williams, Richmond, Virginia) and Michele J. Brace, Donald Lee (of Virginia Capital Representation Resource Center, Richmond, Virginia).[84]

Does all this high-priced talent sound like the oft-heard and tear-stained claim that O'Dell and other "poor people don't have resources to make the justice system work for them…."

Every claim made by the patent-leather crowd was dismissed. "We do not believe," said J. Michael Luttig, U.S. Fourth Circuit Court of Appeals judge, in writing the opinion, "that O'Dell has come even close" to meeting the standards

# An Eye for an Eye
*William T. Harper*

required to make his case. The court bluntly faulted the O'Dell team's contention of, among others, the following:

> 1. How he came to be covered in blood shortly before his apprehension (first he said he vomited all over himself and then he claimed he was in a fight).
> 2. Tire tracks found at the murder scene were not from his truck (the Commonwealth's expert witness in this field said he examined patterns for some two thousand different tires and four or five thousand different design units, and he could not find a single tire, other than O'Dell's, that matched tire tracks found at the scene).
> 3. The testimony from fellow inmate Steve Watson was "untrustworthy" (Watson testified O'Dell confessed to him while in jail that he murdered Helen Schartner after he had picked her up in a bar, "tried to 'get a little' from her and when she refused to 'give it up,' [he] strangled her and dumped her body." It was rejected because "O'Dell was unable to prove a plea agreement existed between Watson and the Commonwealth.")
> 4. O'Dell's team's charge that Watson told his version of the murder in an effort to plea bargain and get lesser sentences for him and his wife on unrelated charges.[85]

It is interesting to note that later the above-mentioned "Lori Urs persuaded inmate Watson to recant and local media had made his recantation public. But when he was threatened with imprisonment for perjury, Watson recanted his recantation."[86] So this obvious liar admits he was lying but when his lies were anti-O'Dell, the defense charged that that liar was "untrustworthy." But, when Watson later recanted his recantation, the defense praised his actions and never mentioned his "untrustworthiness."

# An Eye for an Eye

*William T. Harper*

The court's conclusion in this matter was:

"When viewing all of this evidence – being together at the County Line Lounge, leaving within fifteen minutes of each other, being covered with blood, planning to go suddenly to Florida, having inconsistent alibis, plus the wounds matching his gun, the tracks matching his tires, the hairs, the semen, the spermatozoa, the blood enzymes, the blood DNA on the jacket, the confession, and the nearly identical earlier crime [see below] – we do not believe it can even remotely be claimed that O'Dell has established that it is more likely than not that *no* reasonable juror would have convicted him."[87]

Also, an interesting – and sometimes amusing – facet of the anti-death penalty argument is the way abolitionists constantly bellow like a bull elephant in the jungles of Africa when DNA testing doesn't go their way.[88] But when it favors their "cause," it's acclaimed as the greatest invention since some caveman rounded off a stone and turned it into a wheel. For instance, most of the above defense re-hash of the O'Dell trial excoriates the DNA testing done at that time. But on the other hand, Sister Prejean cries, "the prosecutor did not test [a crime-scene] cigarette for fingerprints [nor did it] conduct a saliva test on [the cigarette]." Obviously, death penalty abolitionists want it both ways: when the State does a DNA test, abolitionists call it unreliable; when it doesn't do a DNA test, it's unjustifiable. Damned if you do. Damned if you don't.

With all the talk about faulty DNA testing, readers of *The Death of Innocents* weren't told "the rest of the story." As noted, O'Dell did ask for and was granted new DNA testing based on new methods then available. O'Dell was even allowed by the Court to select a laboratory of his choosing, in this case, LifeCodes. O'Dell declared "LifeCodes has an

# An Eye for an Eye

*William T. Harper*

impeccable reputation and is used by police departments and prosecution offices all over America..." As a result of O'Dell's request, virtually all evidence was released to LifeCodes for further DNA testing. Results of that testing were disclosed to O'Dell's counsel on August 21, 1990. Notwithstanding the fact that LifeCodes found the blood on the blue jacket matched that of Helen Schartner, O'Dell's counsel consciously chose to suppress that report. Robert S. Smith, O'Dell's attorney, admitted this on June 12, 1997....[89]

Nearly three years after LifeCodes' report was placed in their hands, O'Dell's counsel finally revealed the full report to the Attorney General of Virginia. Having touted LifeCodes as one of the finest DNA laboratories in the country, O'Dell's counsel then reversed their course and proceeded to attack LifeCodes' findings of a DNA match between Helen Schartner's blood and blood stains on O'Dell's jacket! Fortunately neither the United States Fourth Circuit Court of Appeals nor the United States Supreme Court were fooled by this duplicity.[90]

\* \* \*

Wanting it both ways is common in abolitionists' arguments against the death penalty. They constantly wail about prosecutors using "jailhouse snitches" to secure convictions – saying the snitch lies and makes deals to get favorable treatment in the prisons or in the courts. But poster boy O'Dell inadvertently defuses that argument when he says, "Each time [Watson, the snitch who testified against him] gets into trouble, I am told that he calls the prosecutors and threatens to expose what they did to me if they don't help him."[91] It is hard to imagine prosecutors would expose themselves to that kind of career-ending (if not criminal) blackmail.

The susceptible sister goes on to paint the usual picture of a convicted murderer who is merely a victim of society. Writing on page 89 of *The Death of Innocents*, she

# An Eye for an Eye
*William T. Harper*

presents the following (synopsized) page-long paragraph of O'Dell's trials and tribulations and how, as usual, "the devil made him do it:"

> "...At thirteen, he had been arrested in four states. At nineteen, he was convicted of car theft. At twenty-five, he had fourteen felonies on his record. He was sent to the 'brick yard,' the place for incorrigibles. When a homosexual with a knife tried to assault him, he had fought back and killed the attacker. He was indicted for second-degree murder. When another convict lied in court in order to make parole [sound familiar?], the jury believed the convict, and twenty more years were added to O'Dell's twenty-four-year sentence."

Joseph O'Dell's 30 years of criminal activity is passed off as merely store robberies, car theft, and an innocent-by-reason-of-"self-defense" murder. It also almost seems the good nun approves of O'Dell when he "fought back and killed the attacker," the homosexual. No castigation there about "thou shalt not kill." The store robberies are passed off much like a teenager who swipes a cosmetics package from a drug store to give to his impoverished mother as a Christmas gift. The car theft seems like a gang of junior high school kids out on a Halloween prank. And the inmate prison murder is, naturally, a "heroic" self-defense. No wonder we "feel sorry" for poor Joseph O'Dell. Isn't that what we're all supposed to feel?

But wait a minute. What do the abolitionists say that we *can* believe? O'Dell's unvarnished lawlessness is presented in one of his hearings before the United States Court of Appeals for the Fourth Circuit:

> "O'Dell, born in 1941, began his criminal career at age 13 with a juvenile conviction for breaking and entering, followed by five convictions over the next

# An Eye for an Eye
*William T. Harper*

three years for auto theft. By 1958, O'Dell had turned violent. In that year, he was convicted of assault three times and of threatening bodily harm once. The following year, he was convicted of attempted escape from prison. After being released from the penitentiary, he returned five months later when his probation was revoked. He was then convicted of five armed robberies and five unauthorized uses of motor vehicles and sentenced to 24 years in prison. While imprisoned, O'Dell was convicted of second degree murder...."

This is a bit different from that innocent little schoolboy described in *The Death of Innocents*. It was yet another murder, the one that brought O'Dell to the attention of the abolitionists in the first place: the brutal slaying of Helen Schartner. The Fourth Circuit Court's opinion described that murder this way:

"...Schartner had been killed by manual strangulation, with a force sufficient to break bones in her neck and leave finger imprints. She also had eight separate wounds on her head consistent with blows from the barrel of a handgun. About 10 days earlier, a handgun with a barrel that could cause wounds like those found on Schartner's head had been seen in O'Dell's car. Seminal fluid was found in Schartner's vagina and anus. Enzyme tests on that fluid revealed that it was consistent with a mixture of O'Dell's and Schartner's bodily fluids. Spermatozoa also found in Schartner's genital swabs and genital scrapings were consistent with O'Dell's."

Sister Prejean spends 112 pages trying to convince all that Joseph Roger O'Dell, III was a poor, innocent man who died at the hands of the State. To the contrary,

# An Eye for an Eye
*William T. Harper*

"…both the federal district court and now the full *en banc* court have painstakingly canvassed the record, carefully considering every claim that has been advanced by petitioner. Having done so, we are convinced that O'Dell's claims are without merit and his claim of actual innocence not even colorable [plausible]."[92]

The futility of the abolitionists' spirited defense of O'Dell doesn't end with the above opinion. What his defense never mentioned was the incidental (?) fact that O'Dell went to Florida in July of 1974 "and was promptly convicted of kidnapping and robbery, committed just seven months after his release from prison. The victim in that case testified that O'Dell had struck her several times on the head with his gun, choked her, and held a cocked gun to her head in an attempt to force her to submit to sexual advances."[93] Just 14 months later, Helen Schartner was murdered under similar circumstances.

* * *

It is a tragedy that abolitionists will go to any length to present their deceptions, which are later presented as facts by those who knowingly or unknowingly assume them to be the truth. The following account (regarding inmate James Adams who is also referred to in Chapter One is presented verbatim from page 220 of *Dead Man Walking*:

In the last twenty years at least forty-six people have been released from death row because the errors in their convictions were found in time to save their lives.

Some are not so lucky.
James Adams, for example, executed in Florida in 1984.

# An Eye for an Eye
*William T. Harper*

*In 1974 Adams, a black man, was convicted of first degree murder and sentenced to death. Witnesses located Adams' car at the time of the crime at the home of the victim, a white rancher. Some of the victim's jewelry was found in the car trunk. Adams maintained his innocence, claiming that he had loaned the car to his girlfriend. A witness identified Adams as driving the car away from the victim's home shortly after the crime. This witness, however was driving a large truck in the direction opposite to that of Adams' car, and probably could not have had a good look at the driver. It was later discovered that this witness was angry with Adams for allegedly dating his wife. A second witness heard a voice inside the victim's home at the time of the crime and saw someone fleeing.*

*He stated this voice was a woman's; the day after the crime he stated that the fleeing person was positively not Adams. More importantly, a hair sample found clutched in the victim's hand, which in all likelihood had come from the assailant, did not match Adams' hair. Much of this exculpatory information was not discovered until the case was examined by a skilled investigator a month before Adams' execution. Governor Bob Graham, however, refused to grant even a short stay so that these questions could be resolved.*

All the above is enough to make one want to get out and parade up and down in front of any prison death house in the nation and beg to save the life of James Adams. Is there anything the abolitionists say…that we can believe? Put your placards back in storage. Save your shoe leather. It is the "rest of the story" that shows just how misleading abolitionists are as they, in this case and so many others, resort to disreputable journalism to prove their point no matter how dishonest they have to be to do so.

The *facts* in James Adams' case show:

- the above-mentioned hair from the victim (Edgar Brown, not even worthy of having his name

# An Eye for an Eye
*William T. Harper*

mentioned in *Dead Man Walking*) "was *not* in the victim's hand; [i]t was a remnant of a sweeping of the ambulance and so could have come from another source;"

- that a witness who "heard a voice inside the victim's home at the time of the crime" testified the "voice was a woman's." The witness's actual testimony was the voice…"sounded 'kind of like a woman's voice, kind of like strangling or something'."
- "[Also] that upon arrest on the afternoon of the murder Adams was found with some $200 in his pocket – one bill of which 'was stained with type O blood. When Adams was asked about the blood on the money, he said that it came from a cut on his finger. His blood was type AB, however, while the victim's was type O.
- Among the other unmentioned, incriminating details: that the victim's eyeglasses were found in Adams' car along with jewelry belonging to the victim, along with clothing of Adams' stained with type O blood. This is just a sample of the evidence arrayed against this 'innocent'."[94]

One might recommend the abolitionists do as Sergeant Friday (a.k.a. Jack Webb) would: "Just give us the facts, Ma'am." Maybe then they'd get the stories right. But again, that premise is predicated on an idea death penalty abolitionists long ago abandoned: the truth matters.

Do the abolitionists say anything…we can believe?

\* \* \*

# An Eye for an Eye
*William T. Harper*

# An Eye for an Eye
*William T. Harper*

## Chapter Three

### If They're Interred...They're Deterred

*Kenneth Allen McDuff was labeled the "Bad Boy from Rosebud" (his hometown in Texas) in a book with that title by Lone Star State author, teacher and historian Gary Lavergne. If you haven't heard about him, the surviving family members of at least six young women and two boys have. After killing those two boys and one girl in 1966, McDuff was captured, tried and convicted. He was sentenced to die in a Texas electric chair.*

### Kenneth Allen McDuff

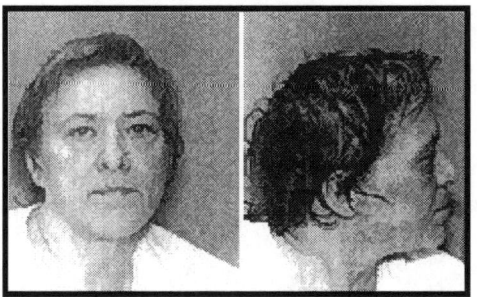

*"Killing a woman's like killing a chicken. They both squawk," McDuff chortled in a CRI report.* [95]

Here's a little more about Kenneth Allen McDuff – who, if the abolitionists had their way, would have never sat in an electric chair. They would have given him their Plan B, their fall-back position: Life-Without-Parole. That's even though, according to a Criminology Research Institute report that corroborates Lavergne's reporting: "(McDuff) didn't just kill his victims; he savaged them in unspeakable ways. He raped them with sadism that made veteran cops cringe. This killer blew off their faces at point-blank range. He slashed and stabbed

# An Eye for an Eye
*William T. Harper*

*with knives, and bludgeoned with clubs and crushed one victim's neck with a broomstick.*

\* \* \*

But, with a perverse denial of justice-deserved that surely would have pleased those in the death penalty abolitionist movement, Lavergne reports:

> "In October of 1989, in a twist of history many in all of Texas and throughout the nation still cannot believe, the State of Texas set Kenneth Allen McDuff, the 'Broomstick Murderer,' free. It was not," the author continued, "just some incredible ruling by an activist, bleeding-heart judge. No trial error dismissed his case. No suspicious California or New York conspiracy set him free. He was *paroled* – by Texans!"[96]

Author Lavergne tabbed McDuff "the poster boy of capital punishment." Indeed, "the Bad Boy" deserved that sobriquet for horror. In his book, Lavergne cites eight known victims of that vicious killer. Others have estimated the count at about 15 murders in all. Here's what happened to the first three according to a sworn statement dated August 8, 1966 by Roy Dale Green, an accomplice in the murders of 18-year-old Robert Brand, his cousin, 16-year-old Mark Dunman, and Robert's girlfriend, vivacious 16-year-old Edna Louise Sullivan.

Green confessed that he and McDuff were cruising two days earlier and spotted a car with three kids parked on a gravel road. Pulling out an ever-present pistol, McDuff "told the kids in the car to get out…and he put them in the trunk of their car." After driving both cars to an empty field, Green said McDuff "told me to put [the girl] in the trunk of his car." McDuff then told Green he didn't want any witnesses and "I'm gonna have to knock [the two boys] off…."

# An Eye for an Eye

*William T. Harper*

Brand and Dunman "were on their knees, begging him not to shoot them. They said, 'We're not going to tell anybody'." Green said McDuff "stuck the gun into the trunk where the boys were and started shooting…. He shot one twice in the head, and he shot the other boy four times in the head." Green's statement continues: "[McDuff] got the girl out of the trunk and put her in the back seat…. He took off his clothes and then he [raped] her. He asked me if I wanted to do it…and I thought he would shoot me if I didn't so I [raped] the girl…. After that, he [raped] her several times."

"[McDuff] made her sit down on the gravel road, and he took about a three-foot piece of broomstick from his car and forced her head back with it until it was on the ground. He started choking her with the piece of broomstick. He mashed down hard, and she started waving her arms and kicking her legs….When she stopped struggling, he had me grab her hands and he grabbed her feet and we heaved her over a fence where he choked her some more." [97]

For that, McDuff received his first death sentence, one of the 558 negated by the Supreme Court's nullification of capital punishment in *Furman v. Georgia* in 1972 – which ultimately, and some say, mysteriously – led to McDuff's parole. Some others say "his mother bribed a parole board official to rubber-stamp Ken's release to murder again…and the State parole system was rife with bad judgment and the potential for corruption…." [98]

According to Lavergne, "the stars were aligned" to free McDuff not only from death row, but from the penitentiary itself. The *Furman v. Georgia* decision was followed by the efforts of the crusading, zealous federal judge William Wayne Justice in Texas who set out to revamp the state's entire Department of Corrections, then led by its Director, W. J. (Jim) Estelle, Jr.

Career criminal David Ruiz' complaints against prison conditions (i.e., *Ruiz v. Estelle*, 1978), resulted in an almost total dismantling of the state's prison system. Ruiz claimed prison management to be "cruel and unusual." Tragically, the

# An Eye for an Eye
*William T. Harper*

state at the time would not spend money to build more prisons and the ensuing over-crowding charges against Texas' prisons opened the front doors for thousands of inmates – including McDuff who was paroled after serving 21 years of his replacement life sentence.

Kenneth Allen McDuff then went out and killed at least five more helpless victims. Had McDuff been executed for his first three murders, he would have been "deterred" from committing his next five or more. Once again, the McDuff tragedy proves, unfortunately, the doors to death row are sometimes revolving, especially when abolitionists are providing "the spin."

Within two years of that 1989 parole, McDuff murdered Brenda Thompson on October 10, 1991, Regina Moore on October 15, 1991, and Colleen Reed on December 29, 1991. Two more of his victims – Valencia Joshua and Melissa Northrup (who was pregnant with her third child) – also were brutally murdered on dates still undetermined.

Kenneth Allen McDuff, and dozens if not hundreds just like him – brutal, vicious, barbaric, unrepentant killers for whom there is absolutely no doubt of their guilt – according to abolitionists, should be spared the death penalty and be sentenced to Life-Without-Parole. There, the anti-death penalty lobby contends, society will be protected from these murderers. McDuff was sentenced to *death* in prison. Yet, at least five more young women paid with their lives because he was not executed the first time.

Thanks to abolitionists' efforts in the Supreme Court's *Furman v. Georgia* decision, the state of Texas could not do what it was supposed to do the first time it had its chance. Kenneth McDuff – believed to be the only inmate ever sentenced to *two* death penalties – was finally executed by lethal injection at the state penitentiary in Huntsville, Texas, on November 17, 1998 – more than 32 years after the first of his many vicious murders.

Sister Prejean and her followers weep and wail before impressionable college audiences, at lavish Hollywood galas

# An Eye for an Eye

*William T. Harper*

and Oscar Award-winners' cocktail parties, before innumerable legislative committees, and on public media about the so-called *Death of Innocents* – such as convicted murderers Dobie Gillis Williams and Joseph Roger O'Dell. Perhaps the weepers and wailers ought to give a modicum of thought to the death of the *real innocents*:

Louise Sullivan, Robert Brand, and Marcus Dunnan were innocents who met up with Kenneth Allen McDuff. As were Brenda Thompson, Regina Moore, Colleen Reed, Valencia Joshua and Melissa Northrup (with her unborn baby). Others that we'll read more about later herein, such as Faith Hathaway, Dennis Hemby, Loretta Bourque, David LeBlanc, Sergeant Louis Wagner III, Sonja Knippers, and Helen Schartner – are those who will never get a reprieve nor a pardon from their death sentences. They are the *real innocents*, the real victims of these crimes and these criminals for whom abolitionists try so hard to garner world-wide sympathy, and reprieve. Unfortunately, life sentences – be they with or without parole – or any other sentence short of the ultimate deterrent, an enacted death sentence – can be commuted, as the McDuff tragedy and others forthcoming here regrettably prove.

\* \* \*

Who says the death penalty isn't a deterrent? The abolitionists do. Their cabal crows from roof-tops like Kansas roosters at sunrise – cock-a-doodling that capital punishment is not a deterrent. Trying to overwhelm us with so-called "facts" and figures, they claim the "evidence that executions do not deter crime is conclusive." They constantly offer bogus and meaningless arguments about murder rates in death penalty states vs. those without it. For instance, they tell us "the homicide rates in Wisconsin and Iowa (non-death penalty states) were half those of then-death penalty-state Illinois between 1990 and 1994." Is that so hard to believe when you compare Keokuk, Iowa to Chicago, Illinois? They cite other

# An Eye for an Eye
*William T. Harper*

"studies" (usually undefined and un-authenticated) to "prove" the elimination of the death penalty does not lead to an increase in murders. They can prove almost anything they want with the right manipulation of the numbers. But one thing they can't disprove. The *applied* death penalty DOES deter murderers.

Yes, we all know those old adages about "lies, damned lies, and statistics" and "statistics don't lie but statisticians do." For instance, when arguing against the death penalty, dissenters frequently cite statistics such as "...58 percent of murder victims are killed by either relatives or acquaintances." They imply almost six of every 10 murders are committed in a momentary fit of rage or passion and society should be more forgiving of these transgressions. But what their statistics fail to tell us (by omission or commission) is "...this so-called 'acquaintance murder' number also includes vicious gang members killing other gang members, drug buyers killing drug pushers, prostitutes and their pimps and their regular clients, and so on. 'Acquaintance' covers a wide range of relationships. The vast majority of murders are not committed by previously law-abiding citizens. Ninety percent of adult murderers have had criminal records as adults."[99]

The abolitionists bombard us with claims that the vast majority of murders are committed "in a fit of passion," such as husband-wife killings and the battered spouse syndrome. Stephen Trattner of Mequon, Wisconsin confessed to killing his wife, Sin Lam Trattner, in January of 2006 "because she pushed him to the breaking point by continually asking for a divorce." He told police "his wife again asked for a divorce Wednesday night, so he slammed her down and banged her head on the floor 10 to 20 times and pummeled her in the face....(Then) he placed his hands around her throat until she stopped moving."[100] Obviously, the threat of the death penalty is not *always* a deterrent.

The death penalty objectors also try to convince us most murders are committed during nickel-and-dime holdups

# An Eye for an Eye

*William T. Harper*

"that went bad" and how other murderers were driven while "under the influence" of alcohol or other controlled substances. They tell us how a homeowner unexpectedly returned home during a burglary and got blown away by the surprised burglar who "really didn't mean to do it." They tell us and how another killer had an IQ of 69 (the cut-off for mental retardation is 70) and "he didn't know what he was doing." Unmentioned are hundreds if not thousands of captured burglars and hold-up men who confess to police they never use a weapon in their crimes for fear of the consequences of murderous action or re-action.

In spite of all this, death penalty objectors insist that "In time, perhaps," Sister Prejean writes, "people will realize that executions do not deter violent crime."[101] And in some cases, she may be right. Fear of the death penalty surely didn't dissuade Kenneth Allen McDuff. If someone believes "killing a woman's like killing a chicken," what would deter such a person?

However, Lynne Abraham, then Philadelphia District Attorney, offers a counter-point to the does-not-deter position. "People are tired of running away from their neighborhoods," she said. "They're tired of little girls raped and murdered and dumped in the bushes…. If you commit the ultimate crime, you pay the ultimate penalty." And, she concludes, "When you are dead, you will no longer kill."[102]

Backing up the DA's statement is the following sample list of a Dirty Dozen killers – which at its best, is hardly even the tip of the iceberg of convicted murderers who were executed in the United States after the reinstatement of the death penalty in 1976 – and the deterrence that followed.

# An Eye for an Eye
*William T. Harper*

| Name | # of Victims Pre-Execution | Date of Execution | # Victims After |
|---|---|---|---|
| Charles Starkweather | 11 | June 25, 1959 | 0 |
| Elmo Patrick Sonnier | 02 | April 5, 1984 | 0 |
| Robert Lee Willie | 03* | Dec. 28, 1984 | 0 |
| Theodore Bundy | 30* | Jan. 24, 1989 | 0 |
| John Wayne Gacy | 33 | May 10, 1994 | 0 |
| William Bonin | 14* | Feb. 23, 1996 | 0 |
| Kenneth McDuff | 08* | Nov. 17, 1998 | 0 |
| Timothy McVeigh | 168 | June 11, 2001 | 0 |
| Aileen C. Wournos | 7 | Oct. 9, 2002 | 0 |
| Carl Junior Isaacs | 6 | May 6, 2003 | 0 |
| Thomas Fortenberry | 4 | Aug. 7, 2003 | 0 |
| Charles Roache | 6 | Oct. 22, 2004 | 0 |

* This number confirmed but probably more.

As the above chart shows, at least 292 murders were committed Pre-execution.

And as the above charts shows, there were Zero murders were committed Post-execution.

Repeat:   Z-E-R-O

\*   \*   \*

Technically speaking, there are two different kinds of criminal deterrence: Specific, where the punishment keeps the individual from repeating his/her crimes; and General, where the punishment keeps *others* from committing crimes.

"Generally" speaking, the threat of the death penalty may not always be a deterrent. But, "specifically" speaking, execution damned-sure is.

The humble chart above received considerable verification in a report in the *Chicago Tribune* on June 10, 2007. Despite the never-ending drumbeat coming from death penalty abolitionists, what "gets little notice, however, is a series of academic studies over the last half-dozen years that

# An Eye for an Eye
*William T. Harper*

claim to settle a once hotly debated argument -- whether the death penalty acts as a deterrent to murder. The analyses say yes. They count between three and 18 lives that would be saved by the execution of each convicted killer.[103]

"'There is no question about it,' said Naci Mocan, an economics professor at the University of Colorado at Denver. 'The conclusion is there is a deterrent effect.' A 2003 study he co-authored and a 2006 study that re-examined the data," the *Chicago Tribune* article continued, "found that each execution results in five fewer homicides, and commuting a death sentence means five more homicides. 'The results are robust, they don't really go away,' [Mocan] said. 'I oppose the death penalty. But my results show that the death penalty (deters) -- what am I going to do, hide them?'"[104]

The *Tribune* story went on to report some supporting conclusions:

- Each execution deters an average of 18 murders, according to a 2003 nationwide study by professors at Emory University. (Other studies have estimated the deterred murders per execution at three, five and 14).
- The Illinois moratorium on executions in 2000 -- imposed by then-Gov. George Ryan and continued by current Gov. Rod Blagojevich -- led to 150 additional homicides over four years following, according to a 2006 study by professors at the University of Houston.
- Speeding up executions would strengthen the deterrent effect. For every 2.75 years cut from time spent on death row, one murder would be prevented, according to a 2004 study by an Emory University professor.[105]

Furthermore, as the *International Herald Tribune* reported a month later, Gary Becker, 1992 Nobel Memorial

# An Eye for an Eye

*William T. Harper*

Prize winner in Economic Science who has followed the debate, added, "'the evidence of a variety of types – not simply the quantitative evidence – has been enough to convince me that capital punishment does deter and is worth using for the worst sorts of offenses'." Even Supreme Court Justice Potter Stewart, hardly a strict constructionist juror in the mold of Antonin Scalia, concluded that "the death penalty undoubtedly is a significant deterrent." [106] One has to wonder, though not too seriously, why the abolitionists never seem to use Stewart's Supreme Court quote vs. Blackmun's?

\* \* \*

Who says the death penalty does not deter murder? One old study shows every execution of a convicted murderer deters 156 murderers. [107] The father of at least one victim doesn't need anybody's study to believes it does – as reported in this story from the *Houston Chronicle* regarding the 1993 murders of teenagers Elizabeth Peña and Jennifer Ertman: "'I've waited 13 years to view an execution,' said Ertman's father, Randy Ertman, who will witness the act.... 'In the grand scheme, it may not mean a whole hell of a lot. But Derrick Sean O'Brien will never kill again'." [108] (Chapter Eight tells some of the horrific details of this gruesome crime.)

 Unwittingly perhaps, one of Sister Prejean's poster boys even helps refute the contention that the death penalty is not a deterrent to murder. Elmo Patrick Sonnier, one of the thugs the nun spiritually counseled, confesses to her, "If I had know then [in 1979 after the Supreme Court ordered the death penalty reinstated] I could get the chair, no matter what they did to me, I would never have confessed." [109] That sounds like a deterrent in itself – if not for murder, then certainly for confession thereto. Following that logic, isn't it also possible Sonnier's fear of the death penalty might have eliminated his murderous rampage in the first place?

 Edward Koch, former mayor of New York City, supports the deterrence argument by saying:

# An Eye for an Eye

*William T. Harper*

"Had the death penalty been a real possibility in the minds of...murderers, they might well have stayed their hand. They might have shown moral awareness before their victims died...Consider the tragic death of Rosa Velez, who happened to be home when a man named Luis Vera burglarized her apartment in Brooklyn. 'Yeah, I shot her,' Vera admitted. '...and I knew I wouldn't go to the chair.'" [110]

Former Massachusetts governor Mitt Romney agrees with the deterrence concept.

"Punishment has an impact on action," he said, "and the idea that a more severe punishment would have an impact on action is obvious to even a schoolchild. There's absolutely no question but that the death penalty would reduce a certain number of heinous crimes." [111]

One can only guess the death penalty demolition derbyites aren't impacted by the governor's logic.

Another supporter of the death penalty as a deterrent is Richard Sitzman, a prosecutor in Norman, Oklahoma. Following the trial of Anthony Sanchez, who was convicted and sentenced to death for murdering University of Oklahoma coed Jewell "Juli" Busken (of Benton, Arkansas), Sitzman said, "There are things people do to other people, so evil, so depraved, that they forfeit their right to walk among us." [112]

In a case with international implications, Dr. David R. Dow, a noted death penalty opponent teaching at the University of Houston Law Center, claims – in the then pending execution of Iraqi dictator Saddam Hussein – that that disgrace to humanity should not be executed. The professor claims that "deterrence is irrelevant," in arguing

# An Eye for an Eye

*William T. Harper*

Saddam's fate because "tyrants are not deterrable."[113] The world in general, and Dr. Dow in particular, can sleep more peacefully now that Saddam was hung high because the Butcher of Baghdad will never, repeat *never*, kill again – order his fanatical minions to slaughter millions of others. Sans execution, Saddam Hussein could, Napoleon Bonaparte-like, escape from a prison on the Isle of Elba and engulf this world in further slaughter.

Dr. Dow goes on to ask "why we must kill" killers when we can merely lock them up and keep society safe from *them* (or did he mean keep them safe from society)? The answer to that pithy question is found over and over again in this book's chapter on why "Life-Without-Parole Is A Joke…But It Isn't Funny." Unwittingly perhaps, the good scholar provides readers with another answer to his mindless question. As murderers languish in their Life-Without-Parole sentences, "time inexorably dulls the impulse to punish" and that, no doubt, gives squeamish pardons boards an excuse for "forgiveness" and commutation. Even worse, with the way society is degenerating today due to video violence, what is horrific now may merely be judged as "poor judgment" in the future – as was the case in Kenneth Allen McDuff.

How aptly Dow supports this argument of why there must be *An Eye for an Eye*: "Because forgetfulness can be the enemy of justice, we fear that if we do not execute people like Saddam, we will one day, many years from now, no longer be capable of apprehending the horrors of their deeds…."

Thank you, Dr. Dow, for your roundabout although helpful, confirmation of the need for the death penalty.

The good doctor and his fellow advocates can speculate all they want that most murders are spur-of-the-moment – where the killers do not give a thought to the consequences of their actions committed in a fit of passion, during a botched holdup or a drug deal "gone bad." But, unless death penalty abolitionists are clairvoyant, how in the world can they possibly *know* what goes on in the minds of hundreds, thousands, perhaps millions of "would-be"

# An Eye for an Eye
*William T. Harper*

murderers; those people who have seriously considered killing someone else but did not because of fear of execution? How can they still contend the threat of retribution via the death penalty flat out is not a deterrent?

How many people, throughout human history, have thought they'd like to kill a cheating spouse or a highly-insured one, a work-place boss who's done them wrong, a rival of any kind, even the killer of a loved one? How many times has one meaningfully uttered silently or out loud, "I'd like to kill that SOB?" Imagine what the consequences would be for many of those people if the death penalty, as a deterrent, was non-existent? How many times have they thought about consequences for themselves and backed off? Do anti-death penalty propagandists know the answer? Surely, it can't be "none." Even if it's only "one," then the death penalty is indeed a deterrent.

To give a further indication of the inanity of the anti-deterrent position, we cite herewith the aforementioned death penalty abolitionist researcher Hugo Bedau (see Chapter Two, et al) wherein he makes the following ridiculous claim:

> "...there are clinically documented cases in which the death penalty actually incited the capital crimes it was supposed to deter. These include instances of the so-called suicide-by-execution syndrome – persons who wanted to die but feared taking their own lives, and committed murder so the state would kill them." [114]

That claim stretches the bounds of credulity to its limits. In case after truly documented case, all anyone wanting to commit suicide-by-cop has to do is point a gun – or even something that looks like a gun – at a law enforcement officer in a perceived life-threatening situation and some police officer will, justifiably so, grant him his death wish. A nut case like that doesn't have to kill someone to be killed in return. And of course, the American Civil Liberties Union for whom

# An Eye for an Eye
### William T. Harper

Bedau was writing in the above instance, comes forth with the canard that Life-Without-Parole is the answer – an answer totally refuted as having more holes than a back-door window-screen in the following chapter.

Saying that Life-Without-Parole is the "answer" because the incarceration would keep killers from killing again is ridiculous. Corrections Officer Susan Canfield, 59, was supervising inmates on a work detail near a Texas Department of Criminal Justice's prison in Huntsville, Texas on September 24, 2007. Two of those inmates – Jerry Duane Martin, 37, and John Falk, 40 – overpowered her, took her weapons, and then ran over her with a truck they had stolen. She died a short time later. Both were captured shortly after the breakout. Falk was serving a life sentence for murder. Tell us again, abolitionists, how keeping killers incarcerated for life really keeps them from killing again.

\* \* \*

Dismissing capital punishment as a non-deterrent begs the additional question: Should all prisons be eliminated as well because, as recidivism rates show, incarceration does not necessarily seem to be any more effective in the deterrence of any crime? Two studies from the U. S. Department of Justice come closest to providing "national" recidivism rates for the United States. One tracked 108,580 State prisoners released from prison in 11 States in 1983. The other tracked 272,111 prisoners released from prison in 15 States in 1994. The prisoners tracked in these studies represent two-thirds of all prisoners released in the United States for those years. In the 15-state study, over two-thirds of released prisoners were re-arrested within three years.[115] To say the death penalty doesn't deter crime is the same as saying "five-to-ten for auto theft" doesn't stop people from stealing cars. However, in both cases, the sentence usually does deter the crime, at least for as long as the sentence – be it death or the five-to-10 years – is carried out.

# An Eye for an Eye
*William T. Harper*

When the death penalty movement proclaims from its lofty pulpits that capital punishment does not deter murder, one need only point to the striking graph below. Drawn by the Bureau of Criminal Justice, the chart gives a general overview of the murder rate compared to the number of executions in the United States up through the end of the 20$^{th}$ Century. It dramatically shows that for the last half of the 20$^{th}$ Century, as the execution rate went up, the murder rate went down in almost perfect ratio. Conversely, when the execution rate went down, as shown in the chart for the years of the enforced moratorium, the murder rate went up. There has to be something more than coincidence in these numbers. That something is called "Deterrence."

During the 16-year period (1980-1995 inclusive), there were 884 executions in the United States. The execution rate rose from an average of 39 per year for the first eight of those years to an average of 71.5 for the last eight of those years. Since 1990, the homicide rate per 100,000 people dropped from 9.4 to 5.5. As the execution rate went up, the murder rate went down.[116]

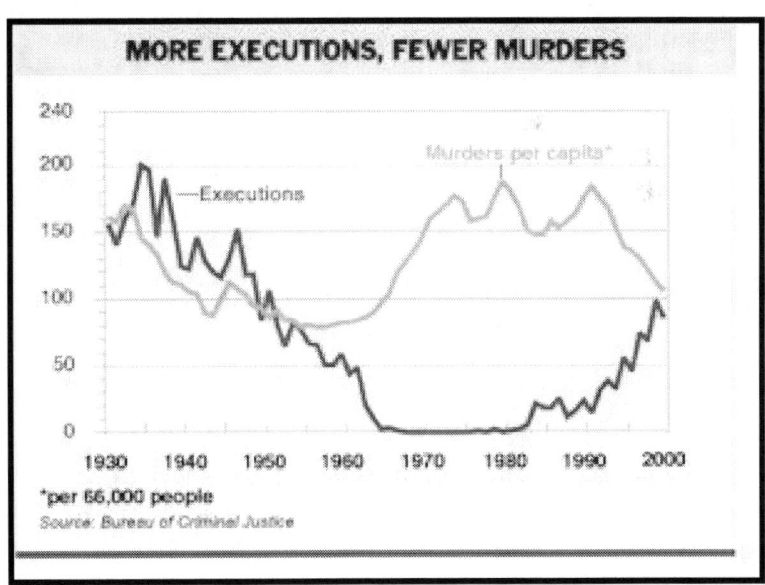

# An Eye for an Eye
*William T. Harper*

Based on those sheer numbers alone, one could say the death penalty is a deterrent – despite what abolitionists would have us believe.

As noted so often, the Lone Star State leads the Nation in providing justice to killers. Since 1977 (when the death penalty was reaffirmed by the U.S. Supreme Court) through the year 2009, Texas sent 448 murderers to their deserved death. As the chart above shows, when the execution rate goes up, the murder rate goes down. So imagine how many potential victims' lives were saved by the elimination of those 448 killers in Texas alone.

Consider further if you will, that during the 1977-2009 period, 1,181 people received the ultimate penalty for their ultimate crimes. As the execution rate goes up, the murder rate goes down. Conversely, as executions go down, murders go up. During the last national moratorium on executions in the United States, 1972-1976, and the five years preceding it with no executions, murders went up by a disastrous one-third (98,320 vs. 74,580) while the Country's population only increased by seven percent (202,212,000 to 216,332,000).[117]

And finally, for now, a study of the men saved from execution by the Supreme Court's *Furman v. Georgia* decision in 1972 shows the 558 men released thereby from death row committed seven more murders and 60 aggravated assaults (aka attempted murder). Had their warranted death sentences been imposed, at least seven lives would have been saved, and 60 more people would have been spared vicious assault.[118]

\* \* \*

With their holier-than-thou attitudes, abolitionists look down their collective noses at we, the masses, and haughtily ask, "is the only thing we can do as a society is to repay evil with evil?" In the first place, who says society is repaying evil with

# An Eye for an Eye

*William T. Harper*

"evil"? Evil must be repaid. Unfortunately, execution isn't the "only thing we can do." Society – through some of its wishy-washy judges, its bleeding-heart pardons boards, its ultra-liberal legislators – has all too often "repaid evil" with plea bargains, reduced sentences, blanket sentence commutations, etc. They have put evil killers back out on the streets where they can and do repeat their evil. Repaying evil with appropriate punishment is the proper thing to do and the punishment must fit the crime. When we look at the Jeffrey Dahmers, the John Wayne Gacys, the Kenneth Allen McDuffs, the Theodore Bundys, and their kind – the appropriate punishment is execution.

These facts prove that for abolitionists to say the death penalty is not a deterrent is a flat-out lie – one often told with malice aforethought. If the threat of being put to death for murder doesn't stop a person from killing, if no sentence – no matter how much lesser than the death penalty – acts as a deterrence, then why have any penalties at all for any crime? What abolitionists are telling us is that not even the ultimate sentence will ever stop the ultimate crime. That's a lie worthy of Pinocchio.

\* \* \*

For those who read the daily newspapers back in the 1970s and 1980s and went beyond the comic pages and the sports section, they were surely familiar with the name Theodore Robert Bundy; "Ted" Bundy, serial killer. No one knows how many young, attractive, dark-haired women he murdered over a 12-year, coast-to-coast span of horror, but here's a partial list of his victims:

WASHINGTON STATE (10)
Lonnie Trumbull; Seattle (6/23/66)
Kathy Devine; Seattle (11/25/73)
Lynda Ann Healy; University of Washington (2/1/74)
Donna Manson; Evergreen State College, Olympia

# An Eye for an Eye
*William T. Harper*

(3/12/74)
Susan Rancourt; Central Washington State College, Ellensburg (4/17/74)
Brenda Baker; Seattle (5/25/74)
Brenda Ball; Burien (6/1/74)
Georgeann Hawkins; University of Washington (6/11/74)
Janice Ott; Lake Sammamish St. Park (7/14/74)
Denise Naslund; Lake Sammamish St. Park (7/14/74)

OREGON (1)
Kathy Parks; Oregon St. (5/6/74)

UTAH (7)
Nancy Wilcox; (10/2/74)
Melissa Smith; Midvale (10/18/74)
Laura Aimee; Lehi (10/31/74)
Debbie Kent; Bountiful (11/8/74)
Susan Curtis; Brigham Young University (6/28/75)
Nancy Baird; Layton (7/4/75)
Debbie Smith; Salt Lake City (2/?/76)

COLORADO (5)
Caryn Campbell; Aspen (1/12/75)
Julie Cunningham; Vail (3/15/75)
Denise Oliverson; Grand Junction (4/6/75)
Melanie Cooley; Nederland (4/15/75)
Shelley Robertson; Golden (7/1/75)

IDAHO (2)
Lynette Culver; Pocatello (5/6/75)
Jane Doe; Boise (9/21/74)

FLORIDA (3)
Lisa Levy; Tallahassee (1/15/78)
Margaret Bowman; Tallahassee (1/15/74)
Kimberly Ann Leach; Lake City (2/9/78) [119]

# An Eye for an Eye

*William T. Harper*

If you look closely, you'll see Theodore savagely murdered 13 females in 1974 alone. That's better than one ferocious killing each and every month!! Yet, death penalty opponents actually proclaim that for the above *partial* string of 28 brutal murders, Theodore Robert Bundy does not deserve the death penalty. How many more would it take? Apparently, as far as abolitionists are concerned, Ted Bundy could have surpassed Adolph Hitler's record of six-million-plus Jews murdered in the Holocaust and he still wouldn't deserve the death penalty. In one sense, the death penalty opponents' opposition did prove itself in the case of Ted Bundy. The threat of the death penalty did not deter Theodore Robert Bundy. But clearly, as shown by the chart early on in this chapter, the *use* of the death penalty finally and most assuredly did for Bundy and many wanton killers.

"Ted Bundy was a Young Republican, law student, avid skier, crisis hotline volunteer and the-boy-next-door. He was also a cannibal, necrophiliac, charismatic sociopath and the man whose name came to define the term 'serial killer' for the 20th century. Though there were at least 57 documented cases of serial killings in America since 1900, Bundy changed the landscape. The man who admitted to killing at least 30 women between 1973 and 1978 – some experts believe he killed more than a hundred – was a remarkable criminal in several ways....

"According to various accounts, he stored severed heads in his home, and was a loner who was simultaneously engaged to two women while he was killing. He incinerated skulls in his fireplace and vacuumed up the ashes. He re-dressed dead victims, ate their flesh, feigned lameness to lure victims and faked accents. He kept one of his victims in his possession for nine days. He was an experienced cat burglar and insisted on strangling his victims while he looked directly into their eyes[120]

# An Eye for an Eye
*William T. Harper*

Theodore Robert Bundy was a sadistic parasite – one for whom the death penalty was designed and one whom the abolitionists would do everything possible to keep from the electric chair, on which he sat on January 24, 1989. Ted Bundy and all other evil killers like him should not be executed, death penalty apologists contend. Rather, Bundy and his ilk should be spared and given Life-Without-Parole terms.

Before his string of murders was uncovered, he was doing one-to-15 years in a Colorado penitentiary for kidnapping an intended murder victim who got away. But, during a recess in a Colorado court house on June 7, 1977, Bundy jumped out of a second-story window. He was recaptured a week later. On December 30, 1977, he hack-sawed his way out of his cell, walked right out the jail's front door, and fled to Florida.

On January 15, 1978, just two weeks after that second escape, Bundy entered the Chi Omega sorority house at Florida State University in Tallahassee and brutally clubbed and strangled Margaret Bowman and Lisa Levy. Bundy crushed Ms. Bowman's skull.

Dr. Robert D. Keppel, founder of the Institute for Forensics in Seattle, Washington, a distinguished detective in the King County Major Crimes Unit where, early in his career, he was chief investigator in the Ted Bundy murder case, was asked: Is it better to execute killers like Bundy or keep them alive? "I know one thing," Dr. Keppel answered after Bundy's execution. "He had a history of always being in escape mode in prison. He had already escaped twice and on two other occasions, he was found with escape implements in his cell.... His whole life was pointed towards escape and once he escaped, he'd kill again. Now he can't do that."[121] Amen.

\* \* \*

# An Eye for an Eye
*William T. Harper*

## Chapter Four

### Life-Without-Parole is a Joke… But it isn't Funny

*Kenneth Allen McDuff – the Sequel.*
*The infamous "Bad Boy from Rosebud" was not the only ogre transferred from death row to a life sentence to parole and back to the streets to murder again. So too was Darryl Kemp.*

**Darryl Kemp**

*Kemp was sentenced to death in 1960 for the 1957 rape and murder of Marjorie Hipperson in Los Angeles County. That sentence was commuted to life by the 1972 Supreme Court ruling in the*

# An Eye for an Eye
*William T. Harper*

Furman v. Georgia *case, as was McDuff's*. Déjà vu *McDuff, Kemp was paroled in the Hipperson killing case in the summer of 1978. Less than four months later, Armida Wiltsey was raped and murdered while out jogging near her home about 20 miles east of downtown San Francisco.*

*Although it took 27 years and some diligent police work, Kemp was finally fingered by DNA evidence in October of 2003. And where was Kemp when he was charged with the Wiltsey murder? He was in the custody of the Texas Department of Criminal Justice, in a Wichita Falls prison serving another life sentence, this time for aggravated rape of yet another woman.*

*In December of 2008, Kemp was finally convicted of Ms. Wiltsey's rape and murder and sentenced to die. However, given his age (76 in 2012), he will most likely die a natural death in the confines of a California penitentiary before his interminable appeals process runs out!*

*What is certain is had Kemp been executed in 1960 as he was sentenced to be for the Hipperson killing, Armida Wiltsey would not have been raped and murdered on November 14, 1978 and her family would not have been forced into facing the agony of her death again and again via the appeals process.*

\* \* \*

In their quest for elimination of the death penalty, revisionists almost always cite Life-Without-Parole (LWP) as the alternative. "Several studies show," Sister Prejean writes "that when jurors know that the defendant will get a true life-without-parole sentence, the number of death sentences drops dramatically." [122] Paraphrasing a famous phrase out of political history, "there she goes again" – saying "several studies show." What studies? By whom? What (if they exist) do those "studies show"? Quoting anonymous studies is often used by the abolitionists to "prove" a point.

The trouble with LWP is, Sister Prejean, most juries don't have the vaguest idea how porous the life-without-parole sentence is (as we shall see later herein) and the death penalty opponents are certainly not going to tell them. Be that

# An Eye for an Eye

*William T. Harper*

as it may, perhaps the number of death sentences *may* drop dramatically, but still, even if it were true…

Life-Without-Parole is a Joke…But it Isn't Funny.

Countless future murders of fellow inmates or prison officers have been and will be committed by convicted vicious inmates serving Life-Without-Parole sentences. Countless inmates serving Life-Without-Parole sentences will literally and figuratively saw their way through prison bars or find other means of escape, only to kill again. Government officials will put them back on the streets.

There's no limit to the imagination of desperate men facing life in prison – with or without parole. According to a Reuters News Service report on October 29, 2007 from Brussels, Belgium, an inmate…

> "made a dramatic escape from jail for the fourth time [yesterday] after his armed accomplices landed in the prison grounds in a hijacked helicopter, prosecutors said [today]. Nordin Benallal, self-styled 'escape king' with several convictions for armed robbery and carjacking, has previously run from a prison van, walked out of jail wearing a wig and sunglasses and scaled a prison wall with a rope ladder…. It marked the second time this year that a prisoner has escaped from a Belgian jail using a helicopter. In April, two men posing as tourists hijacked a helicopter and flew into the yard of a prison near Liege, in the east of the country, to pick up an inmate." [123]

As noted in Chapter Three herein, one federal Department of Justice study reported thousands of prisoners escape or walk away from custody every year.

The previously mentioned Ted Bundy, one of the most infamous of all serial killers (see Chapter Three), was one of those. Another was Richard Lee McNair. He was cracking a safe in a North Dakota Farmers' Union Grain

# An Eye for an Eye
*William T. Harper*

Elevator in November of 1987 when manager Richard Kitzman unexpectedly showed up to assist a trucker with a late load. McNair shot Kitzman three times from behind and left him for dead. McNair reloaded the five-shot revolver, stuck the gun in trucker Jerome Theis' face and emptied it. [124]

Three times in nearly two decades in custody, McNair tasted freedom. Once he spread lip balm on his wrist and slipped out of handcuffs. Another time he crawled to freedom through an air vent. His third escape came as he hid himself under a stack of refurbished mailbags being shipped out of a federal maximum security prison. McNair, a confessed murderer, was serving three life sentences. He was captured by Royal Canadian Mounted Police in Campbellton, New Brunswick, Canada, on October 25, 2007 after they became suspicious of the van he was driving. [125] So what good does it do to sentence him to Life-Without-Parole?. He's currently incarcerated at SuperMax in Florence, Colorado. (Stay tuned for his next escapade.)

\* \* \*

How wrong can the death penalty abolitionists be when they blow their Gabriel-like trumpets blaring to one and all that Life-Without-Parole is the answer? Just lock 'em up and throw away the key, they say. That way, they tell us, the killers don't have to pay *An Eye for an Eye* and everyone is safe – protected by the prison bars from these predatory murderers. That's the message we hear over and over from Sister Helen Prejean, C. S. J., and others.

Let's ask Sister Prejean if she's familiar with the name John J. Geoghan. Here's a clue. He is (make that, was) a member of the same Roman Catholic Church as the nun. He is (or, was) a priest in that church. And he was beaten and strangled to death in 2003 while serving a sentence in one of Massachusetts' most secure prison facilities. A convicted pedophile, Father Geoghan was beaten and strangled to death by Joseph L. Druce, "an admitted neo-Nazi and *convicted killer*

# An Eye for an Eye

*William T. Harper*

*who is already serving a sentence of life without parole* (emphasis added)."[126] Yes, Sister Prejean, Life-Without-Parole is the answer. Ask Father Geoghan – and his family.

Life-Without-Parole is the answer you say? Just lock 'em up and throw away the key. That'll solve the problem, right? Well, what do you do about the David Saucedas of the world? "David Sauceda, 27, walked out of jail early Sunday morning [October 28, 2007] when he gave the name, address, Social Security number, birth date and system ID number of his cellmate, Michael Garcia, according to the Bexar County, Texas sheriff's department."

Sauceda was in a San Antonio jail on a felony auto theft charge and awaiting trial – along with his brother, Jesse – "for the November 2006 killing of a San Antonio man, and with robbing a 59-year-old woman after binding her with duct tape." Sheriff Roland Tafolla said his "department will review its jail release procedures to figure out what went wrong. 'We made an error,' he said."[127] So much for keeping a killer incarcerated via a Life-Without-Parole sentence. Just lock 'em up and throw away the key, right? But, maybe they'll do it right this time. The manhunt for Sauceda ended on January 26, 2008 when U.S. Marshalls found him in Tangancicuaro, Mexico.

There are many ways to get around the Life-Without-Parole sentence. Life-Without-Parole is a joke and if it wasn't so serious, the following fiasco would be funny. A dog trainer who did volunteer work at a Lansing, Michigan prison ran off with a convicted killer and helped him escape after being placed in a dog crate loaded into the back of her van. The woman, Toby Young, was founder of a program that rescued dogs from animal shelters and worked with inmates to train the pets and make them suitable for adoption. Authorities at the state prison said seven inmates apparently helped Young pull off the escape by putting 27-year-old prisoner John Manard into the crate, then hoisting it into Toby Young's vehicle. Two guards who were supposed to check the van

# An Eye for an Eye
### William T. Harper

before it left the prison did not do so, perhaps because they recognized and trusted Young.[128]

Life-Without-Parole is the answer? No, not in the following cases either:

Donald (Peewee) Gaskins and Rudolph Tyner were both serving what amounted to Life-Without-Parole sentences for murder. Tyner was convicted of murdering Tony Cimo's mother and step-father during a robbery in South Carolina. Seeking revenge, Tony Cimo hired Gaskins to kill Gaskins' fellow-inmate Rudolph Tyner, which Gaskins did by giving him a bomb disguised as a radio, right there in the doomed inmate's cell. Gaskins had already been convicted of nine other murders. For one of those murders he had previously been sentenced to death, a sentence subsequently commuted to life imprisonment; for the others, he was serving consecutive life sentences.[129] Had that death sentence not been commuted to Life-Without-Parole, Rudolph Tyner may have lived a lot longer. On September 6, 1991, Gaskins was finally put to death in Columbia, S.C. for Tyner's murder.

Gaskins' murder of Tyner is not an isolated incident. For an idea of how penitent those serving life sentences can be, "the Aryan Brotherhood," reported the *Orange County* (California) *Register* on March 15, 2006, "reputed to be the most violet prison gang [in the country]...was going on trial in what may be the biggest capital-murder case in U. S. history…. It will include more than 120 prosecution witnesses to provide details proving that the white inmate organization carried out the murders and attempted murders of 32 people over 30 years."

These are murders and/or murder attempts that were committed by Brotherhood members while in prison on other inmates and correctional officers and/or those on the outside who crossed them. One can only ask – had these thugs received the death sentence which some of them received but which were never carried out, how many of those 32 people would still be alive today? Did somebody say the death penalty was not a deterrent?

# An Eye for an Eye

*William T. Harper*

A number of similar cases of inmate-on-inmate violence have been recorded. For instance, Warren Bridge, while on death row for shooting store clerk Walter Rose four times with a .38 caliber pistol during a $24 robbery in Galveston, Texas in 1980, was implicated in the bombing of another inmate's cell and the non-fatal stabbing of still another inmate.[130]

Take the case of Conrad Jeffrey, as recorded in *Freed to Kill* by Robert James Bidinotto. After murdering a woman in 1974 by stabbing her 52 times with a pair of scissors, Jeffrey was committed to an institution for the mentally insane. Eight years later, doctors at the institution "decided that Jeffrey had recovered and could be safely released." Subsequently, Jeffrey was convicted 17 times for minor crimes; he sexually attacked a 12-year-old boy and a 14-year-old girl, got a five-year sentence, and served half of it. He was paroled on March 25, 1993. Five weeks later, on May 5, 1993, police – acting on a warning from some of seven-year-old Divina Genao's playmates – burst into Jeffrey's boarding house room where they found "little Divina face-down, naked, bound and gagged. She had been viciously beaten, sexually assaulted, then strangled to death."[131] Similar convoluted circumstances that led to Conrad Jeffrey's release can, and no doubt have, led to the release of other killers who were freed by "the system" to kill again.

Tell us again abolitionists, about Life-Without-Parole being the panacea. While you're telling us that, let us tell you about Glen Stewart Godwin. On August 18, 1980, Godwin stabbed his friend Kim LeValley 26 times. Godwin was later arrested, tried, found guilty of first-degree murder, and sentenced to 26-years-to-life, ending up in California's infamous Folsom State Prison.

On June 5, 1987, Godwin escaped from that maximum security institution. He was recaptured five months later in Mexico when he was caught trafficking cocaine. Convicted on that charge and sent to a Mexican prison in Guadalajara, Godwin escaped again on September 26, 1991 –

# An Eye for an Eye

*William T. Harper*

but not before, according to official reports, he murdered a fellow inmate. [132]

Consider this: 177, 816 people were murdered in this country during the years 2000-2010 inclusive. [133] That's 16,165 people a year; 310 people a week, and 44 murders a day – every single day! Most of this human slaughter was caused by released and paroled criminals. As Morgan Reynolds, a Texas A&M University economics professor and director of criminal justice at the National Center for Policy Analysis in Dallas, Texas reported, "Criminals under supervision commit 15 murders a day in the United States." [134]

There is no direct correlation between those 177,816 victims in the first decade of this Millennium and the 636 killers executed in that same time frame. [135] But even more importantly, had Glen Stewart Godwin been executed for murdering Kim LeValley – as he should have been – another victim might still be alive today. As shown in these cases (and more to come further on in this chapter), Life-Without-Parole or 26-years-to-life sentences do not sound like much of a panacea. These are just a few of the serious flaws in life sentences abolitionists lobby for. There is no doubt whatsoever that keeping some murderers alive in prison for years and years is far, far more dangerous to yet even more innocents.

The most compelling argument against substituting Life-Without-Parole for the death penalty is the never-ending threat that murderers will, one way or another, get out of prison and kill again. The history of penology is rife with examples of such horrid developments. Illustrative of that point is the following extracted article from "The New American" and headlined: "Murders That Could Have Been Averted by Capital Punishment": [136]

The list contains the incidents where 13 convicted killers went on to kill 21 post-conviction victims even after they had been "locked up" but no one had, obviously, "thrown away the key." (Also, some other cases shown in the original "New American" article are not included in the

# An Eye for an Eye

*William T. Harper*

above 13:21 ratio and have been deleted from the list below because they are covered elsewhere in these pages.)

- Some 80 years ago, Charles Fitzgerald killed a deputy sheriff and was given a 100-year prison sentence as a result. He was released after serving just 11 years, and in 1926 murdered a California policeman. He was given "life" for that killing, but was paroled in 1971.
- In 1931, "Gypsy" Bob Harper, who had been convicted of murder, escaped from a Michigan prison and killed two persons. After being recaptured, he then killed the prison warden and his deputy....
- In 1951, Joseph Taborsky was sentenced to death in Connecticut for murder, but was freed when the courts ruled that the chief witness against him (his brother) had been mentally incompetent to testify. In 1957, Taborsky was found guilty for another murder, for which he was electrocuted in May 1960. Before his execution, he confessed to the 1951 murder.
- In 1952, Allen Pruitt was arrested for the knife slaying of a newsstand operator and sentenced to life in prison. In 1965, he was charged with fatally stabbing a prison doctor and an assistant prison superintendent, but was found not guilty by reason of insanity. In 1968, his 1952 conviction was overturned on a technicality by the Virginia Supreme Court. He was re-tried, again found guilty, but given a 20-year sentence instead of life. Since he had already served 18 years, and had some time off for "good behavior," he was released. On December 31, 1971 he was arrested and charged in the murder of two men in Spartanburg, South Carolina.
- In 1957, Richard Biegenwald murdered a store owner during a robbery in New Jersey. He was convicted, but given a life sentence rather than death. After serving 17 years, he was paroled. He violated his

# An Eye for an Eye
*William T. Harper*

parole, was returned to prison, but was again paroled in 1980, after which he shot and killed an 18-year-old Asbury Park, New Jersey girl. He also killed three other 17-year-old New Jersey girls and a 34-year-old man....

- In 1972, Arthur James Julius was convicted of murder and sentenced to life in prison. In 1978, he was given a brief leave from prison, during which he raped and murdered a cousin. He was sentenced to death for that crime and was executed on November 17, 1989.
- In 1976, Jimmy Lee Gray (who was free on parole from an Arizona conviction for killing a 16-year-old high school girl) kidnapped, sodomized, and suffocated a three-year-old Mississippi girl. He was executed for that second killing on September 2, 1983.
- Also in 1976, Timothy Charles Palmes was on probation for an earlier manslaughter conviction when he and two accomplices robbed and brutally murdered a Florida furniture store owner. Palmes was executed for the killing on November 8, 1984. An accomplice, Ronald Straight, was executed on May 20, 1986. (The other accomplice, a woman, was granted immunity for testifying for the prosecution.)
- In 1978, Wayne Robert Felde, while being taken to jail in handcuffs, pulled a gun hidden in his pants and killed a policeman. At the time, he was a fugitive from a work release program in Maryland, where he had been convicted of manslaughter.
- In 1979, Donald Dillbeck was convicted and sentenced to 25 years in prison for murdering a Florida sheriffs deputy. In 1983, he tried to escape. In January of this year he was transferred to a minimum-security facility. On June 22nd, he walked away from a ten-inmate crew catering a school banquet. Two

# An Eye for an Eye

*William T. Harper*

days later, he was arrested and charged with stabbing a woman to death at a Tallahassee shopping mall....

- On October 22, 1983 at the federal penitentiary in Marion, Illinois, two prison guards were murdered in two separate instances by inmates who were both serving life terms for previously murdering inmates. On November 9, 1983 Associate U.S. Attorney General D. Lowell Jensen told a Senate subcommittee that it is impossible to punish or even deter such prison murders because, without a death sentence, a violent life-termer has free rein "to continue to murder as opportunity and his perverse motives dictate."

- On December 7, 1984 Benny Lee Chaffin kidnapped, raped, and murdered a nine-year-old Springfield, Oregon girl. He had been convicted of murder once before in Texas, but not executed. Incredibly, the same jury that convicted him for killing the young girl refused to sentence him to death because two of the 12 jurors said they could not determine whether or not he would be a future threat to society!

- Thomas Eugene Creech, who had been convicted of three murders and had claimed a role in more than 40 killings in 13 states as a paid killer for a motorcycle gang, killed a fellow prison inmate in 1981 and was sentenced to death. In 1986 his execution was stayed by a federal judge and was later reduced to another life sentence.

- When he was 14, Dalton Prejean killed a taxi driver. When he was 17, he gunned down a state trooper in Lafayette, Louisiana. Despite protests from the American Civil Liberties Union and other abolitionist groups, Prejean was executed for the second murder on May 18, 1990.

# An Eye for an Eye
*William T. Harper*

(Author's Note: There's a touch of irony in this list in that it contains the surnames names of two authors with decidedly different views on the death penalty – Prejean and Harper!)

> (As another aside to the "Gypsy" Bob Harper story above, after the killings cited therein, Harper was captured and immediately flogged – legally at the time – by prison authorities. But, when it came time to charge him with those murders, it was determined that any further punishment could not be exacted under the terms of "double jeopardy." Pity the Killers…Forget the Victims!)

The list of cases such as those above goes on – and on…. In its annual report on *Officers Killed and Assaulted, 2004*, the Federal Bureau of Investigation reported that over the 10-year period commencing in 1995, 24 law enforcement officers have been feloniously killed by those having prior arrests for murder.[137] Things have deteriorated vastly, as listed by the Federal Bureau of Investigation in its *Officers Killed and Assaulted* report. For the year 2010 alone, 19 of the alleged offenders killing and assaulting officers were under judicial supervision at the time of the incidents.[138]

In the McConnell prison unit in Beeville, Texas, author Joseph T. Hallinan writes on page seven of his book, *Going Up the River* (Random House, New York City, New York, 2001), "Every day…officers report 10 to 12 assaults. Guards have to wear safety glasses to protect them from feces, urine, and foods that are regularly heaved at them. One guard…was shot with a homemade arrow-launching device that sent a metal shaft three inches into his upper arm, severing an artery." This then is another potential price for warehousing convicted killers.

And the following case isn't a "potential" price for warehousing convicted killers:

Robert Lynn Pruett, 20, was sentenced to 99 years in prison for his role in the 1995 murder of Ray Yarborough.

# An Eye for an Eye

*William T. Harper*

On December 17, 1999, while in prison, Pruett missed getting a hot lunch and was given a sack lunch. He attempted to take his lunch into the recreation area, which was in violation of prison rules. Officer [Daniel] Nagle told Pruett that he needed to eat his lunch before going to the recreation area, and wrote a disciplinary charge against Pruett. Later that afternoon, when Nagle was in his office adjoining a multi-purpose room, Pruett stabbed Nagle eight times with a "shank" made of a metal rod sharpened to a point at one end, and wrapped in tape at the other end....

Nagle died from a heart attack that he suffered as a result of the trauma caused by the stab wounds.... John Lee Davis of the Texas Department of Criminal Justice Office of Inspector General testified that after Pruett was arrested, Pruett stated, "Go ahead and run that disciplinary case on me now. Oop[s], I want to call my first witness, Officer Nagle. Oops, he's dead." Davis said that Pruett then began laughing.[139]

\* \* \*

Another question arises. Is Life-Without-Parole really a punishment or is it, as follows, a reward? The television program "Investigative Reports," with TV journalist and anchor Bill Kurtis narrating, produced a video cassette about the notorious killer Richard Speck. The program is promoted thusly:

> "On the night of July 13, 1966, eight nurses were savagely murdered in their Chicago townhouse. The killer, Richard Speck, eventually became America's symbol of evil. For all his brutality, Speck was careless, and after hearing the chilling testimony of a survivor, the jury took only 45 minutes to convict him. He was sentenced to death, but the execution was never carried out [thanks to *Furman v. Georgia*].

# An Eye for an Eye

*William T. Harper*

Speck settled in to a seedy prison life filled with drugs, sex and money....

"Shocking footage of his life behind bars [has been] uncovered by "Investigative Reports" (in which)...he flashes rolls of money, jokes with his sex partner, and apparently snorts cocaine on this secret video recorded in the maximum security prison. And for the first time ever, Speck admits to the crime and recounts the horrific details. Can life behind bars sufficiently replace the death penalty as just punishment for wanton murder?" [140]

Good question.
This then is Life-Without-Parole, the punishment abolitionists would "inflict" on those topping Dr. Michael Stone's "Scale of Evil," no matter how grave, terrible, outrageous, heinous, cruel) the crime. Speck was convicted of murder (probably only because of good detective work with finger-prints and the one student nurse who faked her death at the scene and thus lived to identify the killer of her eight friends). He was sentenced to death. But he was another of those whose sentence was commuted when the U. S. Supreme Court temporarily voided the death penalty in 1972. Speck, whose "Life of Riley" in the pen was not unique, ultimately did get punishment that was unusual but it certainly wasn't cruel when he died of a heart attack in prison on December 5, 1991.

\* \* \*

Another question concerning "the good life" for those serving Life-Without-Parole might be, How Can This Happen? The "this" in this case comes from the Congressional Record, House of Representatives - May 10, 1996, Page H4805:

# An Eye for an Eye
*William T. Harper*

"Mr. HEFLEY. Mr. Speaker, for over a decade, the Social Security Administration funneled more than $50,000 in benefits into the bank account of serial killer William Bonin.

"Known as the freeway killer, Bonin, who was executed February 23, confessed to murdering 21 people in southern California in 1979 and 1980. He had been receiving Social Security disability insurance checks since he was diagnosed with a mental illness in 1972, but the Government failed to cut off the payments when he took up residency on death row in 1982. Federal law prohibits him from eligibility for these payments, but Bonin continued to receive monthly disability checks ranging from $300 in 1982 to $589 last month...." That $50,000 is probably another number the death penalty opponents facetiously factor in to the cost of executing the death penalty.

\* \* \*

No matter how you slice it, killers do avoid the death penalty, often with help from abolitionists and others. They do – one way or another – get out of prison. The abolitionists assure us that:

"...in a growing number of states...life-without-parole sentences are *true* life sentences. The only way prisoners serving such sentences can be released is by commutation of sentence by the governor, and because of the unpopularity of such commutations, governors now grant them rarely." [141]

Illinois Governor George Ryan did, in fact, grant commutations rarely. But in one of them, he commuted the sentences of 156 murderers in one fell swoop in 2003. And "rarely" wasn't a word used much during the Fergusons'

# An Eye for an Eye
*William T. Harper*

administrations in the Texas governor's mansion. To relieve prison over-crowding early in the Twentieth Century, paroles became popular. But many paroles came with a cost. In an apocryphal story of the times during Governor James E. ("Pa") Ferguson's administration (1915-1917), an inmate's father visiting the Governor's farm admired a mule and was told he could buy it for a mere $10,000. Stunned, the father asked, "What would I do with that mule?" He was told, "Your son could ride it home from the prison in Huntsville."

Nor was "rarely" a word in Louisiana Governor Edwin Edwards' vocabulary, as you'll see later on in this chapter. Take another look at the above statement about the rarity of Commutation. It may be the only way Life-Without-Parole killers can be legally "released" but it's surely not the only way they can "get out." And despite the fact "governors now grant [commutations] rarely," only once could be more than enough.

There are commutations, and there are get-out-of-jail-free passes a governor can issue. One of the latter cases is noted in *Dead Man Walking* via Howard Marsellus' "confession" of malfeasance going on between Louisiana Governor Edwards' office and Marcellus while the latter was chairperson of the Louisiana Pardons Board. Marsellus talked extensively about the Tim Baldwin murder of Mary James Peters, for which Baldwin was eventually executed. Also implicated in that case was Baldwin's girlfriend, Marilyn Hampton. She received a life sentence and, according to Marsellus, "cut a deal" with the state's Department of Corrections and the governor's office that got her released from that life sentence after only eight years and after her official records were apparently tampered with.[142]

So you see, length of a sentence or conditions attached thereto – whether it's "time served" or "life without parole" – can mean little when it comes to carrying out a sentence, even in a murder conviction. What difference does it make in some of these cases what sentence is imposed? There's always a prospect killers will hit the streets again. On

# An Eye for an Eye

*William T. Harper*

May 31, 1984, six death-row inmates took 13 prison personnel hostage, donned guard uniforms and, wielding a fake bomb, bluffed their way out of Mecklenburg Correctional Center in Boydton, Virginia. Fortunately, all of these killers were recaptured before they could kill again. Luck was on the side of the good citizens of America's east coast in this case.

There are many other ways to get out of jail free. According to an Internet article entitled, "What You Won't Find In The Clinton Museum And Library," by Sam Smith, in 1993:

> "Arkansas Governor Jim Guy Tucker comes to Washington to see his old boss [William Jefferson Clinton] sworn in [as 42nd President of the United States], leaving his state under the control of president pro tem of the senate, Little Rock dentist Jerry Jewell. Jewell uses his power as acting governor to issue a number of pardons, one of them for a convicted drug dealer, Tommy McIntosh.
>
> "According to the *Washington Times*," Smith continues, "many in the state 'say it was a political payoff, offered in exchange for dirty tricks Mr. McIntosh played on Clinton political opponents during the presidential campaign.' It seems the elder McIntosh had worked for Clinton in his last state campaign and, according to McIntosh in a 1991 lawsuit, had agreed not only to pay him $25,000 but to help him market his recipe for sweet potato pie and to pardon his son." [143]

As shown in this case of a drug-pusher and the previously-mentioned Kenneth Allen McDuff, there are any number of ways to get out of jail free. And one of the best ways to avoid the death house is to be denied access to it by an abolitionist *prosecutor*. Terence Hallinan, San Francisco district attorney (1995-2003), worked extensively with

# An Eye for an Eye

*William T. Harper*

"...unions, women's organizations, Lesbian, Gay, Bisexual and Transgender associations, environmental organizations, victims rights organizations, and civil rights groups."[144] Nearing the end of his second term as DA, Hallinan "announced a personal moratorium on seeking the death penalty.[145] Amazingly, especially in San Francisco, Mr. Hallinan was defeated when next he came up for election.

\* \* \*

The main stream media is arguably a proponent of the death penalty's abolition. What follows is an edited version of an editorial appearing in the *Asbury Park* (N. J.) *Press* on September 15, 2006, full of innuendo and flimsy "facts" in support of Life-Without-Parole:

> State legislators need no further proof about the merits of the death penalty law than to listen to the families of murder victims. Their pain at the thought that their loved one's killer can walk free after a successful appeal or at the end of his sentence should convince any wary lawmaker that Life-Without-Parole is a far better punishment than a cell on death row. Those cells have become the permanent home of New Jersey's murderers as they await the outcomes of appeal after appeal to their death penalty sentences. As a result, no inmate – as heinous as his crime may have been – has been executed since the state restored the death penalty in 1982.
> [The Death Penalty Study Commission recommended changes to the state legislature with Life-Without-Parole as the best alternative.] That would spare Joanne Barlieb of Atco the fear that her mother's killer in a 1985 convenience store robbery could be free and on the streets in 14 years. "Our family was forced to relive the nightmare three

# An Eye for an Eye
*William T. Harper*

times," Barlieb told the panel of their courtroom appearances.

That penalty would also mean that Robert O. Marshall, 66, of Dover Township, would not be eligible for parole in eight years for his role in the contract murder of his wife in 1984.... Marshall was re-sentenced to life in prison with parole eligibility in 2014 after judges, in one of Marshall's numerous appeals, ruled that his defense was inadequate during the death penalty phase.

...All of these appeals cost money, which was cited by Sen. Raymond Lesniak, D-Union, as another reason to drop the law, which he supported in 1982. Now adopting the stance of death penalty opponents, Lesniak also said "there is no foolproof system to prevent the execution of an innocent person."

The evidence against the death penalty law is convincing. It has to go, with Life-Without-Parole the sentence that serves justice and the families left behind.

Unfortunately, on December 13, 2007, New Jersey became the first U.S. state to legislatively abolish the death penalty since the U.S. Supreme Court reinstated capital punishment in 1976. Lawmakers in the Democrat-controlled state Assembly voted 44-36 in favor of a bill to scrap the death penalty and substitute it with life in prison without the possibility of parole for those found guilty of the most serious crimes.

The vote followed approval by the state Senate and the measure was signed into law the next week by Democratic Governor Jon Corzine, a foe of capital punishment. New Jersey, which had not executed anyone since 1963, then became the then 14th state without a death penalty.... [146]

# An Eye for an Eye
*William T. Harper*

The "will of the people" was aborted in the above story as reported by Reuters News Service, which went on to state:

> An opinion poll published on [December 11, 2007] found 78 percent of New Jersey voters would keep the death penalty for the worst criminals, such as serial killers or child murderers. But a Quinnipiac University poll also found 52 percent preferred Life-Without-Parole for people guilty of first-degree murder. [147]

The results of these actions in Washington and New Jersey cause one to wonder: what ever happened to majority rule there? Likewise, the Garden State voters' views on Life-Without-Parole as a preference only goes to show those polled were ignorant of the consequences of that extremely fallible sentence – thanks, in no small part, to the anti-death penalty propagandists.

This kind of nightmarish editorializing is exactly the reason why *An Eye for an Eye* was written. The arguments presented above are bogus to say the least. Re-read if you will the first paragraph of the editorial. "Their [the families of murder victims] pain," the editorial writer claims, "at the thought that their loved one's killer can walk free after a successful appeal or at the end of his sentence should convince any wary lawmaker that Life-Without-Parole is a far better punishment than a cell on death row." The editorialist needs reminding that had the mandated death sentence for those in "a cell on death row" been carried out, the victims' families would long ago have been relieved of that anticipatory pain and they would no longer need to be "wary."

The writer goes on to note, "no inmate – as heinous as his crime may have been – has been executed since the state [of New Jersey] restored the death penalty in 1982." And the primary reason may very well be too many in this

# An Eye for an Eye

*William T. Harper*

nation's judicial system are buying into the weeping and wailing of abolitionists and editorial writers who tell us nobody should have to pay the ultimate penalty for their ultimate crime. Even worse, in New Jersey, the State's Supreme Court is, according to Kent Scheidegger of the Criminal Justice Legal Foundation, guilty of "pure obstruction of the enforcement of the [death penalty] law simply because a majority of the judges disagree with it, and they are willing to make up new rules without limit to impose their preference on the state." [148]

The newspaper's editorial – just as the vast majority of abolitionists do – stretches facts almost to the breaking point. The editorial writer says Life-Without-Parole "would spare Joanne Barlieb the fear that her mother's killer in a 1985 convenience store robbery could be free and on the streets in 14 years." The writer offers absolutely no verification that is what Ms. Barlieb said. Her only quote in the article was, "Our family was forced to relive the nightmare three times." From what one reads in the *Asbury Park Press*, "the fear" is the anti-death penalty editorial writer's, not Ms. Barlieb's. And wouldn't "that fear" be totally removed for everybody if her mother's killer had gotten the ultimate penalty when he should have?

Other states also have jumped on the abolitionists' bandwagon to the point where there are now 17 states and the District of Columbia without the death penalty option (as of August, 2012). And in at least one more state, Oregon, its governor, John Kitzhaber, announced in 2011 that he would *refuse* to permit any further executions to occur while he served as governor. The Oregon chief executive, putting his personal beliefs ahead of that of the state legislature's enacted law, claimed:

> "In my mind, it is a perversion of justice [and] I refuse to be a part of this compromised and inequitable system any longer and I will not allow further executions while I am governor." [149]

# An Eye for an Eye
*William T. Harper*

Could it be that if Governor Kitzhaber thought surveillance cameras were "a perversion of justice," he would arbitrarily and single-handedly ignore the laws of the state? Is the "will of the people" in the state of Oregon (or any other of the 49 states) to be held hostage by a governor's personal pique? Does any governor get to pick and choose which of his state's laws he will uphold? *"l'état, c'est moi!"*

If the courts and society would stop listening to those bleeding hearts; if they would ignore those who maintain no killer should pay the full penalty of the law for their heinous crimes, if they would expeditiously carry out the mandated sentences of the juries that are consistently *upheld* by courts of appeals, would not then the editorial writer(s)' complaints of excessive costs also be mitigated, to say the least. And since when is the cost of the death penalty process to be equated with a brutally murdered victim?

\* \* \*

Life-Without-Parole is NOT the answer. It does NOT guarantee permanent incarceration. Look at the case of Michael Shepherd noted in Chapter One herein who shot Megan Liebengood to death on September 14, 2004. He was sentenced to Life-Without-Parole – **for twenty-five years**!

You can even kill a cop in cold blood and end up with a Life-Without-Parole sentence but be eligible for parole in 25 years. Ron Parker was a 27-year-old Deputy Beach Marshal in St. Augustine Beach, Florida. On January 12, 1975, Parker was shot and killed by Thomas DeSherlia, who at the time was wanted for bank robbery in Iowa and two murder/kidnappings in Alabama. DeSherlia had a minor automobile accident and Parker was dispatched to investigate. Upon coming in contact with DeSherlia, Parker was shot several times and he died at the scene. DeSherlia was later caught after a running gun fight. He pled guilty to the officer's murder and was sentenced to life in prison with no

# An Eye for an Eye
*William T. Harper*

chance of parole – *for twenty-five years,* that is.[150] And think of this: with varying state regulations that grant inmates those "good-time" bonuses (i.e., one day removed from their prison sentence for each one or two days they behave themselves), a 25-year sentence could be reduced to 12.5 years!

Another case, about which much more is written in Chapter Five is that of Donald Eugene Harding. His court record while on trial for two depraved murders in 1980 showed during a previous incarceration, he was convicted of dangerous or deadly assault by a prisoner on a fellow jail inmate and for which he was sentenced to life imprisonment without possibility of parole – **for twenty-five years**.

The barrier has already been broken; shattered. Where do we draw the line? Will Life-Without-Parole evolve into Life-Without-Parole for 20 years? For 15? For 10? Who is to say in years to come that Life-Without-Parole will not degenerate into "time served" in the county jail while awaiting trial? And again, countless inmates serving Life-Without-Parole have sawed their way through prison bars or found other means of escape, only to kill again.

Even further evidence of the futility of the Life-Without-Parole "panacea" is that sentence gives killers a lifetime pass to kill and kill again while in prison. For those serving Life-Without-Parole, there is, theoretically, no hope. They supposedly never will legally get out of prison – at least not by walking out with a state-purchased bus ticket in hand. And without hope, what incentive is there for even mildly good behavior? To go to the typical extreme, it is – as one Kentucky inmate serving a Life-Without-Parole sentence for murder – put it, very easy for him to kill another inmate simply "because I have nothing to lose." What are the courts supposed to do about that guy? Give him another sentence of Life-Without-Parole? Life-Without-Parole is a ticking time bomb in a prison setting.

Reporting on Louisiana's infamous Angola prison (where Sister Prejean ministered to murderers Elmo Patrick Sonnier and Robert Lee Willie), a newspaper series on

# An Eye for an Eye
*William T. Harper*

possible violence at Angola described a pervasive "sense of hopelessness" that bloomed in this prison's air. In an institution holding more than 4,400 men serving an average sentence of 21 years, and a good portion of these mandatory no-parole sentences, people were giving up hope of getting out. And as the newspaper series pointed out, "A hopeless prisoner is a dangerous prisoner." [151]

There's clairvoyance in that observation. If abolitionists want to claim Life-Without-Parole is the panacea, they should talk to Charles Michael Kastelhun's family. He was stabbed to death in his prison cell on Nov. 10, 1998 by his cellmate, Alex Bennett, who was serving a life sentence for the 1988 murder of a Louisville man during an argument.

Bennett was simply tired of sharing his prison cell with other inmates who didn't give him the "respect" he thought he deserved, according to Michael Cornett, his closest friend in prison. Bennett asked for a cell of his own, and when he didn't get it, something inside him snapped, said Cornett. Bennett turned on Kastelhun, who was his newest cellmate, and brutally stabbed the man 30 times in the head and neck with a home-made knife. "You can only push a dog so far before they will bite you," said Cornett.[152] Bennett's response: "I want to live in a cell by myself.... I have nothing to lose." [153]

Bennett, already serving a life sentence for a previous murder, got a new Life-Without-Parole sentence for killing Kastelhun. (Reports coming out of Kentucky State Penitentiary in Eddyville indicate Bennett's wrist is still sore from the slap he received.) As Sheriff Chris Kirk of Brazos County, Texas put it, "Life-Without-Parole today is like the camel getting its nose under the tent." [154]

Charles Baird, now head of the criminal law section of The Fowler Firm in Austin, Texas and a former Judge of the Texas Court of Criminal Appeals, said the state's mandatory prison requirement for capital killers constitutes "Life-Without-Parole." [And, he continued] "It is very

# An Eye for an Eye
*William T. Harper*

difficult to spend that period of time in confinement for any number of reasons. Prison is a very dangerous place, and the odds of being murdered by other inmates are very high."[155]

> In Palestine, Texas, an inmate was apparently strangled in his cell Monday and officials are preparing to charge his cellmate. Jerry Sinclair, 25, was found unconscious in his cell at the Michael Unit near Palestine just before dawn Monday. He was declared dead less than an hour later. It was the Texas Department of Criminal Justice system's **fourth homicide of the year** [emphasis added]. Sinclair, of Tarrant County (Texas), was serving a five-year sentence for failing to comply as a sex offender. His cellmate is serving a 38-year sentence for murder.[156]

Life-Without-Parole is the answer? On February 2, 1984, Robert Earl O'Neal was serving a life sentence plus 15 years in the Jefferson City, Missouri Correctional Center for a 1980 murder of an elderly man during a burglary. During lunch break, the 23-year-old inmate, a member of the white-supremacist Aryan Nation prison gang, attacked another inmate, Arthur Dade. O'Neal stabbed Dade, an African-American, in the heart and chest four times with an ice pick-like shiv. Dade died.[157] It was another case of an inmate serving a lifetime-plus sentence for murder who then killed again. Had O'Neal paid the death penalty sentence he deserved for his first murder, Arthur Dade might still be alive today. So much for Life-Without-Parole.

\* \* \*

Even at one of the Nation's fortress-like super maximum-security prisons, SuperMax in Florence, Colorado, the threat of inmate violence is prevalent. Cory Hodge was a prison guard for less than three years at Supermax — home of

# An Eye for an Eye
*William T. Harper*

America's most feared and notorious criminals — before he decided he had had enough. He left to take a job as a train conductor. "I felt like staffing levels were coming to a point where it was getting ridiculously dangerous to be there," said Hodge, who was stabbed in the head and arms at another prison before going to Supermax. "I have a wife and children. I want to be around for them."[158] Officer Hodge had good reason for concern. "In 1970, inmates at California's Soledad Prison attacked and killed a guard...in July, they killed another. Over the next two years, five more guards were murdered."[159]

Guards at Supermax complain that because of cost-cutting, staffing levels are perilously low, and as a result, prisoners are growing angrier and threats and assaults against the staff are on the rise at the Alcatraz of the Rockies. Unfortunately, almost all prison systems in the country today are facing similar financial crunches and are again facing potential mandatory release programs that could put hundreds of violent criminals back on the streets. Overcrowding is — as it was when the same problem sent Kenneth Allen McDuff back on the streets to kill again — an even greater threat today than it was then.

According to the U. S. Department of Justice figures, at midyear 2011, there were 748,728 inmates in custody in America's prisons and jails.[160] "Prison guard shortage called a risk" blared a *Houston Chronicle* headline in the April 15, 2007 editions.

> "I'm told," said one Texas lawmaker quoted in the article, "that where you need two (correctional officers), you've got one, and sometime you have none. It means," he continued, "the public is at risk of a breakout. It means you endanger corrections officers, and you potentially endanger inmates."

# An Eye for an Eye
*William T. Harper*

We're not being totally facetious nor overly callous here when we suggest one way to somewhat relieve prison over-crowding would be to comply with the sentences facing the thousands of those on death row across the nation.

* * *

The $60 million Supermax is the nation's most secure prison, reserved for the worst of the worst. Unabomber Ted Kaczynski, al-Qaeda conspirator Zacarias Moussaoui, terrorist cleric Omar Abdel-Rahman, would-be shoe-bomber Richard Reid and Oklahoma City bombing conspirator Terry Nichols are all there, locked up in solitary. As prison guard Hodge noted above, it is getting "ridiculously dangerous" to be in almost any prison – on either side of the bars.

On October 22, 1983 at the federal penitentiary in Marion, Illinois, two prison guards were murdered in two separate instances by inmates who were both serving life terms for previously murdering inmates. On November 9, 1983 Associate U.S. Attorney General D. Lowell Jensen told a Senate subcommittee *it is impossible to punish or even deter* [emphasis added] such prison murders because, without a death sentence, a violent life-termer has free rein "to continue to murder as opportunity and his perverse motives dictate."[161]

When asked for later information, the United States Department of Justice reported that "in the 12 months ending June 30, 1999, nearly 9,300 inmate assaults on jail employees took place, including four that resulted in staff deaths."[162] When inmates "have nothing to lose," it is, indeed, "a jungle in there." In that "jungle" is where abolitionists strive mightily to put their poster-boy (and -girl) killers. If abolitionists had half the heart and the sensitivity they profess to have, they might – for the convicts' sake – want rather to see them face the ultimate penalty as opposed to living the rest of one's life behind bars, especially in a place such as Supermax. But, it's the "cause" that really matters and

# An Eye for an Eye
*William T. Harper*

Kevin Scudders, whose off-color observation about how little the abolitionists care for his "cause" is seen elsewhere in these pages, no doubt has seen right through their crocodile tears.

Similar super maximum security prisons have been growing rapidly over the last twenty years and by now, almost every state and the Federal government has at least one. They are, as noted, used to house "the worst of the worst" convicts and to keep them from inflicting even more evil on their fellow inmates and prison staffs. The following is extracted from a National Public Radio program on July 26, 2006 describing life in Supermax:

> These places have many names – Supermax, intensive-management units, secure housing – but the meaning is the same: years alone, out of the public view and away from public oversight. Isolation today means 23 hours a day in a concrete cell no bigger than a bathroom. One hour a day is spent alone in a concrete exercise pen, about the length and width of two cars. Most inmates held in solitary have no contact with the outside world other than the U.S. mail. Depending on the state, inmates have limited access to visitors. Most can't watch television, call anyone on the phone or even touch another person while in the units.

The exercise pens are basically chain-linked enclosures, "cages" some call them. "Put the monkey in the cage and let 'im get some air," complained one inmate therein. It's where you have to wear plastic "spit masks" so you can't spit on a correctional officer who has to enter your cell for some reason. Some prisons allow those in "the hole" (or the SHU, the security housing unit as it's called in California prisons) to have only one five-minute shower per week. What used to be called "solitary confinement" is in our politically correct world now called "ad-seg" (Administrative

# An Eye for an Eye
*William T. Harper*

Segregation).

It's interesting to speculate on the noble desires of death penalty opponents. In their adamant efforts to spare murderers from their justly deserved punishment, they may very well be condemning them to what even some inmates consider a lifetime of hell on earth via an eternity pent up in a six-by-twelve-foot SuperMax-like cubicle behind bars. With friends like that, who needs enemies?

Without facetiousness, this concept could be carried a step further for inmates who, as true believers, seek forgiveness for their crimes from their higher power. Having then been granted that forgiveness, those killers could look forward to a heavenly eternity following their execution. Instead, they waste away in a penitentiary in fear that any day, any night they could become a murdered murderer.

Understand. Again, this is not a plea for more lenient treatment for murderous inmates. Far from it. They get what they deserve (or at least, they should); what they brought on upon themselves. Faced with that kind of a "life" for 20 or 30 or 50 years, a painless prick from a needle in your arm in a prison death house sounds infinitely more appealing. At least, you "get it over with."

\* \* \*

For those who still believe Life-Without-Parole is the answer, is the panacea, read this story about Clarence Ray Allen. In 1978, he was convicted of murdering Mary Sue Kitts and instead of getting the death penalty, he was sentenced to *Life-Without-Parole* at San Quentin State Prison in California. While serving his *Life-Without-Parole* sentence, he conspired with a fellow inmate, Billy Ray Hamilton, to kill witnesses who testified against him in the Kitts trial. The objective was to "get rid of" anyone who might be able to testify against him in a subsequent re-trial Allen was seeking through the appeals process.

# An Eye for an Eye
*William T. Harper*

After Hamilton was paroled, he did Allen's bidding and murdered three more people. Again, Allen was tried for murder and this time was sentenced to death, a sentence which was carried out on January 17, 2006 – almost 30 years after killing Kitts. [163] Had Allen paid the proper price for the first murder, those other three people would not have been shot-gun-blasted into eternity. So much for *Life-Without-Parole*.

Life-Without-Parole is a Joke…But it Isn't Funny.

Furthermore, killings outside the walls plotted by those inside the walls are not as uncommon as one might think. Even the Chief Justice of the United States Supreme Court reportedly was a target for Mafia inmates. "Languishing at the federal penitentiary in Lewisburg, Pa., mobsters from three Mafia families allegedly had murder on their minds in 1979, according to recently released FBI documents. The intended victim was Warren Burger." [164]

Another thing about Life-Without-Parole that isn't funny is the phony confessions emanating from those serving such sentences. It's the ploy attempted by Elmo Patrick Sonnier's little brother Eddie after both were convicted of murdering Loretta Bourque and David LeBlanc. With the older Sonnier facing the death penalty, the younger brother, after getting a life sentence, declared, "I want to tell the truth and get everything off my chest."

He then "confessed" it was he and he alone who murdered the two kids. But, the prosecutor in the case "…discredits this confession of guilt, arguing that Eddie Sonnier, his death sentence now overturned by the court, is transparently trying to save his brother from the electric chair. The jury readily agrees with the prosecutor and re-sentences Patrick Sonnier to death." [165] In other words, since Eddie was serving a "life" sentence, the courts would have to wait until that "life" (his) was over before it could exact a death penalty. Eddie Sonnier had nothing to lose. This same bogus ploy was not and is not unique to the brothers Sonnier.

Life-Without-Parole? A life in a maximum security

# An Eye for an Eye
*William T. Harper*

prison today can be a lot shorter; a lot shorter than the Justice Department's Bureau of Justice Statistics says the average stay for inmates on death row in 2004 was 11 years through the death penalty appeals process. And when an inmate "with nothing to lose" or a gang of inmates decided to "hit" another inmate, the end of that Life-Without-Parole sentence is going to be a lot more brutal, a lot more bloodier, and not nearly as antiseptic as when the State carries out a death sentence.

Giving some of these heinous killers a Life-Without-Parole sentence is like throwing a bucket of blood-soaked chum into a school of starving sharks. Maximum security prisons like California's San Quentin are exactly that – "a shark-tank," as one lifer put it during an interview on a "National Geographic Channel Presents" program aired in July 2006. It's survival of the fittest with no holds barred. The ingenuity and creativity of those serving lifetime sentences would find a cure for the common cold and solve the Nation's energy crisis if the convicts turned their talents in those directions.

It is amazing to discover what inmates can turn into lethal weapons that can be used in an escape effort or other mayhem. A convict should be allowed to read a newspaper in his cell, right? It's frightening to know how a long-termer "with nothing to lose" can patiently fold a newspaper so tight that it becomes a menacing, life-threatening club. Or, put a sharp, pointed object – such as a filed-down toothbrush handle – in the end of that newspaper club and it becomes a spear. Some of those long-termers even make dangerous darts out of staples that hold their prison magazines together. It's a shark tank in there.

Nobody's saying prison chow comes close to rivaling that served in fancy French restaurants in New York City or Cajun cuisine in pre-Katrina New Orleans. But, as mediocre as prison food is, it used to be better in some ways. Inmates were occasionally served t-bone steaks. Not anymore. Some of the more clever convicts "with nothing to lose" would

# An Eye for an Eye
*William T. Harper*

gobble down their steaks and pocket the t-bone. That leftover from a Texas steer soon would be filed down into a deadly shank or shiv and there's only one purpose for a shank or a shiv in a prison; it's to penetrate somebody's body, either another inmate's or a member of the prison staff.

In the shark tanks that confine the brutal, despicable Life-Without-Parole prisoners, it's the "feeder" (the correctional officers and other maintenance professionals) that quickly become the ante for those killers in there who "have nothing to lose." According to now retired warden Nancy Doom at Kentucky State Penitentiary in Eddyville, Victor Hiatt, Inmate ID 151701, was the most menacing inmate in that penitentiary. He is, as of August 2012, serving a life sentence elsewhere for murder. Grimly, Hiatt lays it on the line. "I've accepted my own death," the killer says quietly, "so I don't worry about dying. I don't respect life – my own or anybody's." [166] He has made it known, said Ms. Doom, he would like to kill a staff member.

\* \* \*

Some inmates even enter prison with a bulls-eye on their back. They're immediately identified as targets by some of their new prison partners. Some, like the notorious Jeffrey Dahmer are labeled as a "trophy" as soon as the prison door slams shut behind them.

You remember Jeffrey Dahmer, don't you? If not, neither do any of these people – because they're all dead:

- ☐ June 1978      - Stephen Hicks
- ☐ September 1987      - Steven Toumi
- ☐ October 1987      - Jamie Doxtator
- ☐ March 1988      - Richard Guerrero
- ☐ February 1989      - Anthony Sears
- ☐ June 1990      - Eddie Smith
- ☐ July 1990      - Ricky Beeks
- ☐ September 1990      - Ernest Miller

# An Eye for an Eye
*William T. Harper*

☐ September 1990    - David Thomas
☐ February 1991    - Curtis Straughter
☐ April 1991    - Errol Lindsey
☐ May 1991    - Tony Hughes
☐ May 1991    - Konerak Sinthasomphone
☐ June 1991    - Matt Turner
☐ July 1991    - Jeremiah Weinberger
☐ July 1991    - Oliver Lacy
☐ July 1991    - Joseph Bradeholt

These are the young men Dahmer murdered, dismembered and, in some cases, cannibalized. He was sentenced to 15 consecutive life terms in prison for 15 of the above murders. Life-Without-Parole in other words. The abolitionists didn't want him to get the death penalty. Instead, a fellow inmate imposed it. Dahmer became a "target" the minute he walked into the Columbia Correctional Institute in Portage, Wisconsin. (Inmates at San Quentin anointed Scott Peterson with a similar "honor" after he arrived there in 2005 following his conviction in the Christmas Eve 2004 murder of his wife and unborn son.) On November 28, 1994, Dahmer was beaten to death with an iron bar by fellow inmate, Christopher Scarver, another murderer serving a life sentence. Justice can be much swifter and more deadly inside the cellblocks.

The list of fallacies about Life-Without-Parole grows longer than a fisherman's catch. Herb Alexander, Robert Lee Willie's trial prosecutor for his murder of Faith Hathaway, thusly answered the defense's contention the world would be safe because Willie would spend the rest of his life in prison if given a Life-Without-Parole sentence:

> "The statute does say no probation, no parole, no suspension of sentence, but have you ever heard of a pardon or commutation? Those are two things that are given to the governor by the Constitution of the State of Louisiana and they can't

# An Eye for an Eye
*William T. Harper*

be taken away by statute. As a result, a governor, whoever the governor is eight, ten, twelve years from now, can take it upon himself to let Robert Lee Willie back out onto the streets and back out into society because that governor more than likely will not know the facts of this case. So don't think that life really ever means life, because it doesn't." [167]

Speaking of Louisiana and pardons and its governors, the flamboyant Edwin Edwards again comes to mind. According to one report:

"...from 1975 to the end of his second term, [Edwards] granted clemency in 1,199 cases, including 125 murder cases..." and he "used his executive clemency power for his own political and perhaps financial benefit, while endangering the public safety by turning loose hundreds of dangerous criminals." [168]

Edwards' above clemency record benefited an average of 21 murderers a year, almost two a month for five years! And in a most horrible coincidence, Governor Edwards' brother Nolan was shot to death by an inmate the governor had previously pardoned via influence brought by his brother's law firm. [169]

What good is a Life-Without-Parole sentence when you have a governor who has installed a revolving door for murderers in the state's penitentiary? (Ironically, in 2001, Edwards was himself sentenced to 10 years in prison on racketeering charges. So far, none of his successors in the governor's office in Baton Rouge has granted him clemency.) The citizens of the State of Illinois might ask the same question after Governor George Ryan, because of his personal and political beliefs, granted blanket commutation of sentence to all 156 Illinois death row inmates in January, 2003.

# An Eye for an Eye

*William T. Harper*

Yet another Interstate Highway to the Freedom Trail is the sometimes preposterous legal system that has failed so many times in the past and abolitionists want to weaken further in the future. Consider this:

> "Edward Harvey Stokes, a convicted child molester who successfully appealed his life sentence, is a free man. He was released from the Orange County [California] Men's Jail last week. Stokes' conviction was overturned by the 4th District Court of Appeals, which ruled his right to cross-examine was compromised because the 16-year-old boy he allegedly molested killed himself before trial."[170]

Some of the more absolute abolitionists would have, no doubt, freed Stokes merely on his "rehabilitation" statement when he said "he felt like a monster for molesting 212 victims."

Life-Without-Parole is a Joke...But it Isn't Funny.

\* \* \*

Another example shows why life with or without parole is a farce. JoAnne Chesimard, now 62 and living [in Cuba] under the name Assata Shakur, was convicted in 1977 of murdering State Trooper Werner Foerster during a gun battle on the New Jersey Turnpike. A second trooper, James Harper, was wounded. The shootout began after Harper pulled over Chesimard and two companions for a faulty tail light, according to State Police files. Foerster, patrolling nearby, responded to provide back up.

The troopers asked the driver, Clark Squire, to step out of the vehicle after his license did not match the sedan's registration, the files show. As Foerster questioned Squire, Harper walked around the car to speak with Chesimard and her brother-in-law, James Costan. Shots were fired from within the car and both troopers returned fire, according to

# An Eye for an Eye
*William T. Harper*

police. After Foerster was hit and incapacitated, "Chesimard then took the weapon away from Foerster and shot him in the neck and head," [police] said. "This isn't the result of a toe-to-toe exchange. This is an execution and there's a clear distinction."[171]

Sentenced to life in prison, Chesimard escaped from the Clinton Correctional Institution for Women in Hunterdon County (New Jersey) on November 2, 1979 when three gunmen posing as visitors took two guards hostage and drove her out of the facility's maximum-security unit in a van.[172] She fled to Cuba and the United States Department of Justice has offered a one-million dollar bounty for her capture and return to the U. S. The cop-killer escaped the death penalty and then escaped – period. Now, she basks in Castro's Cuba listening to and watching her life story as it has been glowingly portrayed in literature, film and song.[173]

So much for life with, or without parole.

\* \* \*

Escapes, political misconduct, botched prosecutions, and socially liberal judges, juries and parole and pardons boards are not the only ways to circumvent the abysmal Life-Without-Parole sentence. Hurricanes Katrina and Rita devastated parts of Louisiana, Texas and Mississippi in 2005, and left some law enforcement and judicial agencies with many of their records destroyed, thereby throwing open doors for defense lawyers' renewed appeals at taxpayers' expense. And if the defendant in these appeals (i.e., the State) can't produce the records, it loses and inmates walk – right out the prison doors.

What is even more threatening about the Life-Without-Parole panacea is if abolitionists get their way and it does indeed become the ultimate penalty for even the most heinous of crimes, the next step for them might be to see the abolition of Life-Without-Parole – claiming it too is "cruel and unusual" because it leaves murderers with no hope for

# An Eye for an Eye
*William T. Harper*

release! Who knows where efforts to protect killers may end. What we do know is:

Life-Without-Parole is a Joke...But it Isn't Funny.

If Life-Without-Parole really meant there was no possible way for murderers to get out of prison or no possible way they could continue their mayhem even within the confines of the walls, anti-death penalty advocates might have a case. And if Life-Without-Parole really meant what it says – which it obviously doesn't – imagine what incarcerating these killers forever would do to the currently epidemic problem of prison over-crowding. However, there are more loop-holes in the Life-Without-Parole panacea than you'll find in a crocheting contest in an old-folks home. Yet another is, as even abolitionist professor David Dow at the University of Houston tells us, "When evil-doers are not put to death, they grow old in prison, and our passions recede."

Those receding passions showed up as "the dissent [in *Ayers v. Belmontes* where the U.S. Supreme Court upheld California's death penalty law in a 5-4 decision on Nov. 13, 2006] stated that the state's need for an execution was greatly diminished by the fact that this case was now 25 years old, and, hence, the people would gain little by having an execution carried out now, whereas the defendant had everything to lose by an unfair decision...."[174]

This is exactly what has been talked about when killers have extended their time on death row for so long they become old and feeble-looking which brings sympathy from those who judge them today for crimes committed decades ago and about which contemporary judges and parole board members know little of the horror of the time.

That fact in itself could well be a goal of the multi-appeals driven lawyers: let the killers grow old and feeble in prison and then they won't pay the penalty they deserve. Dr. Dow continues and writes about Adolph Hitler's second-in-command (but he could be talking about any mass-murderer), Rudolph Hess:

# An Eye for an Eye
*William T. Harper*

...a "former Nazi who was the sole resident of Spandau prison in France [sic] until he died at the age of 94, these aged monsters can become sympathetic figures, old men with walkers shuffling around prison yards who seem too gray and infirm to have committed the atrocities we know they did. We may not forgive them – some crimes are truly unforgivable – but time inexorably dulls the impulse to punish. Vengeance is a primal and proximate urge. The further we are from the moment of the crime, the less powerful is its pull.

"Because forgetfulness can be the enemy of justice," the professor continues, "we fear that if we do not execute [these] people…, we will one day, many years from now, no longer be capable of apprehending the horrors of their deeds, of feeling the compulsion to punish…. We execute, therefore, because we do not trust the strength of our own moral convictions, because we lack faith in our own memories, because we have no confidence in our power to continue to condemn the actions of a tyrant who remains imprisoned, yet alive." [175]

\* \* \*

Four cases cited here, with or without Life-Without-Parole sentences and even no sentence at all, vividly show how easily human frailty can get anyone out of prison – no matter what sentence they may or may not be serving:

> Mount Clemens, Michigan – A man who killed three people after being mistakenly released from prison pleaded guilty Friday to murdering two of them, a pregnant woman and her husband. Patrick Selepak, 27, faces a mandatory life term in prison without parole for first-degree murder when

# An Eye for an Eye
*William T. Harper*

sentenced Aug. 1. He previously received a life sentence for the third killing.... State corrections officials have acknowledged he should still have been imprisoned at the time of the killings. Several parole workers were disciplined and state release rules tightened. [176]

Centennial, Colorado – Valerie Barnes left her job 3 1/2 years ago, but her refusal to complete final tasks could land her in jail and spring several felons from prison. Barnes was a court reporter in the Arapahoe County courthouse. For three years, she has been unable – or unwilling – to finish transcripts of trials awaiting appeals in Colorado's higher courts. Without the full trial records, the criminal convictions in the eight cases may be voided, which could free the defendants convicted of charges ranging from child molestation to manslaughter...because they do not have complete records of their trials. [177]

Washington, DC – Convicted murderer Robin Lovitt is scheduled to die by injection at Virginia's Greensville Correctional Center on Wednesday night. Only Governor Mark Warner can save his life...and he has never granted clemency to a condemned killer. But now, as Warner [was] considering a run for the 2008 Democratic presidential nomination, he must make a decision on the most controversial death-penalty case of his four-year term. Lovitt's attorneys argue – who has maintained his innocence – should be spared because an Arlington [Virginia] Circuit Court clerk mistakenly threw away DNA evidence that could have proved his claim. [178]

Houston, TX – Four or five deputies – and

# An Eye for an Eye

*William T. Harper*

possibly more – had opportunities to stop condemned murderer Charles Victor Thompson before he walked out of the Harris County Jail, a sheriff's spokesman said today. As the hunt for the 35-year-old multi-murderer widened, Lt. John Martin said Thompson encountered deputies in at least three places in the downtown jail as he made his way to freedom. "This was 100 percent human error," Martin said. [179]

Nonetheless, there are even some anti-death penalty activists who are against the Life-Without-Parole sentence. "Some argue against the measure on legal and philosophical grounds. Stephen Bright, a liberal death penalty lawyer in Atlanta, thinks it should be adopted only as a substitute for capital punishment. Life-Without-Parole is a bad thing," Bright was quoted as saying in a newspaper article by Mike Tolson. "Once you have it on the books, it is given to too many people. There will be overcharging. The state will file death on everybody so that the defendant will plead to life.[180] (For more on Mr. Bright, see this book's Epilogue.)

"Houston defense attorney Rusty Hardin, a longtime prosecutor under former Harris County District Attorney Johnny Holmes, also dislikes the idea. 'It's a stalking horse for the abolition of the death penalty,' Hardin said.... Hardin fears an inevitable expansion of Life-Without-Parole should it go on the books [in Texas]. Repeat offenders and those who commit sex crimes are obvious targets.... 'It has a certain allure to people, but they will really regret it if they get it,' Hardin said. 'There will end up being thousands of those. That punishment will be the end-all, be-all. Every crime will develop its own constituency for Life-Without-Parole. It's terrible social policy.'[181]

"Georgia, which passed a series of life-without-parole laws in the mid-1990s, has seen approximately 250 defendants sentenced under them. The number has increased rapidly, in part because the sentence is not limited to

# An Eye for an Eye
*William T. Harper*

murderers. Any defendant is subject to Life-Without-Parole if he has been convicted twice of the most serious crimes, including rape, armed robbery and aggravated child molestation. Four-time felons also can get it."[182]

William Alford, former prosecutor of Faith Hathaway murderer Robert Lee Willie and now a staunch opponent to capital punishment and a retired (to private practice) public defender in St. Tammany Parish, La., said of murderers he's now working with...

> "While they've done horrible things, they still have redeeming qualities. I've come to believe the thing to do with these people is warehouse them, put them away for life where they can't kill or wreak havoc on society ever again. Some people say, 'Jail is too good for them.' To that, I say, 'you've never been to Angola'."[183]

That may be the case but no matter how bad Louisiana's Angola state prison may be today, it isn't nearly as bad as it was 50 years ago nor, if the do-gooders have their way, is it nearly as good as it will be 50 years from now – leading those same some people to wonder, "where's the punishment?"

\* \* \*

Here's another example of the fallacy of Life-Without-Parole. On November 8, 1988, Fayette County (Kentucky) Deputy Sheriff Joseph Angelucci was shot and killed by William Bennett, 33, while the officer was attempting to serve a warrant on Bennett. The killer was sentenced to 120 years, of which the jury said he had to serve at least half before being eligible for parole. Sixty years plus his 33 years of age would have made him 93 years old before he could even apply. That's pretty close to Life-Without-Parole. But, four years after the officer's murder, the Kentucky Supreme Court

# An Eye for an Eye
*William T. Harper*

issued an opinion saying Bennett would be eligible after serving only 12 years.[184] So much for Life-Without-Parole.

Republican delegate Frank D. Hargrove, Sr. of Virginia stunned his fellow lawmakers by declaring, "One of the responsibilities of government is to protect the public. I have voted for the death penalty over the years numerous times.... But now that we have Life-Without-Parole, I believe that addresses the [public safety] situation without a sentence that is irreversible.... This eliminates the possibility of the awful mistake."[185] Does Life-Without-Parole really "eliminate the possibility of the awful mistake"? Obviously, Delegate Hargrove never heard of Kenneth Allen McDuff...as well as others of his ilk.

Speaking of "awful mistakes," look at this case and think about Life-Without-Parole: Willie Joe McAdams was sentenced to 40 years in prison for shooting a man in the head in 2003. The man survived, although he lost an eye (he could very easily have died). McAdams served exactly two years of his 40-year sentence and was officially released because of what the Texas Department of Criminal Justice admitted was a "human" error. If a "human" error can be made in McAdams' case, could not another "human" error put any heinous killer back out on the streets, whether s/he is serving a Life-Without-Parole or a 40-year sentence? Isn't that what happened with Kenneth Allen McDuff after he killed three people and a "human" error sent him back out to commit at least five more murders? Life-Without-Parole is the answer? Is it, as Mr. Hargrove of Virginia said, a sentence that is "irreversible"?

And finally, consider this: If repealing the death penalty in favor of Life-Without-Parole isn't bad enough, take a look at Critical Resistance, a national grassroots prison abolition group. According to its website, "Critical Resistance works to build an International movement to end the Prison Industrial Complex by challenging the belief that caging and controlling people makes us safe. We believe that basic necessities such as food, shelter, and freedom are what really

# An Eye for an Eye
*William T. Harper*

make our communities secure. As such, our work is part of global struggles against inequality and powerlessness." [186]

But before Critical Resistance ends the prison system "as we know it," consider this "benefit" available to those killers serving Life-Without-Parole:

> State prison officials in Massachusetts must provide taxpayer-funded sex-reassignment surgery to a transgender inmate serving life in prison for murder, because it is the only way to treat her "serious medical need," a federal judge ruled on September 4, 2012. Michelle Kosilek was born male but has received hormone treatments and now lives as a woman in an all-male prison. Kosilek was named Robert when married to Cheryl Kosilek and was convicted of murdering her in 1990. U.S. District Judge Mark Wolf is believed to be the first federal judge to order prison officials to provide sex-reassignment surgery for a transgender inmate. [187]

Yes, just "lock 'em up and throw away the key and everybody will be safe," – transsexual or not, right? Wrong! Again!

Here's another reason why. As reported in a *Houston Chronicle* article appearing on September 3, 2012:

> "With four months still remaining, 2012 is already the deadliest year in more than a decade in Texas prisons. The Texas Department of Criminal Justice has reported 10 homicides this year, up from only three in 2011. There were five in 2010 and just one in 2009, according to agency figures...."
>
> "Unfortunately, offenders serving prison sentences can become aggressive and act out violently against not only staff but also other offenders," prison department spokesman Jason

# An Eye for an Eye
*William T. Harper*

Clark said. In 1985, 27 inmates were killed and hundreds of others hurt in attacks...."

Yeah, nobody has to worry about these killers once they're sentenced Life-Without-Parole....

After all of this, it is revolting to listen to the rest of the anti-death penalty cabal weep and wail with multiple tissues daubing their eyes as they tell us that killing the killers won't bring their victims back to life. Neither will their alternative to execution — the benevolent Life-Without-Parole. So where is the justice in their argument for substituting one penalty for another?

Life-Without-Parole is a Joke...But it Isn't Funny.

\* \* \*

# An Eye for an Eye
*William T. Harper*

## Chapter Five

### It Isn't the Law...It's the Lawyers

*On January 25, 1980, probably by posing as a security guard, Donald Eugene Harding managed to gain entrance to the Tucson (AZ) motel room of Robert Wise and Martin Concannon. Wise was district supervisor for KAR Car Products Inc. Concannon was the corporation's area sales representative in Tucson. Their bodies were discovered in Wise's motel room the following morning.*

*Wise was found on the floor next to the bed, tethered to a bedpost by a restraint wrapped around his neck. He had been bound with his hands behind his back, with his ankles tied together and secured to his hand ligatures. Wise had been shot once in the chest from a few inches distance with a .25 caliber pistol. This wound perforated his spinal cord and was the cause of death. In addition, he had been shot in the left temple from a distance of no more than three inches. He had been further bludgeoned with a motel lamp, causing abrasions of the head and skull, broken teeth and multiple fractures of the right side of the jaw. Chips broken from the wooden lamp were removed from this victim's right temple and mouth.*

*Concannon's body was found in the bathroom area of the room. Like Wise, he had been shot in the left chest region at close range, and the chest wound similarly perforated his spinal cord. As was Wise, Concannon had been shot near the temple from no more than three inches distance. Unlike Wise, however, Concannon did not die instantaneously from these wounds. According to the medical examiner, this victim lived a short time after being shot. The examiner testified to three other findings concerning Concannon. He found hemorrhages at the base of Concannon's neck caused by bindings secured there. Second, he found evidence of "defensive wounds" in the form of black and blue marks over Concannon's knuckles of the sort sustained while trying to ward off*

# An Eye for an Eye
## William T. Harper

*blows. Finally, he had removed a pair of calf-length men's dress stockings from the mouth of this victim, socks which had been pushed to the back of his throat, thereby obstructing his breathing passage.*

*The two victims had been bound and otherwise restrained with dozens of strips of bedding material, shoelaces and their own clothing before their executions. Their bodies were covered with blankets. Robert Wise's briefcase, containing his credit cards, was removed from the motel. Mark Concannon's borrowed Oldsmobile was taken from the motel parking lot.* [188]

\* \* \*

Donald Eugene Harding, who was arrested the day after these murders, represents just about everything that's wrong with the abolitionists' case against the death penalty. He was a heinous and depraved killer. He was sentenced to Life-Without-Parole *for twenty-five years*. He attempted murder while serving that Life-Without-Parole sentence. He escaped from prison and went on a killing rampage.

**Donald E. Harding**

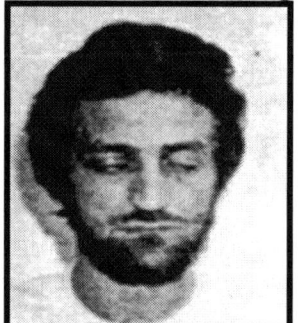

One of his attorneys tried to circumvent the law by lying. He made a mockery out of the judicial appeals process.

The only thing right about the Donald Eugene Harding story is his gas-chamber execution lasted 10 minutes and 31 seconds [189] (no one knows exactly how long it took his

# An Eye for an Eye
*William T. Harper*

tortured victims to die) and it caused Arizonans to vote for lethal injection for all future executions.

Here is an official list of crimes Harding is accused of committing (the Concannon and Wise murders excluded) after he broke out of a Little Rock, Arkansas jail on Sept. 17, 1979 where he was being held for first-degree murder and battery:

- Attempting to rob a prostitute in Chicago on Sept. 27, 1979.
- Robbing a steakhouse in Omaha of $83,000 in cash and jewels, and pistol-whipping a patron on September 30, 1979.
- Holding up a Knoxville, Tennessee bank on October 23, 1979.
- The murder of Stanton Winston Blanton in Dallas on December 10, 1979.
- The kidnapping and robbery of the B.R. Baker family in their north Dallas home on December 11, 1979.
- Using a phony security guard's badge to enter insurance agent Ronald Svetgoff's motel room in Waco, Texas, before tying and gagging him, and stealing his car on December 18, 1979.
- Tying up Clayton Hall, his wife and another couple, and robbing them in Dallas on December 24, 1979.
- Robbing, hog-tying and gagging Phillip Buss in a Salt Lake City hotel on December 31, 1979, and stealing his car.
- Robbing and murdering Charles Dickerson on January 3, 1980, in a motel in South Lake Tahoe, California. Dickerson was found beneath a bed, bound and gagged, and dead of asphyxiation.

# An Eye for an Eye
*William T. Harper*

- Pulling a .25-caliber automatic pistol on Frank Palmer of Sacramento, and tying him with cord and neckties from Palmer's apartment before stealing his car and credit card on January 5, 1980.
- Asking to rent an apartment from Lyle and Margaret Murphy of Bakersfield, California, and then stealing their money and their car.
- Forcing Joseph Wohlers and his uncle, Robert Stoick, into their Los Angeles hotel room at gunpoint on January 6, 1980, and hog-tying them before taking their credit cards, luggage and car.
- Murdering and stealing a car from Gerald Huth, a businessman from Minnesota, on U.S. 101 near Paso Robles, California on January 10, 1980.
- Kidnapping and robbing Shirley Land and four others in her husband's San Diego optometry clinic, January 21, 1980.
- Using adhesive tape from Allan Gage's *colostomy bag* [emphasis added] to tie his hands and feet while robbing him in a Phoenix motel room on January 25, 1980. Gage suffocated on a sock stuffed in his mouth and secured with tape....[190]

Harding is another of those animals the anti-death penalty types weep and wail about; saying this pillar of society does not deserve the ultimate punishment for his multitude of ultimate crimes. They moan that his extended death in the Arizona gas chamber was "cruel and unusual punishment" – while never saying a word about the cruelty he viciously inflicted on his murder victims Stanton Winston Blanton, Charles Dickerson, Gerald Huth, Allen Gage, Robert Wise and Martin Concannon.

# An Eye for an Eye

*William T. Harper*

This person (the noun "man" doesn't quite fit here) colluded with his unscrupulous lawyer to lie in court, circumvent the law through a phony claim of fear of bodily harm, and get yet another, last-minute stay of his much-deserved execution. That stay was based on the revelation that "the convicted killer's original attorney [Dan Cooper] had admitted in an affidavit he told Harding that Harding's best hope was to create errors in the trial [while acting as his own attorney].... Harding virtually presented no defense, made no opening or closing statements and asked only one question during the trial."[191]

To carry this travesty of justice to its ultimate extreme, "...Cooper was defended by his boss, County Public Defender Fred Dardis, who said while obviously putting his personal belief ahead of the law he was sworn to uphold, 'We support Dan and his fight to keep Mr. Harding from being put to death'." Cooper continued the charade by claiming, in effect, it's alright to lie to a judge and jury. "...I don't think I've done anything unethical," he said. "[Harding's] only chance was to create an error and the best chance for that was for him to defend himself."[192] Is that in itself not a punishable crime? Is that conspiracy?

This all begs the question: What is the bonafide role of a defense attorney, court-appointed or not? Is it to simply get the client off no matter how much cheating, manipulation, fabrication and deception is necessary? If bald-faced lying in a court of law by a lawyer isn't "unethical," what is? Evidently, as far as Messrs Cooper and Dardis are concerned, anything goes in a court of law – no matter how disreputable and despicable. Harding, and his co-conspirators Cooper and Dardis, are about as dishonest as a heavyweight boxing champion throwing a fight so he can get another big financial payoff via a re-match.

According to attorney Cooper, "The state now alleges that Don Harding has confessed to committing the Tucson homicides as well as other crimes."[193] Still, the following condensed list of appeals were made on Harding's behalf, all

# An Eye for an Eye
*William T. Harper*

of which were ultimately denied, some summarily, thereby showing how ridiculous were some of those charges.[194] These extended appeals in a case in which there was no doubt of the viciousness of the murders and the depravity of the murderer are, no doubt, similar to those in many other cases. They, in turn, lead to excessive delays and burgeoning costs inherent in the appeals processes, all of which are used by death penalty abolitionists in defense of their "cause."

- January 28, 1980, the Pima County Grand Jury indicted Donald Eugene Harding on two counts of first-degree murder, two counts of armed robbery, two counts of kidnapping, and theft of property valued at over $1,000. For two years while awaiting trial, Harding was represented by public defender Cooper. During this period, Cooper filed 30 motions seeking to exclude evidence, delay the trial, and develop an insanity defense....
- March 15, 1982, Harding asked the state court to allow him to represent himself on an unrelated charge of deadly assault by a prisoner. The trial court granted that request and appointed Cooper as advisory counsel.
- March 23, 1982, Cooper requested he be allowed to withdraw because Harding wanted to act as his own attorney. The court denied the request when Harding refused to sign the waiver of counsel form. Cooper apparently told Harding that he would be relieved as counsel only if Harding threatened him. Harding told Cooper to consider himself "threatened."
- April 15, 1982, Harding again requested to represent himself and Cooper filed a motion to withdraw. The judge permitted Harding's request but appointed Cooper as advisory counsel, stating "the problem of threats" would persist no matter who represented Harding or acted as advisory counsel. Cooper

# An Eye for an Eye
*William T. Harper*

continued to pursue some pretrial motions he had filed and served as advisory counsel throughout the trial, which began on April 20, 1982. Harding was convicted by a Pima County Superior Court jury of all counts named in the indictment on April 27, 1982.

- May 26, 1982, an aggravation hearing was held before the trial court. Harding refused to present mitigating evidence. The court found four aggravating and no mitigating circumstances. The court sentenced Harding to death for the two counts of first-degree murder, two consecutive 21-year terms for robbery, two consecutive 21-year terms for kidnapping and a consecutive five-year term for theft of property [for a total of 89 years, consecutively].
- September 6, 1983, the Arizona Supreme Court affirmed the convictions and sentences on appeal and it denied a petition for rehearing.
- January 10, 1984, the United States Supreme Court denied *certiorari*.
- March 20, 1984, Harding filed for post-conviction relief and his requested stay of execution was granted on March 23, 1984.
- August 7 and October 30, 1984, evidentiary hearings on this issue were held.
- December 28, 1984, after making extensive Findings of Fact and Conclusions of Law, the trial court denied post-conviction relief and dissolved the stay of execution on January 3, 1985.
- March 20, 1985, a petition for reconsideration was denied.
- June 5, 1985, The Arizona Supreme Court denied review of the post-conviction proceedings; and on June 12, 1985, scheduled Harding's execution for August 7, 1985.

# An Eye for an Eye

*William T. Harper*

- August 2, 1985, Harding's first petition for writ of *habeas corpus* and a motion for stay of execution was granted.
- October 16, 1985, Harding's appointed counsel, Francisco Leon, filed an amended petition for writ of *habeas corpus*, which was denied on April 30, 1986.
- December 21, 1987, Ninth Circuit affirmed this Court's denial of all relief.
- October 3, 1988, United States Supreme Court denied *certiorari*.
- December 22, 1988, Arizona Supreme Court issued a warrant of execution, scheduling Harding's execution for February 22, 1989.
- February 2, 1989, Harding filed his second state petition for post-conviction relief.
- February 8, 1989, Arizona Supreme Court stayed Harding's execution.
- On October 5, 1990, after the United States Supreme Court denied *certiorari,* the state appellate court lifted the stay and granted Harding leave to file an amended petition for post-conviction relief.
- November 7, 1990, Harding filed an amended petition for post-conviction relief.
- May 22, 1991, trial court dismissed the petition and issued Findings of Fact and Conclusions of Law holding every issue precluded and dismissed the second petition and request for an evidentiary hearing. The trial court denied Harding's motion for rehearing.
- August 19, 1991, Harding petitioned Arizona Supreme Court for review.
- October 24, 1991, Arizona Supreme Court gran
- ted the state's request to issue a warrant of execution and scheduled Harding's execution for January 3, 1992.

# An Eye for an Eye
*William T. Harper*

- November 13, 1991, Harding's defense counsel filed a petition for writ of *habeas corpus* in Arizona Supreme Court.
- December 18, 1991, Arizona Supreme Court stayed pending execution "to fully consider all of the medical, psychological and psychiatric exhibits submitted."
- March 18, 1992, Arizona Supreme Court denied Harding's motion to remand for an evidentiary hearing, petition for review of post conviction petition, petition for writ of *habeas corpus* and various pending motions.
- March 19, 1992, Arizona Supreme Court issued a warrant scheduling Harding's execution for April 6, 1992.
- March 27, 1992, Harding filed this second Petition for Writ of *Habeas Corpus* with this Court.
- April 6, 1992, Harding executed.

Don't bother to count the number of questionable appeals cited above. Just count the pages!

This legal "three-ring circus" took more than 12 years between indictment and execution! One can only imagine how many chuckles killers like Harding and attorneys like Cooper have when they make such jokes out of these life-and-death matters. They even went to the extreme – given the list of crimes the killer committed as shown above – of filing a motion to have multiple-murderer Donald Eugene Harding released from jail on his own recognizance! Cooper must have felt that too was not "unethical."

For 12 years – from capture to execution – Harding and his defense counsels were granted hearing after hearing, no matter how trivial their claims apparently were. For 12 years, justice that was due Harding was delayed. For 12 years, skyrocketing costs for these frivolous claims were heaped on the backs of law-abiding, tax-paying citizens of Arizona and

# An Eye for an Eye
## William T. Harper

the other 49 states. And when all was said and done, what was the result? Donald Eugene Harding finally paid the ultimate penalty for his multiple ultimate crimes and, death penalty abolitionists had another phony charge that the cost of execution is too high!

\* \* \*

Whether these delaying tactics are by coincidence or design, they are more the rule than the exception. But, consider also this case: Condemned murderer Donald Beardslee, who killed two young San Francisco-area women in 1981 while on parole from an earlier murder conviction, was executed by lethal injection on January 19, 2005 at San Quentin State Prison. He killed Laura Griffin, 54, in her apartment in December, 1969, the same night the two met at a St. Louis-area bar. She was stabbed, choked and drowned in a bathtub. Beardslee pled guilty to second-degree murder, got an 18-year sentence, and was paroled in 1977. He was still on parole when he murdered Stacey Benjamin, 19, and Patty Geddling, 23, in a drug deal in April of 1981. Beardslee got the death sentence for Geddling's murder and Life-Without-Parole for Benjamin's murder. His appeals questioned the competence of one of his trial lawyers, who reportedly read "Bon Appetit" magazine during part of Beardslee's testimony.[195] Although it will never be proven, one has to wonder if this defense attorney was up to another frivolous, fraudulent and outrageous sham (as the Cooper above appeared to be) in a blatantly false effort to delay his client's deserved justice or at least give him an unwarranted cause for appeal.

Perception, as well as beauty, is in the eye of the beholder. How else can courts like the Fourth and Fifth Circuits rule when they are constantly besieged with frivolous appeals brought by death row appellants and their justice-delaying suits from big law firms of New York, Chicago, and Washington, DC?

# An Eye for an Eye
*William T. Harper*

As Harris County (Texas) District Attorney, C. A. (Chuck) Rosenthal said the whole appeals system is driven by the defendant because it's obviously to his benefit to take as much time as possible. "Until 1995 in Texas," he related, "you could file as many writs as you wanted to in a capital case. We've had people go through four or five writs. And one writ means [going through] the trial court, the appeals court, the Federal District court, the Fifth Circuit, and the Supreme Court. And they would go through that five times. We even had claims on the day of execution regarding *voir dire* [jury selection] and that goes all the way back to the first day of the trial." [196]

According to the Barry Latzer/James Cauthen study mentioned herein Chapter Two, et al., "…roughly 60% of all death penalty case reversals on appeal concern the sentence only. This means the guilt of the murder is unaffected by the reversal. The reason for this high sentence-reversal rate," the study continues, "is that death cases use juries to sentence in separate sentencing trials, as required by the Supreme Court. Any proceeding that uses juries is more prone to reversal, not because juries make more mistakes, but because the appeals process focuses on the kinds of mistakes that occur in such proceedings. It is these sentencing trials that account for most of the death penalty reversals."

An example of such tactics is found in an opinion filed by the United States Court of Appeals for the Fourth Circuit on June 27, 1995, on behalf of Willie Lloyd Turner. Five lawyers from New York City and Washington, DC firms "… filed a single-issue petition for a writ of *habeas corpus* (his fourth federal *habeas* petition overall) arguing that the Commonwealth of Virginia would violate the Eighth Amendment's prohibition against cruel and unusual punishment by executing him after the 15 years he has spent on death row under allegedly torturous conditions. The district court dismissed his petition. We hold," the court ruled "that Turner has *inexcusably abused the writ* [emphasis added], and therefore we affirm the judgment of the district court." [197]

# An Eye for an Eye

*William T. Harper*

In summarizing the history in Turner's case, the Court noted, "On July 12, 1978, Turner murdered W. Jack Smith, Jr., during an armed robbery of Mr. Smith's jewelry store. In December 1979 a Virginia jury convicted him and fixed his sentence at death. The trial court imposed the death penalty on February 6, 1980." In writing his concurrence with the Fourth Circuit Court's affirmation of Turner's death sentence, Circuit Judge J. Michael Luttig took additional time to deservedly blast the appellant and his lawyers and others like them, to wit:

> It is a mockery of our system of justice, and an affront to law-abiding citizens who are already rightly disillusioned with that system, for a convicted murderer, who, through his own interminable efforts of delay and systemic abuse has secured the almost-indefinite postponement of his sentence, to then claim that the almost-indefinite postponement renders his sentence unconstitutional. This is the crowning argument on behalf of those who have politicized capital punishment even within the judiciary. With this argument, we have indeed entered the theater of the absurd, where politics disguised as "intellectualism" occupies center stage, no argument is acknowledged to be frivolous, and common sense and judgment play no role. And while this predictable plot unfolds with our acquiescence, if not our participation, we lament the continuing decline in respect for the courts and for the law.
> 
> Petitioner does not contest his guilt. He concedes, as he says he must, that his death sentence was constitutionally permissible when imposed. He even concedes that, until a month and a half ago, he himself did not wish to pursue further appeals. He has brought four state *habeas* petitions and this is his fourth federal *habeas* petition. His

# An Eye for an Eye
*William T. Harper*

> various claims have now been reviewed *in at least twenty different federal and state proceedings* [emphasis added]. He has been accorded every possible opportunity to test the legitimacy of his conviction and sentence. The delay of which he now complains is a direct consequence of his own litigation strategy, coupled (ironically, although not surprisingly) with the customary leniency allowed him by the courts to press his claims as effectively as possible.
>
> This is not -- or at least it should not be -- a political game. The object is to apply the law, not to defeat it through subterfuge. Petitioner's claim should be recognized for the frivolous claim that it is, and his delay in raising it, for the manipulation that it is.... As long as the courts indulge such sophistic arguments, then such arguments will be made, and the politicization of capital punishment within the courts will continue.[198]

Here we have lawyers for a confessed murderer who have spent 14 years going up and down court house steps – dragging victims' families with them to hear and rehear gory details – "in at least 20 different federal and state proceedings" and with this latest appeal, to claim that to keep Turner on death row any longer would be "cruel and unusual punishment." Turner himself has said he "did not wish to pursue further appeals" but the legal eagles keep pushing the courts to the extremes with "sophistic arguments" that make one wonder about the legal subterfuge. Do they really care about Willie Lloyd Turner or have they written him off for their own personal and corporate gains and discarded him to the outhouse, as Ohio death-row inmate Kevin Scudder declared in his own case in Chapter Two of this book? Furthermore, is it any wonder that the costs for litigation in death penalty cases runs high?

\* \* \*

# An Eye for an Eye
*William T. Harper*

Legal and social theorists are quick to excoriate some judges who, they claim, "are all too happy to appoint inadequate defense attorneys, thus assuring a guilty verdict and a death sentence...[and who] may be all too prone to side with the prosecution: supporting their motions, sustaining their objections, and – no small thing in a public forum – addressing them politely and with respect, while belittling and berating the defense."[199] On the other hand, they never do mention their bleeding-heart brethren like Dan Cooper at the courtroom defense tables or sitting on the bench who do everything in their power not just to defend them, but to shield and protect killers from the rights of justice.

Take, for instance, the case of James Free who raped and murdered Bonnie Serpico in 1979. At Free's trial, the presiding judge forced the victim's husband, Andy Serpico, and his daughters to sit in the back of the courtroom while Free's weeping mother was allowed to sit next to the jury. The judge also denied the jury the knowledge that Ms. Serpico was indeed the victim's mother because, he said, "that would be prejudicial."[200]

Let us not forget either federal District Court Judge Robert N. Chatigny in Connecticut. In August of 1987, Michael Ross was given the death penalty unanimously by a jury of his peers after being convicted of the rape and murder of seven women and the murder of an eighth over three years starting in 1981. Even the U. S. Supreme Court upheld the sentence. But, interventionist Judge Chatigny stayed Ross' execution because, the judge charged, Ross' sexual sadism was "clearly a mitigating factor."[201] Was the judge suggesting the more sadistic a killer is the lighter his sentence should be? If you're just an "ordinary" killer-rapist you don't get off; if you're a "sadistic" killer-rapist, you do? Had Judge (the word is used advisedly) Chatigny presided over the trial of the infamous bank-robber Willie Sutton, he probably would have awarded that thief the keys to the U. S. gold repository at Ft. Knox, Kentucky.

# An Eye for an Eye

*William T. Harper*

But this story doesn't end there. Ross, who confessed to murdering the eight women, faced another execution deadline and again, Judge (?) Chatigny intervened. This time he called the killer's court-appointed attorney on the eve of the execution and told him, "I'll have your law license" if the lawyer didn't file another last-minute appeal based on the defendant's competency.[202] This unheard-of interference from the bench brought many in the Constitution State's legal community up in arms with one of them saying, "He clearly stretched the bounds of propriety, if not judicial ethics."[203]

And still this story of "anything goes" with those opposed to the death penalty doesn't end there. Chatigny, when he was asked during a hearing questioning his actions if they had anything to do with "his partiality with respect to the implementation or execution of a death sentence in any litigation," he answered "No," and that he was free to decide these issues according to his "own conscience."[204] What the jurist didn't disclose was that he "was an advocate in the Ross case in 1992, before he became a judge."[205] This guy is just about in the same league as Howard Marsellus – chair of the Louisiana Pardons Board who went to federal prison for accepting bribes (see Chapter Four) – and whom Sister Prejean heaps so much scorn and later praise upon in her books.

As that great American composer Cole Porter wrote for the 1934 Broadway musical *Anything Goes*:

> The world has gone mad today
> And good's bad today,
> And black's white today,
> And day's night today....
> *Anything Goes*

\* \* \*

As shown above, over and over defense attorneys launch counterfeit claims and stop at nothing to keep their clients

# An Eye for an Eye
*William T. Harper*

from getting the justice they deserve. The case of Porfirio Jimenez is another example. Jimenez was given a Life-Without-Parole sentence after confessing to the May 2001 murder of 10-year-old Walter Contreras Valenzuela in Morristown, New Jersey. Later, a New Jersey appeals court said in October 2005 that Morris County *prosecutors* "must prove to a jury that the accused child-killer is not mentally retarded before they can ask jurors to impose a death sentence."[206] In other words, the *prosecution* must prove a negative. The prosecution had to appeal the ruling – just as defense attorneys knew it would – thereby, of course, causing further delay in scheduling the trial.

Some semblance of sanity did prevail as the state Supreme Court, however, overruled this, saying "it is the burden of the defense to prove, by preponderance of evidence, that a person is mentally retarded to avoid the death penalty.[207] It is the role of the defense to prove retardation, as per New Jersey's highest court."[208] But, as was its aim, the defense got one more delay in administration of justice and the continuance could go on *ad infinitum*. "Justice delayed is justice denied."

On the other hand, death penalty abolitionists never mention nor castigate sympathetic and conniving defense lawyers such as, for instance, the aforementioned Dan Cooper in Arizona and a counterpart in Ohio, Keith Yeazel. Yeazel was even more creative in debasing the criminal justice system by asking the Ohio Supreme Court to spare his client, Phillip E. Elmore, from the death penalty. Elmore was convicted of kidnapping, aggravated robbery and the aggravated murder of his former girlfriend by beating her to death. The rationale for Yeazel's August 8, 2006 appeal was that Elmore's jurors "were not allowed to smoke while deliberating."[209]

While "defense attorneys concede that as many as three quarters of the requests may be frivolous,"[210] even some killers who seemingly have more ethics than their liberal-leaning defense attorneys get fed up with some of the

# An Eye for an Eye
*William T. Harper*

inconsequential appeals process.

Paul Dennis Reid was a dishwasher in a Donelson, Tennessee restaurant who was fired on February 15, 1997. The next day, he launched a killing spree that lasted three months. He murdered Steve Hampton, 25, and Sarah Jackson, 16, execution style. Ronald Santiago, 27, Robert A. Sewell Jr., 23, and Andrea Brown, 17, were shot and killed in a midnight robbery (in which Jose Alfredo Ramirez Gonzalez, was stabbed 17 times but survived). Angela Holmes, 21, and Michelle Mace, 16, were kidnapped and their throats were slashed.

He was later arrested, tried and convicted in three separate trials and sentenced to death. Over Reid's objections, his attorneys tried to stop his execution, contending he was mentally ill and couldn't comprehend the gravity of his decisions. Twice, however, Reid implored Tennessee courts to disregard those appeals.

In a letter to the State's Supreme Court, he wrote:

> "'May I please reiterate my meticulous, yet adamant conscious choice not to pursue any post-conviction appeals.... Defense attorneys," he continued, "have admonished me that they intend to petition the high courts with frivolous relentless appeals...." Therefore, he concluded, "I elect to no furtherance [of] any post-conviction appeals." [211]

If Reid is truthful here, even his defense attorneys are admitting their flagrant use of "frivolous relentless appeals."

Some would say Reid's attorney and Messrs Cooper and Yeazel should also be labeled as incompetent as were the figuratively-speaking and aforementioned herein "sleeping lawyers." These frivolous, inconsequential appeals did nothing more than waste everyone's time, increase the needless cost of the appeals system (thereby bolstering the abolitionists' claims of exorbitant death penalty costs), and bring added grief to families of the victims. Justice delayed is

# An Eye for an Eye
*William T. Harper*

justice denied, no matter from which side of the legal bar the irresponsible delay comes.

This all brings to mind an attempt on then President-elect Franklin Delano Roosevelt's life on February 15, 1933. The 33rd President was to give a speech in Miami, Florida. Giuseppe Zangara fired five pistol shots at the dais, missed Roosevelt, but he hit Chicago Mayor Anton Cernak and five other people, one of whom died. Less than a month later, Cernak also died. Zangara, who pleaded guilty to murder, was electrocuted on March 20 – one month and five days after the attack. Justice delayed is justice denied. That being the case, justice surely was not denied in this case.

\* \* \*

One might be tempted to agree with the abolitionists' implied indictment of appeals lawyers where they contend that just about every murderer who ever entered a prison death row was put there by inept, corrupt, and maybe even "sleeping lawyers." Yet when some of those same "incompetent" lawyers resort to skullduggery on the other side of the fence, never is there a hue and cry from the death penalty apologists of the world.

Remember the lawyer who lied to the judge and told him he was fearful his client would harm him? Remember the no-smoking-while-deliberating joke? How about the "cold sandwiches" appeal? One defendant's appeal was based on the fact that he was given "bologna sandwiches during lunch breaks at his trial."[212] Remember the "Bon Appetit" magazine-reading defense lawyer? When those things happen, when defense lawyers resort to every unethical trick in the book to falsify the record, to raise the costs, to delay the inevitable, they're seen by some as "crusaders" who will stop at nothing to keep their clients from the death chamber – *even those proved guilty of terrible crimes.*[213]

While never mentioning tactics used by their surrogates in the legal system such as those listed above, just

# An Eye for an Eye
*William T. Harper*

about all other defense attorneys who do not keep or get their clients off death row (i.e., the "sleeping lawyers" – all *one* of him), are demeaned as "shamefully inadequate" or "less than competent" or as "abysmally inept." They are consigned by abolitionists to the junk heap of the legal system. And just about every prosecutor who ever tried to get a murderer the justice he deserved, is lumped into a bag of those who "deliberately" mislead juries and those who will "win at all costs" in an effort to go down the road that will lead to that state's governor's mansion.

But when crusading legal-eagles resort to questionable tactics in the courtroom (ala Dan Cooper), they are lauded. When defense lawyers don't raise any objections during a murder trial, abolitionists quickly claim "criminal courts, overwhelmed with the sheer number of cases, resort to 'bargain basement' justice."[26] On the other hand, when an attorney, Ronald J. Tabak, "whose Wall Street firm [hardly 'bargain basement'] has volunteered" to participate in a death penalty defense, and it then clutters a court calendar with frivolous appeal petitions, then all's fair in love and war.[214] In this case, Tabak's appeal (made on behalf of multi-murderer Robert Lee Willie who was convicted of savaging Faith Hathaway) was lavishly praised in *Dead Man Walking* as "a thick document, 170 pages, bound with a blue cardboard cover" containing "fourteen arguments on Robert's behalf."

The hot-shot Wall Street lawyer cites pretrial publicity and demands a change of venue. He claims the media had the effrontery to call this horrific murder "the worst crime in the history of Washington Parish." That's exactly what it was. He claims the district attorney in the case called Robert Lee Willie and Joseph Vaccaro "animals". Knowing what they did to Faith Hathaway, it would be hard to find a more appropriate noun for them in the entire English language.

The pin-striped suit from the Big Apple even charged "the fact that Vaccaro had received life and Willie death [left] the impression that Willie was more culpable than Vaccaro." What difference does that make? The fact that both were

# An Eye for an Eye
*William T. Harper*

equally culpable in the unspeakable rape and murder of Faith Hathaway makes them equally guilty. Instead of bemoaning Willie's fate, had they been perhaps honest, they would have admitted Vaccaro's sentence should have been equal to Willie's.

And, of course, Tabak throws in the old war-horse: "claims of ineffectiveness of counsel."[215] At least he didn't claim Willie's lawyer was asleep throughout the trial. Needless to say, "in August 1984, the Fifth Circuit Court of Appeals denied the petition and a request for rehearing, and on November 12, the U. S. Supreme Court refused to hear the case."[216]

\* \* \*

Anti-death penalty proponents constantly cite the cost of death penalty litigation vs. the cost of keeping a killer in prison for life as a reason for promoting Life-Without-Parole. We won't bother with the ethical question of whether dollars should matter in a life vs. death situation or the value of a murdered victim's life vs. court costs. But, as Sister Prejean notes, the "execution of a prisoner costs more than life imprisonment. That's because," she writes, "capital trials require more expert witnesses and more investigators, a longer jury-selection process (those who oppose the death penalty must be screened out), the expenses of sequestering a jury, not one but two trials because of the required separate sentencing trial, and appeals in state and federal courts...."

"In Florida," she continues, "which may be typical, each death sentence is estimated to cost approximately $3.18 million, compared to the cost of life imprisonment (40 years) of about $516,000."[217] Perhaps if hot-shot lawyers wouldn't keep cluttering court dockets with frivolous appeals such as the above-cited, if anti-death penalty attorneys stopped lying to the courts, if no-smoking-while-deliberating appeals weren't offered as a delaying tactic, if cold bologna sandwiches weren't such baloney, it wouldn't cost the claimed

# An Eye for an Eye

*William T. Harper*

but herein disputed $3.18 million to finally give murderers the quick justice they deserve. All this assumes the nebulous claim that murderers will, indeed, spend the rest of their lives passively in prison and not rape and kill again – inside prison walls or out.

Specific dollar claims notwithstanding, why does it cost so much to finalize an execution sentence? James B. Hubbard is an example of an answer to that question. He was convicted of murdering 62-year-old Lillian Montgomery on January 10, 1977 – less than a year after he was released from prison for another murder. Ms. Montgomery died after being shot three times, once in the face, once in the head, and once in the shoulder. Hubbard, who was living with Ms. Montgomery at the time, said the woman *committed suicide*.[218]

For the next 27 years, Hubbard and his lawyers filed appeal after appeal in court after court. Twenty-seven years – and, other than some grandchildren who probably never met her personally – who's left to know or care about Lillian Montgomery? The anguish of her rape and the horror of her death are only remembered by some jaded attorneys and in some faded newspaper clippings. Her 97th birthday anniversary would have occurred this year (2012). Who's left to sing "Happy Birthday to you"?

After his final appeal was rejected by the U. S. Supreme Court, Hubbard was finally executed by lethal injection on August 5, 2004. For almost three decades (not even counting the 20 years he previously served in prison for his first murder), James B. Hubbard was a financial burden to the state and people of Alabama – because Ms. Montgomery "committed suicide." That's why it costs so much to bring justice to murderers.

\* \* \*

Arguing against the abolitionists' claim that death sentences typically "cost approximately $3.18 million, compared to the cost of life imprisonment (40 years) of about $516,000,"

# An Eye for an Eye
*William T. Harper*

former Harris County District Attorney Rosenthal responded:

> "It all depends on how you do the math. Some of the significant figures the abolitionists throw in as part of the cost of the death penalty process," he noted, "actually includes salaries for the prosecutors – which would have to be paid whether or not they were involved in that particular case. The abolitionists, to pad their point, sometimes even add in the cost of the building the prosecutors work in! It all depends on how and who is doing the math."[219]

One who did the math is Ray Larson, Fayette (Kentucky) Commonwealth Attorney. He too has heard these claims by abolitionists regarding comparative costs of incarceration vs. execution. He had a merry time refuting them. Responding to a newspaper article of March 8, 2005 in which public defender Ernie Lewis says, "It has cost taxpayers 'perhaps' $50 million for each of Kentucky's two executions," Larson wrote:

> "There he goes again. State public defender Ernie Lewis is throwing around 'statistics' again. Let's look at his latest claim. This time it's about the death penalty and his 'guess' at the cost of executing some condemned killers. Only this time he uses terms like 'he guesses' or 'perhaps' it costs $50 million for each execution. Let's take a closer look at Ernie's latest 'statistic' to see if his latest claim bears any resemblance to fact.

# An Eye for an Eye

*William T. Harper*

**"Harold McQueen   Sentenced   Executed   16 Years**
              **to death, 1981      1997      on Appeal**

"So maybe:
"2 public defenders @ $75,000 per year to
    represent killer X 16 years                = $2,400,000
"Annual cost of incarceration @ $40,000
    per year X 16 years                        =    640,000
"Total for 16 years                            = $3,040,000

"At these costs we are about $47 million short of Ernie's $50 million. Based on Ernie's $50 million 'statistic' and our estimate of the annual costs of $190,000, Harold McQueen's appeal should have lasted 263 years, not 16 years. But we know the appeal lasted 16 years, so our annual costs must be wrong. So maybe there were:

"2 public defenders @ $250,000 per year
    to represent killer X 16 years             = $4,000,000
"Annual cost of incarceration @ $50,000
    per year X 16 years                        =   $800,000
"Total for 16 years                            = $4,800,000

"We are still $45.2 million short. So maybe there were:

"2 public defenders @ $1,000,000/year
    to represent killer X 16 years             = $32,000,000
"Annual cost of incarceration @ $100,000
    per year X 16 years                        =   1,600,000
"Total for 16 years                            = $33,600,000

"Even at these costs we are still $16,400,000 short of the $50 million guess. So maybe there were:

# An Eye for an Eye

*William T. Harper*

"30.25 public defenders @ $100,000 per year
   to represent killer X 16 years =$48,400,000
"Annual cost of incarceration @ $100,000
   per year X 16 years = 1,600,000
"Total for 16 years =$50,000,000

"There it is -- $50 million. We've finally figured it out. It's just that simple. 30.25 public defenders whose annual salary is $100,000 per year, representing one condemned killer, plus the annual cost of $100,000 to keep that murderer on death row for a year, all multiplied by the seemingly endless appeal process of 16 years. Now, why in the world would anyone not believe the statistics Ernie Lewis quotes?" [220]

As might be expected vis-à-vis many abolitionists claims, Ernie's latest "statistic" bears (very) little resemblance to fact.

\* \* \*

When death penalty abolitionists calculate the cost of incarceration versus capital punishment, they naturally rely only on incarceration's minimal, bare-bones figures (i.e., prisons and their basic costs for personnel, meals, etc.). But they never go beyond that to real-world costs – such as serious medical costs for aging, ailing and infirmed inmates that come with years of imprisonment. They never talk about the enormous cost for building newer and more secure maximum security prisons needed to house these brutal murderers.

\* \* \*

Another reason the cost of the death penalty process runs so high is because in many cases it behooves defense lawyers

# An Eye for an Eye
*William T. Harper*

financially to drag the process out as long as possible. In a C-Span program taped on October 15, 2004, Donald A. McCartin, Superior Court Judge in Orange County, California (1978-1993) and author Don Lasseter (*Perfect Justice: Death Row and the Appeals Process*) discussed the topic of incarceration vs. execution costs and used the case of Randy Stephen Kraft as an example. Kraft, known as "The Angel of Darkness" was convicted on May 13, 1989 of one of 16 homosexual murders (and he is suspected in another 35). According to Lasseter, it has since cost over $10,000,000 for Kraft's appeal process.

This begs the question: Assuming most of that money went for legal fees and expert witnesses, can we also assume lawyers really don't care about guilt or innocence? Are they more interested in prolonging the process and thereby increasing the fees? Judge McCartin seemed to agree when he told the story of the lawyer who asked a judge that a jury be sequestered "because that's the only way we can make money." The judge sequestered the jury.

In an another case, Lawrence Sigmund Bittaker and Roy Lewis Norris were tried and convicted for the rape, torture and murder of five women in Southern California in 1979. (Go here for the gory details of those beastly acts – http://news.google.com/newspapers?id=4y8dAAAAIBAJ&sjid=054EAAAAIBAJ&dq=norris%20roy%20lewis&pg=6593%2C4087049). Norris, who turned state's evidence, was sentenced to 45-years-to-life. Bittaker received the death penalty on February 17, 1981. As of the summer of 2012, he still sits in a California prison – after 31 years and counting.

Since his conviction, Bittaker has filed appeal after appeal. And, "when Bittaker was not busy drafting appeals, he amused himself by filing frivolous suits against the state prison system.... In one case, where he claimed he had been subjected to 'cruel and unusual punishment' by receipt of a broken cookie on his lunch tray, it cost state officials $5,000 to have the suit dismissed.... It was all great fun and cost Bittaker nothing, since California prisoners are permitted to

# An Eye for an Eye
*William T. Harper*

file their suits for free."²²¹ Is it any wonder death penalty cases and their attendant appeals can get expensive?

When bewailing the cost of a finalized death penalty sentence versus Life-Without-Parole, another thing the abolitionists never seem to mention is the sky-rocketing costs of keeping the medically-challenged in prison for years and years. According to an Associated Press report, "Razor wire topping the fences seems almost a joke at the Men's State Prison [at Hardwick Georgia], where many inmates are slumped in wheelchairs, or leaning on walkers or canes. It's becoming an increasingly common sight: geriatric inmates spending their waning days behind bars. The soaring number of aging inmates is now outpacing the prison growth as a whole.... It's all fueling an explosion in inmate health costs for cash-strapped states.

> "Rising prison health care costs," the AP report continues, "– particularly for elderly inmates – helped fuel a 10 percent jump in state prison spending from fiscal year 2005 to 2006, according to the National Conference of State Legislatures. The graying of the nation's prisons mirrors the population as whole. But many inmates arrive in prison after years of unhealthy living, such as drug use and risky sex. The stress of life behind bars can often make them even sicker. And once they enter prison walls, they aren't eligible for Medicaid or Medicare, where the costs are shared between the state and federal government, meaning a state shoulders the burden of inmate health care on its own."²²²

\* \* \*

One more F grade in high school mathematics for the abolitionists is that their cost analysis figures for incarceration always seem to assume that those who are serving a life

# An Eye for an Eye
*William T. Harper*

sentence – versus those in the death penalty appeals process – will never cost the state (and tax-payers) another nickel in legal expenses. Do they mean that convicts serving life sentences will be so grateful to escape the death chamber they will drop any claims of innocence and never file an appeal for sentence reduction and/or freedom? That assumption, like so many of their others, is patently false.

Furthermore, as those inflated figures become more and more a phoney argument for abolition, more and more abolitionist defense attorneys may continue using the appeals process to extend and expand their delaying tactics in the courtroom and thereby raise the cost of appeals hearings to further justify that bogus cost claim. Consider also the case of Clarence Ray Allen (see Chapter Four) who spent 27 years on death row launching appeal after appeal. His final one came when his lawyers claimed Allen was now **too old** to be executed!!

Likewise, it behooves the defense to seek delay after delay after delay because the longer a case can be stretched out, the better chance there is an existing law can or will be changed – legislatively, judiciously, or by executive fiat.

It is hardly a coincidence that Bureau of Justice Statistics figures show 43 percent of those sentenced to death between 1973 and 2005 were still in prison awaiting application of the sentence. Where the sentence was carried out, it took, on average, 12 years to do so. Something is seriously wrong with the appeals process if it provides so many obstacles to the carrying-out of sentences. When abolitionists cry for the poor death row murderer because of his/her agony of living under the cloud of years of litigation during the appeals process, they need to be reminded that it is neither the State nor the People that bring on those oft-times phony claims that only prolong the "agony."

Sister Prejean says when it comes to arguing against the death penalty, "the argument I always save for last is this one: if we believe that murder is wrong and not admissible in our society, then it has to be wrong for everyone, not just

# An Eye for an Eye
*William T. Harper*

individuals but governments as well. And I end by challenging people to ask themselves whether we can continue to allow the government, subject as it is to every imaginable form of inefficiency and corruption, to have such power to kill." [223]

That being her primary argument, then one must ask in return: If, as she suggests, we cannot "allow the government, subject as it is to every imaginable form of inefficiency and corruption, to have such power to kill," what legal remedies can we entrust to government? Was the government inefficient and corrupt when it brought in the Enron bankruptcy convictions? Was the government inefficient and corrupt when it declared a system of national time zones or established daylight savings time? Was the government inefficient and corrupt when it put copyright laws into effect to protect authors?

Was it not, one might ask the Good Sister in rebuttal, that very same "government, subject as it is to every imaginable form of inefficiency and corruption," that enacted the very same laws she so passionately defends for the never-ending right of the appeals process?

And oh, by the way, it is not the government that sentences criminals to death; that has the power to kill. That is a role reserved only for juries; 12 citizens good and true. The government carries out the will of the people. Isn't that what government is supposed to do?

\* \* \*

Looking at costs of incarceration versus execution, according to Joshua K. Marquis, district attorney in Clatsop County, Oregon who is mentioned earlier in this text, "I have both prosecuted and defended death penalty cases. I am outspent 20-1. If you are charged with capital murder in Oregon for the last 15 to 20 years, you will get a defense that costs at least $250,000." **Allen Tanner**, a former prosecutor in Houston who crossed the great divide and is now a noted defense

# An Eye for an Eye
*William T. Harper*

attorney who helped defend the infamous "Railway Killer," Angel Maturino Resendez, the 39-year-old drifter tied to nine slayings and charged in four in 2000, agreed with Mr. Marquis when he said courts "give me as much money as I need" when representing an indigent client. [224]

While castigating Illinois governor George Ryan's blanket commutation of all death row inmates in the Land of Lincoln in 2003, Marquis' rebuttal to charges there of inadequate defense was:

> "I think...the Cook County [Chicago area] public defender's office does a superb job," he said in a televised debate.
>
> "A lot of these cases [the abolitionists are] talking about happened in 1978, in 1981, frankly, a generation ago legally. They're focusing on some horror stories. We can talk about horror stories on the other side. We can talk about people like Henry Brisbon (see Chapter One), who wasn't on death row for the first person he murdered, or the second or third person he murdered. He was on death row because of the inmate he killed." [225]

Continuing the discussion about charges of inept legal representation on that televised death penalty debate, Kim Ogg, former chief felony prosecutor who put two convicted killers on Texas's death row and a Justice for All board member (a Texas-based victims-rights group), said:

> "I work in Texas, which is in the deep South. And I would dispute that quality-of-counsel argument. Death row inmates here, when they are defendants charged with capital murder, receive what I would say is the best representation in Houston, in Harris County. There is probably less danger of an innocent person being convicted in a capital crime, because each side takes such care in preparation."

# An Eye for an Eye
*William T. Harper*

Even some of the staunchest advocates of the judicious use of the death penalty readily concede abolitionists' charges of ineptitude by some court-appointed defense attorneys may have been in fact true – 20 years ago or more (i.e., pre-1980-85). "But," as former Harris County District Attorney Rosenthal quickly added, "the judicial system has changed precisely because what was 'the shamefully inadequate legal counsel' and the 'over-worked and under-funded' court-appointed defense counsel system. Now," it was pointed out, "court-appointed defense attorneys must attend classes and take qualifying examinations." [226]

Surprising as it must be to most abolitionists, "The DAs want to make sure that the defense lawyers are competent," attorney Allen Tanner told this writer, "because they don't want trials coming back into the system." Rosenthal adds an amen to that, saying "there are any number of court-appointed defense attorneys out there today that I would rather have defend me in a capital case than a lot of the big-name lawyers we read about every day." [227]

To which might be added in the immortal words of Walter Cronkite, "That's the way it is," today; not back in the dinosauric legal generations of the 1970s and 1980s and before that death penalty abolitionists cite in all their biased horror story arguments against the death penalty. In countering abolitionists' legalistic arguments about the constitutionality of the death penalty and whether or not it is cruel and unusual, retentionists argue the Constitution of the United States banned cruel and unusual punishment when that document was written in the 18$^{th}$ Century. The Constitution still bans cruel and unusual punishment as it is conceived today. The Constitution hasn't changed; only the definition of "cruel and unusual" has. Two-hundred years ago, death by hanging or firing squad was not cruel and unusual punishment; nor are they today. Two-hundred years ago death by burning at the stake or use of the stock was not considered cruel and unusual punishment but it is today.

# An Eye for an Eye

*William T. Harper*

Only the definition has changed, not the concept.

\* \* \*

An old cliché says "All is fair in love and war." The political, cultural and social elites, those with their "insularity, their sense of moral superiority, and mostly their smug certainty that they're a lot smarter than the rest of us," [228] certainly have bought into that axiom. "Faced with the irrefutable evidence of the Baldus study," Sister Prejean writes:

> "*McCleskey* gave the Supreme Court the opportunity to address the problem of race in the death penalty in a definitive way. But in its narrow 5-4 ruling in *McCleskey v. Kemp,* the Court not only ignored the consequences of the race studies, it did something worse: It legitimized racial discrimination in the application of the death penalty, declaring racial disparities 'an inevitable part of our criminal justice system'." [229]

According to Professor Barry Latzer at the John Jay College of Criminal Justice in New York, "…virtually all the statistical studies now show no discrimination against black defendants. In fact, whites stand a better chance of a death sentence than blacks for the same crime. There is also proof that those who kill whites are more likely to get the death penalty than those who kill blacks. But since the killers of whites usually are white (86% of the time) and the killers of blacks are black (94%), this means that whites get more death sentences…." [230]

It would also do little good to point out to death penalty abolitionists that "a recent RAND Corporation study of the federal death penalty from 1995 to 2000 similarly found no evidence of racial bias." What is more important, however, is the readily-apparent fairness of this study versus the *McCleskey* claims made above. "Our findings," noted

# An Eye for an Eye
*William T. Harper*

Stephen Klein, a RAND senior research scientist and co-leader of the project, "support the idea that race was not a factor in the decision to seek the death penalty once we adjusted for the circumstance of the crime."

The authors of the study noted its limitations and "agreed that their analytic methods cannot provide definitive answers about race effects in death-penalty cases. Analyses of observational data can support a thesis and may be useful for that purpose, but such analyses can seldom prove or disprove causation."[231] It would behoove us all if abolitionists were as frank, forthcoming and unbiased as is the RAND study.

It really isn't the law. It's the lawyers.

\* \* \*

Death penalty opponents are relentless in their search high and low, trying desperately to find just one "victim" of their never-proven claim of an innocent being executed. We went through this same process with scam artist Roger Keith Coleman (see Chapter Two) proclaiming his "innocence" even as he was strapped on a death house gurney. Mr. Coleman fooled almost everyone, except the DNA practitioners who – at his followers' insistence – found the evidence proving not only was he a killer, he was a lying killer.

Now we have another making the same death-bed claim and whose cause has been taken up by, among many others, David Atwood, President of the Houston Peace and Justice Center. In the latest incidence of that innocence proclamation, Atwood lists Cameron Willingham as one of those "people who were *probably* [emphasis added] innocent" when executed by the State of Texas.[232] The Office of the Clark County (Indiana) Prosecuting Attorney looked at Willingham's case. Maybe we should too.

According to the Clark County prosecuting attorney's website,[233] on December 23, 1991, Cameron Willingham poured a combustible liquid throughout his home and intentionally set the house on fire, resulting in the death of his

# An Eye for an Eye
*William T. Harper*

two-year-old daughter Amber, and his one-year-old twins Karmon and Kameron. Neighbors testified Willingham was "crouched down" in the front yard when the house fire started and despite their pleas, refused to make any attempt to rescue the children. An expert State witness testified the floors, front threshold, and front concrete porch were burned, which only occurs when an accelerant is used to purposely burn these areas. Trial testimony demonstrated that Willingham neither showed remorse nor grieved the loss of his three children.

Willingham's neighbors testified that when the fire "blew out" the windows, Willingham "hollered about his car" and ran to move it to avoid its damage. A fire fighter also testified Willingham was upset his dart board was burned. An investigation revealed the fire was intentionally set with a flammable liquid. Willingham's claims of heroic effort to save the girls were not borne out by his unscathed escape with little smoke in his lungs."

Barry Scheck (again of the O. J. Simpson trial fame) is another who protests, claiming his latest batch of arson "experts" have refuted the testimony of arson "experts" at Willingham's trial. In particular, Scheck's experts cite something called "glazing" of glass which they say, *could have* come from the fire-fighters hoses spewing water on the hot glass. The original experts said it came from the extreme temperature of the fire, such as that caused by an arsonist using an inflammatory agent. In other words, it *could have* come from either source. Once again, we're in the he-said-she-said field of criminal justice. Atwood and the field of apologists for Willingham never mention the eye-witness testimony at the scene.

Are the media "in the tank" for the anti-death penalty cause? You decide in this example from a newspaper report dated August 4, 2012.[234] It's another dredging up of old news in the Cameron Todd Willingham arson case from 1991. The Willingham case and that of Ruben Cantu (below) are the abolitionists' best hopes (out of thousands of other murderer

# An Eye for an Eye
*William T. Harper*

executions) of making their point that there was at least one Death of Innocents.

In a usual display of "objective" media reporting, the *Fort Worth Star Telegram* writer refers to "the junk science" that was used in the Cameron Todd Willingham conviction. Despite outrage from the abolitionists in their agreement with that label, it has yet to be proven that the methods used in that arson investigation were "junk." At best, they might be able to claim the methods weren't as good as methods developed in the intervening two decades. But that's like charging that DNA testing 20 years ago is not as good as it is today. No kidding? And computers of 20 years ago are not nearly as efficient as they were two decades ago, either.

\* \* \*

One other case Atwood cited was that of Ruben Cantu. Death penalty abolitionists have spent more than 25 years trying to make Cantu their poster boy for the death of an innocent. On November 8, 1984, Pedro Gomez, 25, was fatally shot and Juan Moreno, 19, was wounded during a burglary and robbery in a San Antonio, Texas home. Two days later, Ruben Cantu confessed his involvement in the murder to Ramiro Reyes. A month later, Reyes told police of Cantu's confession. On March 1, 1985, Cantu shot a San Antonio police officer, was arrested and later indicted for Gomez' murder. Cantu was tried and convicted in July, 1985 of Gomez' murder, was sentenced to death on August 1, 1985 with said sentence carried out on August 24, 1993.

In a 183-page 2007 report entitled, "In the Matter of Juan Moreno, Investigation Relating to *The State of Texas v. Ruben Cantu*, Cause No. 85-CR-1303," issued by Susan D. Reed, Criminal District Attorney for Bexar County (San Antonio), the conclusion is:

> "Based on the available evidence, which has been compromised to some degree by the passage of

# An Eye for an Eye
*William T. Harper*

nearly two decades since the offense, this investigation concludes that Ruben Cantu was guilty of the capital murder of Pedro Gomez and the intentional shooting of Juan Moreno. The claims of Cantu's innocence, made more than 12 years after his execution, do not withstand the scrutiny of close review and analysis, and lack any credible supporting witnesses or verifiable facts.

"On the contrary, when the claims supporting Cantu's asserted alibi that were capable of verification were investigated, the evidence negated or fatally undermined Cantu's alibi. Inextricably coupled with the lack of supporting evidence is the admitted bias of those asserting Cantu's innocence and the absence of credibility of Cantu's friends and associates who have told various contradictory versions of the story through the years depending on which version benefited them the most at the time.

"Finally, and most convincingly, Ruben Cantu's admissions of guilt both before and after his trial and conviction put to rest any reasonable doubt concerning the police investigation and tactics used, the skills and strategy of the prosecution and defense attorneys, and the verdict of guilty rendered by an impartial jury." [235]

But, "Nay," sayeth the likes of Mr. Atwood. Apparently, in their view, everyone in the criminal justice system was wrong – the witnesses, the juries, the judges, the prosecutors, the appeals courts, the hearing boards – everyone else was wrong and they are right in claiming that Ruben Cantu *probably* was innocent. And Al Capone was *probably* only guilty of income tax evasion.

Once again we ask the question: If Ruben Cantu, Cameron Willingham, Roger Coleman – along with Roger O'Dell and Dobie Williams, et al., had been given Life-

# An Eye for an Eye
*William T. Harper*

Without-Parole sentences for their murder convictions, would we ever have heard of any one of them? Are their defenders really trying to save "innocent" men or are they only trying to use them to advance their "cause" – the elimination of the death penalty?

\* \* \*

And if you want to hear the granddaddy of all lawyer-generated phony pleas for allowing a cold-blooded killer to avoid his rightful death sentence, read on about this one.

> David Headley, one of Darryl Kemp's two attorneys [in the Wiltsey murder trial covered above in Chapter Four], urged jurors to remain analytical as they listened to what was expected to be emotionally upsetting testimony from Wiltsey's family and from Kemp's surviving victims.
>
> Headley did not dispute that his client was a serial rapist and said he was guilty of "probably a dozen rapes," including some in which he broke into women's homes to rape them, but argued that Kemp *never intended to kill his victims.*
>
> Over the years, he developed a clear pattern of behavior, Headley said. He would knock his victims unconscious, rape and sodomize them and then, when they woke up, he would talk to them, asking them embarrassing questions.[236]

Did defense attorney Headley actually make this plea with a straight face? Was he saying that poor Mr. Kemp was upset by the raped Ms. Wiltsey's reluctance to enter into chat sessions with the man who had just sexually assaulted her? That he got somewhat peeved so, not being able to help himself, he strangled her to death, "leaving her with injuries to her mouth, neck and vaginal area and ligature marks on her wrists from being tied up?"[237]

# An Eye for an Eye
*William T. Harper*

## Chapter Six

### Pity the Killers...Forget the Victims

*[Eighteen-year-old Faith Colleen Hathaway] is completely nude. Her arms are outstretched over her head, her legs are spread wide apart, her knees drawn up with her feet on the ground. Blood and gore cover her face, throat and chest. She has been stabbed seventeen times. Two of the fingers on her right hand are missing and lie nearby on the sandy floor of the cave. Already, insects are gathering, the smell of death and imminent decay a call to feast on this unexpected presence in their midst. Faith's face is turned to the side, and her mouth is wide-open. Her eyes too are open, frozen in a mask of pain and horror as her life ebbed away. Her face is bruised and bloody. Several of her teeth are missing, and most of them are loose from the battering she has suffered. Her inner thighs are scraped raw, and her vagina is torn and ravaged.*

*All of these wounds are now starting to attract the attention of the flies that buzz around her body. Soon they will begin to deposit their eggs in these bloody receptacles, and maggots will begin to multiply and commence the body's inevitable descent into decay and decomposition.*[238]

\* \* \*

That is what Detective Michael L. Varnado saw and described in *Victims of Dead Man Walking*, his 2003 book (co-authored with D. P. Smith) in which he described his discovery of what was left of Faith Colleen Hathaway, a beautiful high school graduate of but two weeks. It was on June 4, 1980, deep in the piney woods near Franklinton, Louisiana, about 70 miles due north of New Orleans. One week earlier she had been

# An Eye for an Eye
*William T. Harper*

brutally raped and savagely murdered at the blood-stained hands of Robert Lee Willie and Joseph Jesse Vaccaro.

Detective Varnado asked for and received permission from Faith Hathaway's mother, Elizabeth Harvey, to publish the gruesome pictures of what was left of her daughter at the time of her body's discovery. Ms. Harvey gave that permission because:

> "...after Faith's murder, people often hesitated to even say Faith's name, as if she had never existed. Instead, all the attention was focused on Robert Lee Willie – his rights, his last visit, his last meal, his last minutes on earth.

**Robert Lee Willie**

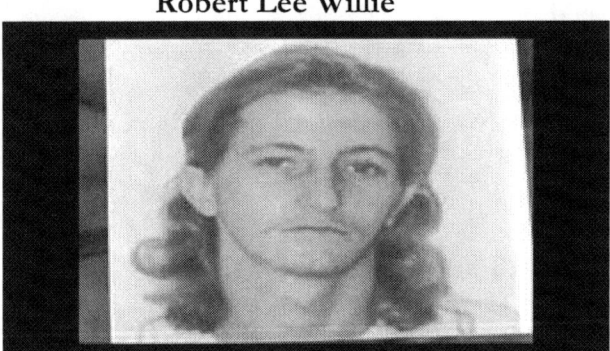

Ms. Harvey felt that it was important to include the crime scene photos 'to show what Faith's last of everything was like'." [239]

Ms. Harvey was, perhaps unbeknownst to her, vocalizing the pain and horror so many family members of the murdered encounter – the victimization of their loved ones and attempts at canonization of the killers. The scenario of death penalty opponents, with variations on the theme, goes something like this:

"The killers (the poor, misunderstood, miscreants, who were generally 'abused as children'), really didn't mean to

# An Eye for an Eye
*William T. Harper*

do it. They actually are warm, fun-loving, good-natured, family men who were driven to these heinous crimes by circumstances beyond their control." Robert Lee Willie was described thusly:

> "There's a child sitting inside this tough, macho dude."[240]

That "child" (as Sister Prejean viewed him) was arrested 30 times between 1972 and 1979.[241] Imagine, if you will, how any killer must have "suffered" through his depraved up-bringing punctuated with a brutal beating (a spanking, perhaps) received for stealing that lousy piece of candy when he was 10 years old. And can you believe it, the poor killer was deprived in his youth. He couldn't even have a brand-new, $143,675 Mercedes-Benz S600 as a middle-school graduation gift. "All the other guys in the gang got one." It was his dysfunctional family that turned him bad. Then, there's that person, you know, the one who stepped in front of the killer's Uzi when it erupted into a hail of gunfire; the one who had no business being there during that minor drive-by shooting.

Pity the killers...Forget the victims.

\* \* \*

Hardly a day goes by that a newspaper story, editorial or television report appears about some anti-death penalty group's attempt to prevent a heinous murderer on death row from being executed. Because the killer – so it goes – had a hard life or a sad childhood, he shouldn't have to face a death sentence for the brutal slaying of an innocent human being.

In what appears to be *not* a rare act of hubris, Sister Prejean regrets her late arrival at Patrick Elmo Sonnier's death row cell. "By the time I sought remedial legal help for him it was too late. If I had acted sooner, I believe he would be alive today," she wrote.[242] Not even Clarence Darrow nor

# An Eye for an Eye
*William T. Harper*

his "Monkey Trial" adversary William Jennings Bryan could have ameliorated the horror of the Sonnier brothers' murders. The Sonniers were unarguably guilty of the deliberate, brutal and reprehensible murders of two innocent teenagers.

What kind of mitigating circumstances could there possibly be for such acts? Are these two guys the only ones in the history of mankind to have been raised in an impoverished home? Millions and millions have had similar upbringing and they didn't go out and blow the brains out of a couple of kids. And unfortunately, not enough prosecutors write books to bring this point to the public. That's probably because they're too overwhelmed battling frivolous appeal hearings by unscrupulous defense attorneys with "a cause." And unfortunately, that "cause" many times is not to save the life of their duly-convicted client. It is only to abolish the nation's death penalty.

Over and over we are told by these anti-death penalty activists that a grim upbringing somehow explains and excuses a vicious, brutal and senseless murder. Unless we read Horatio Alger stories or The Hardy Boys books, we never hear from abolitionists about the millions and millions, the tens and hundreds of millions of young people who also had a grim upbringing but who never harmed a hair on a single head of anyone throughout their lives. We hardly ever hear one word from death penalty opponents about innocent victims of these killers; only that we should show sympathy and understanding for the murderer, and that we should agree the death penalty should be abolished.

Where is their compassion for the lost life of their victims, or the families and friends whose lives have been permanently shattered by the murderer? The revisionists appear to believe that we, as a society, should show more concern for the killer than the killed. They somehow feel the lives of killers are worth more than the lives they snuffed out. By executing Oklahoma City bomber Timothy McVeigh,

# An Eye for an Eye
*William T. Harper*

death penalty opponents charge, society is just as guilty for taking his one miserable life as he was in taking 168.

Pity the Killer...Forget the Victims – all 168 of them.

Sometimes death penalty revisionists purposely make it very hard to know who the victim really is.

Who is next to join these notorious killers the abolitionists would enshrine in a Heinous Hall of Fame? Jesse James was a renegade, a bank-robber, a train-robber – and a wanton killer who terrorized the Midwest during the 1870s. But apologists of then and now have built James into a Robin Hood-like character and an avenger of the lost Confederate cause. Countless western dime novels have been written about his "heroic" escapades. Many movies have been made (even one titled, "Jesse James Meets Frankenstein"). A huge sign hovering alongside Interstate Highway 35 north of Kansas City, Missouri proclaims a touristy Jesse James Farm and Museum in Kearney, Missouri, near his Clay County birthplace. There is no sign there (nor anywhere else) proclaiming the birthplaces of Jesse James' innocent victims.

Famed author Larry (*Lonesome Dove*) McMurtry wrote a book called *Anything for Billy* in which he tells about "the escapades of the legendary outlaw and gunman, Billy the Kid and his colorful gang," as one reviewer put it. What makes a gang of killers "colorful"? Known by some as William H. Bonney, Billy the Kid actually was a vicious and ruthless killer who died at the age of 21, not before he took the lives of 21 men, one for each year of his life, the first one when he was just 12 years old. He killed without reason. He too is listed by some among the pantheon of "heroes" in American folklore, hoisted to his lofty place by those who make "victims" out of killers. More contemporary history: the 1930s bring additional brutal, sadistic, glorified killers: Bonnie and Clyde, John Dillinger, Charles "Pretty Boy" Floyd, Lester Gillis a.k.a. "Baby Face" Nelson, George "Machine Gun" Kelly, et al.

This bunch, all *nice* kids who were *victimized* by society, would share their fame with the latest batch of "legendary outlaws" of the 1970s and beyond: Robert Lee Willie, Elmo

# An Eye for an Eye

*William T. Harper*

Patrick Sonnier, Kenneth Allen McDuff, John Wayne Gacy, Jeffrey Dahmer and the rest of those despicable killers the abolitionists would have us believe don't deserve the ultimate penalty for their ultimate, multiple crimes. The anti-death penalty advocates no doubt also have pedestals waiting for Jack the Ripper and Attila the Hun. Fifty years from now, there will no doubt be similar apologists for Saddam Hussein and Osama bin Laden.

\* \* \*

Robert Lee Willie – the non-fiction "hero" or "victim" or both – was among those disgusting killers Sister Prejean counseled while he was on death row at Angola Prison in Louisiana and then wrote about. His case would never pass a lie-detector test either. In her extensive story about Willie, she was then and still is seeking abolition of the death penalty – no matter what the justification for its implementation. Her unabashed pleas for forgiveness for convicted killers no matter how heinous their crimes, her innumerable personal presentations, and other "on-message" interviews, are unfortunately, littered with questionable "facts."

She immediately comes to the defense of Dobie Gillis Williams – another convicted killer she befriended – when she writes:

> "I can tell [the warden] wants the [execution] to go quickly so he and the Tactical Unit—the team responsible for the physical details of killing Dobie—can get it over with as soon as possible." [243]

Is that a "fact"? Did Warden Cain want to "get it over with as soon as possible?" Or is that a supposition?

Another "fact" is presented when the nun quotes teen-killer Willie as saying, "I let Joe Vaccaro call all the shots and I went along." [244] That "fact" is refuted in a book telling about another victim of the Willie-Vaccaro reign of terror – a

# An Eye for an Eye
*William T. Harper*

victim who managed to live (barely) and tell her story. "Contrary to what Helen Prejean writes in her book based on her death row conversations with Willie," Christopher Buchanan says, "Debbie Morris (another Willie rape victim) testified that Willie was clearly in charge [in her case]. 'Joe was so brain dead from drugs, [Morris said] he couldn't figure anything out.... There's no question in my mind that Willie was in charge'."[245] Sister Prejean has "a cause." Debbie Morris does not. (See below for more about Debbie Morris' "encounter" with Willie and friend.)

Among those also questioning some of those "facts" are Detective Michael Varnado (now an investigative consultant in his own firm) and assistant district attorney William Alford, Jr. who were deeply involved with Sister Prejean's pet Willie project. They are "united in their disdain for Prejean." Alford, who has since changed his mind about the death penalty, said he "does not appreciate at all the sensationalism that Prejean has brought to the case."[246] He also said…

> "Sister Prejean got in to see Robert Lee Willie, claiming to be his spiritual advisor. She didn't advise him, she just got his story. She wasn't worried about his soul; she was worried about her cause. His last words come from her. His last words were 'The death penalty is wrong.' Huh? It should have been more like, 'Please forgive me for all that I've done.' She just got his story and made money off it."[247]

Pity the Killer…Forget the Victim.

Varnado says Prejean's book incorrectly stated he possibly moved Hathaway's body before experts could examine it – opening the possibility that Willie was not the killer. Varnado adds Prejean also incorrectly wrote that he coaxed the confession from Willie in exchange for leniency for his mother, who was jailed for helping the fugitives. Varnado recalls his anger at Prejean was especially strong in

# An Eye for an Eye
*William T. Harper*

the Angola witness room, the night Willie was executed. "In that witness room," he says, "I came real close to slapping a nun in the face."[248] The detective concludes by saying he also "believes the book and the movie turned Willie into the victim and gave short shrift to those on the receiving end of his crimes."[249]

Could it possibly be that Detective Varnado and Attorney Alford are/were claiming Sister Prejean is a fraud?

\* \* \*

Following the execution of her daughter Faith's murderer, Mrs. Harvey said:

> "There's always these sob-sister groups that show up and burn candles talking about their opposition to the death penalty, but they don't know how it feels to lose someone you love to these fiends. They say," she continued about the death penalty, "it's cruel and unusual punishment. But I'd like for the newspapers to publish the coroner's report on the death of Faith next to the story of Willie's execution and show how she suffered before she died at the hands of Robert Lee Willie and (co-defendant) Joseph Jesse Vaccaro."[250]

Sister Helen Prejean makes Robert Lee Willie one of her poster boys for mercy, protesting he should not get the death penalty juries gave him and multiple appeals courts upheld. No one, she professes, no one – not even a savage killer like Robert Lee Willie – should get the death penalty.

> "I tell [Willie, later she says] that despite his crime, despite the terrible pain he has caused, he is a human being and he has a dignity that no one can take from him, that he is a son of God."[251]

# An Eye for an Eye

*William T. Harper*

Even though the crime, she says, "sounds like it is straight out of Truman Capote's *In Cold Blood*," she practically dismisses its horror by saying merely: "The eighteen-year-old Hathaway girl had been brutally raped and stabbed and left to die in the woods."[252] The "Hathaway girl," indeed. Even for Mike Varnado, a seasoned detective, "the Hathaway case [became] a major source of a strain on his personal life that descended into alcoholism."[253]

Pity the Killer…Forget the Victim.

The nun even goes so far as to suggest the "Hathaway girl" brought on her own demise. On May 28, 1980, the day when her life was ripped from her body, Faith Hathaway was only hours away from starting her enlistment in the U. S. Army. She went out to mark the occasion with her friends and say goodbye (certainly, not knowing how permanent that "goodbye" would be). She, with her mother's permission, met her friends at the Lakefront Disco in her hometown of Mandeville, Louisiana, after she finished her final night of work as a waitress at Bossier's Restaurant.

Not too subtly in her effort to ameliorate Robert Willie's horrendous crime and offer the usual "mitigating circumstances," Sister Prejean (almost cruelly it appears here – as it does also to Varnado on page 99 in his book) then condescendingly insinuates that the tragedy of the girl's multiple rapes and her ensuing murder by Robert Lee Willie and Joseph Vaccaro could have been partially Faith's fault:

> As panic mounted [the nun writes], had she tried shutting her eyes tight, fighting to throw off the *sluggish effects of the alcohol?* [emphasis added] It was a time when a woman needed her sharpest wits about her, a time to think clearly and keenly about escape. Or perhaps it was better that *her wits were not so sharp.* [*emphasis* added] Better, maybe, for the *anesthesia of the alcohol* [emphasis added] to dull the pain and horror soon to be hers.[254]

# An Eye for an Eye
*William T. Harper*

Detective Varnado offers a different view:

"Faith Hathaway was a sensible girl, a girl with a sense of purpose in life, a very mature eighteen-year-old. She was not a wild girl, out partying all the time. She rarely dated, rarely stayed out late. She was focused on her life, ready to join the Army, excited about the future. Would she have asked for or voluntarily accepted a ride from Willie and Vaccaro? Absolutely not! ...Add to this the lateness of the hour and the short distance Faith had to walk home, if indeed she was walking when she came into contact with Willie and Vaccaro." [255]

The detective goes on to use Willie's own words not only to refute the killer's story of the initial encounter with Faith, but he uses those very same words to destroy the nun's hypothesis. Willie told Varnado he and Vaccaro picked Faith up "by the Corner Pack Store." The Corner Pack Store is almost directly in front of Ms. Hathaway's apartment! Why would she need a ride from there?

Nonetheless, the suggestion that Faith might have been suffering from the "sluggish effects of alcohol," is once again, a favorite tactic of abolitionists – find some way to reverse the roles, to turn killers into victims. Woe is me. The poor murderer. The Devil made me do it. In one notorious case, it wasn't the Devil; it was Tupac Shakur's rap music that made poor boy felon Ron Howard murder a state trooper (see Chapter Nine).

\* \* \*

And it doesn't stop there. In her telling of the Sonnier brothers' murders of Loretta Bourque and David LeBlanc, Sister Prejean quotes Elmo Sonnier talking about his brother Eddie prior to the killings: "Something I think the boy David

# An Eye for an Eye
*William T. Harper*

[LeBlanc] said to [Eddie] teed him off."[256] Here we go again. Naturally, in Sister Prejean's account, "the boy David" is at fault for the murders. Never does she note that this kind of rape was a frequent sinister act with the Sonnier brothers, prior to and after the Bourque/LeBlanc murders.

Pity the Killers…Forget the Victims.

Then, the crowning indignity is heaped upon Loretta and David and their families. After Sonnier's execution for murder, the *New Orleans Times-Picayune*, according to the nun's glowing account…

> "had run the [Associated Press] story on Pat's [Sonnier] burial with the headline: 'Executed Killer Blessed with Burial for the Elite,' and the article had said, that this executed murderer 'received in death what few Catholics ever achieve – a funeral Mass conducted by a bishop and burial within the shadow of graves of other bishops.' There is no mistaking the thrust of the article – Pat Sonnier was buried as a hero."[257]

"As for the bishop's presence," Sister Prejean was quoted later in a newspaper interview, 'the bishops are taking more and more stands for human rights. They are very much against capital punishment. That's why he was here.' Sonnier was buried in a special plot at Roselawn Cemetery set aside for nuns. Just across the narrow gravel road is the plot where bishops and noted priests are buried."[258]

Why, one might ask, was this murderer given such honors at his burial? If it is just because nuns and bishops are opposed to capital punishment, then why – one might also ask – are not all those executed by the state not given similar honors? The *Picayune's* revealing account brings to mind some other questions:

# An Eye for an Eye
*William T. Harper*

Other than the families of those murdered kids Loretta Bourque and David LeBlanc, does anyone know where *they* are buried?

What about nuns and bishops taking stands for the victims' human rights?

Did any bishop or other high official of the Church participate in the *victims'* funerals?

Why, why was Elmo Patrick Sonnier alone so honored by the Catholic Church?

Why didn't the ultra-liberal, death penalty revisionists in Hollywood make a sympathetic movie about Loretta and David instead of the glorified portrayal of Sonnier/Willie composite played by actor-activist Sean Penn in the film?

Once again – Who are the victims in these horrific crimes?

\* \* \*

Sister Prejean is almost rhapsodic in her descriptions of the evil villain, Robert Lee Willie – an ogre who previously had been involved in the murder of one of his drug-dealers, and a week later, the killing of police Sergeant Louis H. Wagner III. This is the same monster who – along with his fellow fiend, Joseph Vaccaro – a week after kidnapping, raping and murdering Faith Hathaway, kidnapped and repeatedly raped 16-year-old Debbie Lynn Cuevas (*nee* Morris) and tried hard to kill her boyfriend, Mark Brewster. "They hung him from a tree, stabbed him in the side, cut his throat, burned him with cigarettes, and shot him in the back of the head at close range. They left him for dead...."[259] He miraculously survived, no thanks to Robert Lee Willie – an animal who, according to Sister Prejean, should not get the penalty he deserves. People shoot pit bulls for less.

Fortunately for pit bulls, we're led to assume, they don't have to "suffer the indignities" of life on death row.

# An Eye for an Eye
*William T. Harper*

The abolitionists decry "situations in which human beings [those on death row] are forced to sit in a cage while they wait to be taken to their deaths...." At least the cage they sit in is clean and dry. And when they are taken to their deaths, they go – if they so care to – with the comfort of a "spiritual advisor" or other member of the cloth to comfort them in a surgically-clean environment. The go with the chance to say that last goodbye to friends and loved ones. They go with the pleasure of "their last meal."

Pity the killer...Forget the victim.

Faith Hathaway didn't have those luxuries in her maggot-infested shallow grave. Neither did Loretta Bourque nor did David LeBlanc as they buried their faces in dirt when three bullets plowed into the back of each of their heads. Nor did Dennis Hemby as he died face-down in a swampy river under Robert Lee Willie's heel. Nor did back-shot police Sergeant Louis H. Wagner. Nor, presumably, did any of the other victims of the one-thousand-plus killers who were deservedly electrocuted, lethally injected, hung, shot or gassed to death in the United States since the 1976 re-establishment of the death penalty.

\* \* \*

As was mentioned, the public constantly hears about the plight of killers of innocents facing the so-called cruel and inhuman punishment for their heinous crimes. And rarely do we hear about those innocents themselves and almost never about their survivors who also have to spend a real life without parole in suffering. And when we do, we're left to wonder. The case of James Vernon Allridge brings this point vividly to mind.

The entire Epilogue of *The Death of Innocents* – except for the last five short paragraphs – is given over to James Allridge's suffering through rejections from various appeals hearings while awaiting and receiving the ultimate punishment. Only once in all 1,299 words of that mournful

# An Eye for an Eye
*William T. Harper*

plea – as he went to his death he "asked pardon of the victim's family" – does the reader have a clue who James Vernon Allridge is. Or who his victim was. Or how his victim was murdered. Or how his victim's family has suffered through the years and years since Allridge blew his victim's brains out on Sunday night, February 3, 1985.

But, what the reader did hear about was how Academy Award-winning, glamorous actress Susan Sarandon (i.e., "Sister Helen Prejean" in the movie "Dead Man Walking") was "shaken" by Allridge's pending execution. Sarandon had been corresponding with "James" for eight years and she "had come to know him as a person, alive and filled with insight."[260] She had been buying "James" artwork and, no doubt, displaying it proudly in her Hollywood mansion for all her bleeding-heart glitterati friends to ogle over. (Allridge had more than 360 colored-pencil works hanging in other private collections the world over.) The actress even traveled from Hollywood, California to Livingston, Texas to chat with and console Allridge for two hours while he sat on death row ("No cameras, please").

We read all these things about "James" and Susan and others who have bought his art, including activist and author Gloria Steinem and Sting (an English musician, singer-songwriter, multi-instrumentalist, activist, actor and philanthropist). We read of letters of support Allridge received from actor Robert Redford, businessman Ted Turner, and actress Elizabeth Taylor.[261] What we don't read about in those 1,299 words is a single thing about James Vernon Allridge's victim, the 21-year-old Fort Worth, Texas convenience store clerk Brian Clendennen – not even his name.

We don't find anything there about the .25-caliber bullet Allridge slammed into Clendennen's brain, execution style, while he knelt on his knees bound hand and foot. We don't read anything there about Brian Clendennen's mother and his brother who have been painfully grieving for more than two decades – while Allridge sat in jail reading and

# An Eye for an Eye
*William T. Harper*

showing off his mail from Redford, Turner, Taylor, and others. We're not told how his mother was seated in her car outside her son's convenience store waiting to drive him home after work on that midnight; how when he didn't come out of the store when he was expected, she went in and stumbled upon the grisly scene of her son laying in a pool of his own blood.

As Cindy Horswell wrote in another *Houston Chronicle* story, "For 17 years, Shane Clendennen has waited for justice after his brother's killer was sent to death row.... Clendennen cannot understand why Academy Award-winning actress Susan Sarandon made a special trip to death row to visit Allridge.... How would she feel if someone tied up her child and shot him in the back of the head, then she had to watch him on life support for three days until he died?" asked Shane Clendennen.... "She should not have a voice in this unless she has gone through that kind of pain and loss."[262]

Nowhere do we read in *The Death of Innocents* that James Allridge and his brother, Ronald, his partner-in-crime in Brian Clendennen's murder, were also involved in the fatal shooting during another robbery that same year of a 19-year-old diner at a fast-food restaurant because she was "penniless." Ronald had spent *three-and-one-half years* in prison in the late 1970s for killing a high school student and had been accused of killing the store manager of a pizza-delivery business where he worked. We're not told by abolitionists, as Ms. Horswell reported, that "in 1985, the two brothers had gone on a spree of robberies and killings. Each was driving the getaway cars for the other when their capital murders happened...." What pretty "colored-pencil works" James Vernon Allridge could have made from those scenes.

Sister Prejean concludes this additional death of an "innocent" by saying she hoped she "could go to [her] death with a tiny fraction of the poise and grace James Allridge possessed as he stepped into eternity." We didn't hear about the "poise and grace" that Brian Clendennen exhibited when he was on his knees with a .25-caliber bullet ripping into the

# An Eye for an Eye
*William T. Harper*

back of his skull.

\* \* \*

Another case of "cruel and unusual punishment" comes to mind with the murders in the Douglass family in Okarche, Oklahoma in 1979. Brooks Douglass remembers it well. His parents and he were hog-tied in their home by two drifters, Glen Burton Ake and Steven Keith Hatch. The Douglass family was forced to listen while their 12-year-old daughter/sister Leslie was raped. After the rapists ate the family's dinner, Ake shot all four of them in the back of the head. The parents, Dr. Richard Douglass and Marilyn Sue Douglass, died but Leslie and Brooks survived. "Two bullets had torn through Leslie's back, piercing a lung and a kidney and ripping her intestines. Brooks had suffered a severed esophagus, a collapsed lung and puncturing of the pericardial sac protecting his heart." [263]

[In] "reviewing crime scene photos for the first time, did Douglass see that his father had summoned enough strength for one final gesture: 'My dad had somehow made his way over to my mother and put his head on her shoulder'." [264]

Ake and Hatch were captured, tried and convicted for the murders of Mr. and Mrs. Douglas. But, Brooks and Leslie had to relive the nightmare again and again – as they still do today. "Brooks testified seven times in the [seventeen] years after the attack, reliving that terrible night each time." He went on to election to the Oklahoma State Senate and when he championed victims' rights legislation, he "was criticized for fostering revenge." [265]

That "revenge" was legislation that gave some degree of closure to family members as it enabled them to witness the execution of those who have murdered their loved ones.

It doesn't take long for abolitionists to turn victims' survivors into killers' equals. The revisionists like to blur the lines between killers and the killed; to turn public sympathy

# An Eye for an Eye
*William T. Harper*

from the latter to the former.
Pity the killers…Forget the victims.

* * *

The abolitionists like to say those on death row are being "tortured" by their presence there as they sit for 10, 15, 20 years and more during their self-perpetuated appeals process. Are they more "tortured" in their cells and dining halls and exercise areas and courtrooms than was nine-year-old Jessica Lunsford who was suffocated in a plastic bag in a dumpster by John Evander Couey? Are they more "tortured" than 33 men and boys who were raped, tortured, and murdered by the "Killer Clown," John Wayne Gacy? Are they more "tortured" than the nine female victims of the "BTK – bind, torture and kill" murderer, Dennis Rader? Are they more "tortured" than the eight young nursing students – who while waiting their turn to die, tried to hide under beds – until Richard Speck found them and sexually brutalized, stabbed, and strangled them to death in 1966?

In lethal injection procedures, a three-drug "cocktail" is used: The first is a sedative, sodium thiopental to induce unconsciousness; the second is a paralytic agent, pancuronium bromide, which collapses the lungs and diaphragm, and the third, potassium chloride, stops the heart from functioning. The abolitionists' latest claim is in the lethal injection process, "pancuronium bromide, one of the drugs used in the deadly cocktail, paralyzes persons being killed, which makes it impossible for them to cry out if they are in pain…[and it] serves no real function other than to mask distress." [266]

(Don't bother to ask how the killers can "cry out" if they're already sedated heavily with sodium thiopenithal.)

Do they ever ask what difference it made to Robert Lee Willie and Joseph Jesse Vaccaro when Faith Hathaway cried out in pain? What difference did it make to Elmo and Eddie Sonnier when Loretta Bourque and David LeBlanc

# An Eye for an Eye
*William T. Harper*

cried out in pain as the first of three rifle bullets crashed into their skulls? Again, as Faith Hathaway's mother Elizabeth Harvey noted, we hear so much about the rights and "dignity" of killers while their victims' rights and dignity are buried with them in their graves.

Joining his wife in her unrelenting grief was her husband, Vernon, who added his own bitterness.

"'The SOB, Vaccaro, got a life sentence,' Vernon says, and he is crying again, 'and it's been four years and they haven't fried Willie's ass yet. We've been waiting and waiting for justice to be done. I can't rest until justice is done. All you hear about these days is the rights of the criminal. What about our rights? Don't we have a right to see this chapter closed?'" [267]

The anti-death penalty lobby enforces and re-enforces the concept that through state-sponsored execution, the family of the murderer suffers the same loss as the family of the victim. That's not true. At least the family of the murderer knows their loved one committed a heinous crime, inflicted life-long misery on a surviving family, and in some logical measure, the criminal – even though a loved one – deserved the punishment. Even Robert Lee Willie's father, John Kelton Willie, a convicted killer himself, said he "believes that his son deserves to die if he did rape and murder Faith Hathaway." [268] Which he did.

Many murderers have admitted they deserved to die for their crimes. So said George Rivas, on death row for murdering police officer Aubrey Hawkins, who had 11 bullets pumped into his head and body on Christmas Eve, 2000 in Irving, Texas. "I'm guilty. I'm prepared for it," said the ringleader of a gang of seven inmates who escaped from a Texas prison and were confronted by the policeman during their robbery of a sporting goods store. "It's what I deserve," Rivas admitted. [269] Some tiny form of rationalization of guilt –

# An Eye for an Eye
*William T. Harper*

and punishment — is there for Rivas and his family. The families of innocent victims like Aubrey Hawkins don't have even that small measure of solace. Their only comfort — and pain — is in their memories.

Whereas the family of Officer Hawkins just woke up on Christmas morning 2000 with the stunning realization that the son, father, brother who had been there every day was suddenly gone; that he would never be there again. At least families of killers know for months and years of the fate that awaits them and they have time to prepare, to adapt, to say their final farewells. It is not the same loss for the killers and the killed; no matter how many times the abolitionists try to say it is.

\* \* \*

The lament coming from death penalty opponents, the age-old sob-story about "cruel and unusual" punishment, continues. They tell us about David Lawson who was executed on June 16, 1984 by the state of North Carolina for murdering Wayne Shinn. "It took thirteen minutes for the gas to kill [Lawson]," was the lament.[270] We weren't told by the abolitionists that in December 1980, Lawson shot Wayne Shinn in the back of the head after being interrupted during a burglary in Shinn's home; that Lawson also shot Shinn's father, Buren, in the back of the head and left him for dead. They didn't tell us that Wayne Shinn, an electrician, was married and left behind a 10-year-old son and a three-year-old daughter. We weren't told how long it took Wayne Shinn to die or how long his father lay beside his dead son waiting to die. But, we're supposed to weep for the cold-blooded killer, poor David Lawson.

As usual, abolitionists go to great lengths to tell the horrors of the death chamber while totally ignoring the horrors suffered by the victims that brought the murderers to the chamber in the first place. Sister Prejean, as abolitionists often do, cites cases where executions have been botched; i.e.,

# An Eye for an Eye

*William T. Harper*

"Prison officials had to stop the process, open the chamber, and strap [Leandress Riley] in again." What they didn't tell us was on July 18, 1949 during a holdup in a Sacramento, California restaurant, Leandress Riley – while fleeing the scene – shot Walter Hills, a laundry delivery man, in the back and through his heart, killing him instantly.

In yet another case, we're told "it took nine guards to lift [Lewis Williams, Jr.] from his knees, pry his hands loose from the edge of the table, and strap him down."[271] What abolitionists don't tell the public, for instance, is on January 21, 1983, Lewis Williams, Jr. shot Leoma Chmielewski, a 76-year-old lady, in the face from close range (approximately two feet or less) and killed her after he had inflicted multiple blunt force injuries to her head and neck. One can only wonder if that 76-year-old lady would have preferred a needle full of pancuronium bromide before she was beaten and shot to death. But that's a question abolitionists don't ask. The revisionists are too busy worrying about David Lawson, Leandress Riley, Lewis Williams, Jr., et al.

In *Dead Man Walking*, we read "there remains, however, one dimension of suffering that can never be eliminated when death is imposed on a conscious human being: the horror of being put to death against your will and the agony of anticipation." How many times did Faith Hathaway have to endure "the agony of anticipation?" One for each time she was stabbed? Was it 14 times? Fifteen times? Sixteen times? Seventeen times?

Pity the killer…Forget the victim.

\* \* \*

Abolitionists in their zeal to do away with the death penalty, seek to enlist sympathy not only for killers (but never, it seems, for the victims of the killers), but they also try to drag in everyone else. A favorite group deserving their pity appears to be the "strap-down" teams – those correctional officers who have the job of tying down the inmate to the death room

# An Eye for an Eye

*William T. Harper*

gurney. Sometimes convicts go quietly; sometimes they battle like a drug cartel member in a Mexican turf war. It is, admittedly, "a dirty job but someone has to do it."

The public is told by the protesters "strap-down teams have to take human beings out of a cell and strap them down and kill them and they're told, 'You're only doing your job'." [272] Once again, however, abolitionists only tell one part of the story. There is another side. Not all prison staff members condemn the system and their role as part of the strap-down team. In the first place, just about all strap-down team members are there voluntarily and if they feel they can't do that job, they are re-assigned with no malice attached. Captain Terry Green, a participant in 31 executions in the state's death house in Huntsville, Texas, says it is "Just another part of doing what I do as a correctional officer. It's something that the vast majority of the people want done."

Ron Ward, director of the Oklahoma Department of Corrections, speaking at the American Correctional Association's 2004 winter conference, defended the execution teams.

> "Although the duty is strictly voluntary," he noted, "for those who do choose to be a part of the execution team, there is a large bond that is formed among the members. …whatever happens," he told his audience of correctional officers from across the country. "Whatever the public perception or whatever the media's perception is, is not the perception of those of us that deal with this on a daily basis. This is a duty."

Texas Department of Criminal Justice Major Kenneth Dean, who has participated in and witnessed approximately 120 executions, puts it this way:

> "It's a very unique job. Very unique.… I do believe in what I do. If I didn't and I felt that it was

# An Eye for an Eye
*William T. Harper*

morally wrong or ethically wrong, then I wouldn't participate in it. And that's something we are not required to do – participate in it. But I do this voluntarily." [273]

It is an unpleasant job but it's also a dirty job for law enforcement officers to have to go digging in a molding, stinking landfill in search of a body put there by one of those heinous killers strapped down on that antiseptic gurney.

Authorities talk about recovering Lori Hacking's remains from a landfill on October 1, 2004 after her husband Mark shot her while she was sleeping and disposed of her body in a trash bin along with other evidence that ended up in a garbage landfill. The woman's remains were found in an area of the landfill that had been overlooked by cadaver dogs during an initial search for her body.

Another dirty job someone had to do was to go surfing in the Pacific Ocean – looking for Laci Peterson's dismembered body and that of her unborn son Conner. They were reportedly put into that cold ocean by their husband and father, convicted murderer Scott Peterson, on or about Christmas Eve, 2002. The bodies of mother and child were found and removed in body bags by police authorities three-and-one-half months later. Laci's body had no head, no hands, and no lower legs. Yes, again. Working in law enforcement whether in an antiseptic death chamber, in a stinking landfill, or on a Pacific Ocean beach can be a dirty job but somebody has to do it – and they do. But, nobody *has* to do what was done to Lori Hacking, Laci Peterson or Faith Hathaway.

\* \* \*

On page 198 of *Dead Man Walking,* Sister Prejean starts on a 13-page description of Robert Lee Willie's last day on death row in Louisiana's Angola prison. She talks about seeing Willie's mother visit her son along with his three step-

# An Eye for an Eye
*William T. Harper*

brothers, one of whom is gleefully "teasing Robert, accusing him of trying to steal his girlfriend...."[274] They all chat about "all the girlfriends Robert has had" and the conversation shifts to camping trips. This causes Sister Prejean "to smile, remembering when I was kid and all the times we set out to spend the night in the back yard."[275] What about Faith Hathaway's backyard camping trips? Was her family sitting around that night (or any night since her murder) gleefully "teasing" each other?

When the warden comes by to, prematurely it is suggested, tell the family it's time for them to go, the nun comments:

> "Robert could protest this and I would join him in it. He's being cut out of three hours with his family on the last day of his life and [she says with obvious admiration] for some reason he isn't upset."[276]

Faith Hathaway was "cut out of" a lot more than "three hours with [her] family on the last day of [her] life."

Pity the killer...Forget the victim.

\* \* \*

Willie gives all his worldly possessions to step-brother Mick "except for my boots from Marion [the federal penitentiary in Illinois, where he served time and joined the Aryan Brotherhood]. I'm going to walk to the chair in them boots. No cryin' now," he says. "I don't want no cryin'."[277] (Nonetheless, tough-guy Willie didn't go "out with my boots on." He went out the same way other executed murderers in Louisiana went out at the time: wearing prison-issue diapers and white terry-cloth slippers.) Talk about a tough guy. Sister Prejean calls him "the Marlboro Man"[278] and tells his family, "He has a lot of spunk, a lot of inner strength."[279]

# An Eye for an Eye
*William T. Harper*

It's one thing to have "a cause," to really believe the death penalty should be abolished. But it's quite something else to be speaking so adoringly of a malignant killer. Did it take a lot of "inner strength" and "spunk" for Willie to stab the helpless Faith Hathaway 17 times while another brute held her down and left her battered body to the maggots on May 28, 1980?

Now, in Willie's cell in the Angola prison, the nun starts to worry if the killer will "rage and fight all the way to the chair" or "what if his tough veneer cracks and he sobs or faints?"

The nun and killer rehash his earlier comments about "niggers, spics, and chinks." He complains about "blacks being lazy (and) harpin' on what a bad deal they've had." Prejean relates "stories about black people I know...good, hard-working people" and how it's President Ronald "Reagan's economic policies...to see if poor blacks are the real culprits 'gobbling up' our tax dollars." [280]

(And speaking of America's 40th President, the nun – as early as page nine of *Dead Man Walking* – attacks Ronald Reagan when she launches immediately into politics saying, "then I watch Reagan slash funds for prenatal and child care...." Notice: No courtesy reference to *President* Reagan here. Is her cause about the death penalty or is there a political agenda here?)

Now it's chow time and they share a table for Willie's last supper of "fried fish, oysters, shrimp, French-fried potatoes and a salad," according to Warden Frank Blackburn.[281] Poor Willie, the nun tells her readers, had a tough time eating this sumptuous meal because he had handcuffs on. Faith Hathaway had two fingers sliced off one of her hands by her sadistic killers in her struggle to live and, if she had had "fried fish, oysters, shrimp, French-fried

# An Eye for an Eye
*William T. Harper*

potatoes and a salad", it would have been hard too for her to manage her last meal.

While interspersing bravado comments about how "the electric chair don't scare me," Willie continues chatting with the nun about how he grew marijuana and sold it ("there's big money in drugs…"), and about how he could never hold a job for long (it was dangerous work on river tow-boats and barges where whip-lashing cables cut a man "in two like a knife"). That, of course, reminded Sister Prejean of her cousins who worked on oil rigs out in the Gulf of Mexico.[282] One has to wonder what kind of friendly, reminiscing chat Willie had with Faith Hathaway on her last day on earth.

Pity the killers…Forget the victims.

The Sister, having witnessed Elmo Patrick Sonnier's execution, obligingly walks the killer through the procedures of his coming execution because "he doesn't want to be surprised. He wants to be prepared." How prepared was Faith Hathaway? Did anyone walk her through her execution procedures? Willie tells Sister Prejean how he would like to have his execution televised. "It would be a good thing for the people to see what they are really doing" to him, he tells her.[283] That's exactly what Ms. Harvey had in mind when she gave permission for Detective Varnado to show photograph's of her daughter's brutalized body. It would have been a good thing for "the people to see" what Robert Lee Willie did to Faith Hathaway, too.

Maybe Robert Lee Willie was right! Why not have a side-by-side of Willie's antiseptic death right next to the ghastly sight Detective Varnado discovered of the maggot-infested body of Faith Hathaway? How about it, Sister Prejean? "Let's make a deal!"

As Sister Prejean points out when quoting Elizabeth Harvey's description of her dentist brother who identified his niece's remains, he "was pretty tore up when he came back from the funeral home. Before he reached his hand into that bag with all the lime in it and fished out Faith's jaw, he said

# An Eye for an Eye
*William T. Harper*

he had always been against the death penalty. But, boy, after that, he was for it."[284] Yes, Robert Lee Willie was right when he said, "It would be a good thing for the people to see...."

The nun and the killer Willie laugh and joke and talk about his tattoos and the earring in his left ear (which means "I'm no homo," he explains).[285] Faith Hathaway's jewelry was scattered all over her killing ground as she fought frantically and hysterically against two brutes who stole her life. It is hard to believe Sister Prejean, or anyone else, would tell Robert Lee Willie: "You have a dignity, Robert, that no one can take away from you."[286] Faith Hathaway also had a dignity – and a life. Robert Lee Willie, with help from his jailhouse junkie friend Joseph Jesse Vaccaro, took both away from her.

\* \* \*

"Dignity" – for murderers – is a word death penalty revisionists constantly assign to their poster-boy killers. According to most dictionaries, dignity means "the quality or state of being worthy, honored, or esteemed." How were Willie or Sonnier entitled to be called "worthy, honored, or esteemed"? Without reviewing again the horrid details of Faith Hathaway's murder, Sister Prejean says Faith. Hathaway's murderer "was a human being and deserved to be treated with dignity." Is a human being with dignity one who "raped [a teenager] long after her death," as Elizabeth Harvey revealed?[287] The answer to that question is a resounding "No!" Worthy? Honored? Esteemed? Robert Lee Willie? What about Faith Colleen Hathaway's dignity? Her honor? Go to the start of this chapter and detective Varnado's description of the murder scene and see what "dignity" you can find there. There's no doubt Robert Lee Willie took every semblance of dignity away from her. But Willie, we're told by Sister Prejean, "deserved to be treated with dignity."

Pity the killers...Forget the victims.

# An Eye for an Eye
*William T. Harper*

This kind of weeping and wailing about the plight of the condemned murderer goes on and on for 13 pages in *Dead Man Walking*. Robert Lee Willie, the man the Sister sat by "holding his hand at times" at his Louisiana Board of Pardons hearing [288] was a consummate con artist and a liar. Even Sister Prejean seemed to suspect that – although she blithely and quickly shrugged it off.

Willie and Vaccaro – true friends to the end – both squealed like pigs in a sty filled with slop that "the other guy" killed Faith Hathaway. The nun cites "a discrepancy in the physical evidence of [Willie's] case that's been bothering me…. Robert claims that Vaccaro, positioned behind Faith Hathaway, her head in his lap, suddenly began stabbing her, and he, Robert, kneeling in front facing her, had held her hands. But the victim's body was found with her arms above her head and her legs up, knees bent, feet on the ground. To hold her hands, then, Robert would have had to reach across her body, blocking Vaccaro from stabbing her. The pathologist had testified that the victim's hands and feet had to have been held in spread-eagled fashion before she died." [289]

But Sister Prejean quotes Willie:

> "'When we left her, her hands were laying on her stomach and her legs were down flat and her knees together.' There are," she writes, "three possible explanations that occur to me [and one of them is] Robert is lying." [290]

The supposition that Willie is a (shock) liar was, not surprisingly, confirmed at one of his appeals hearings. Paul McGarry, the pathologist who performed the autopsy on Ms. Hathaway's body, was asked, "is it your expert opinion that Faith Hathaway was held in that first-mentioned position until she died or was very close to death?" Dr. McGarry said, "Yes." [291]

# An Eye for an Eye
*William T. Harper*

At the end of the nun's tale of this last day, death row, Pollyannaish story, it's hard to square the nun's account of those seemingly pleasant, innocuous, and picnic-like conversations with Robert Lee Willie – the same guy who helped drown drug-dealer Dennis Hemby on May 23, 1978 when he hits him "in the back of the head and pushes him into the river," according to Detective Mike Varnado, until "...the thrashing weakens and then stops entirely." [292]

Willie, the same thug the Sister was worried about, just one week after drowning Hemby, participated in the back-shooting murder of police Sergeant Louis H. Wagner, III. Again writes Detective Mike Varnado, "In the moment before his death, Louis thinks of [his pregnant wife] Donna, who is asleep in their bed just a few miles away. He thinks of his precious little [first-born] whom he had kissed goodbye that morning. His last conscious thought is of the child he will never know and who will never know him. 'I love you,' he whispers. Then he is still." Willie "kicks at Louis's body with the toe of his boot. He laughs. 'Yeah, he's not moving. He's dead'." [293]

Willie, this supposedly kindly-talking, concerned, family man in the death house on December 28, 1984 as he chatted with the nun, came across 16-year-old Debbie Cuevas and her 20-year-old boyfriend, Mark Brewster, who were parked along a riverfront near Mandeville, La. The young couple was sipping milkshakes and listening to the car radio when Willie, along with his infamous friend Joe Vaccaro, kidnapped them. Brewster was tortured, stabbed, had his throat cut, was shot and left for dead in a remote area. Debbie was forced to go with the foul-smelling pair, who terrorized and raped her repeatedly over a two-day ordeal from hell. In short, the nun's portrayal of Robert Lee Willie outraged Detective Mike Varnado who wrote:

"Sister Prejean says that although Willie acted tough and macho, she can still see the child inside him. To me, this is outrageous.... And she has the gall to call

# An Eye for an Eye
*William T. Harper*

upon the soft, tender feelings of those who would support Willie and say he's just a child." [294]

Pity the killers…Forget the victims.

* * *

Elmo Patrick Sonnier had on "a clean white T-shirt" and a doctor was in attendance at his execution. He writes "loving words" in a Bible for Sister Prejean. [295] Members of his support team, including his spiritual advisor making small talk and reading from Isaiah, were with him at the end in an antiseptic death house with its freshly-polished oak chair. An "old priest raises his hand in blessing." Sonnier asks the warden, "Can Sister Helen touch my arm?" [296]

These were niceties Sonnier and his brother didn't afford David LeBlanc and Loretta Bourque when they executed those two kids as they lay face down in dirt, helpless and alone. There was no nun there for them; no old priest, no support team. There were no readings from the Bible. No chance to say "any last words," as the Warden asked Sonnier. Just three gun shots blasted into the back of each of their heads out there that dark, moonless night. Who really are the victims? Is Elmo Patrick Sonnier's execution *The Death of Innocents*?

As noted, Sister Prejean was present at five executions and ensuing funerals including Robert Lee Willie's. She dedicates 508 words of mournful prose to that scene. She talks of comforting the killer's mother, about how "brave" Willie was; how aunt Bessie "waving her shoe chased away a reporter," how Willie's mother fainted after kissing her son in his casket in the funeral parlor, and of a minister's sermon asking "God to spare Robert Lee Willie the pains of everlasting hellfire." [297] We're not told if the minister even mentioned the name of his victim, Faith Colleen Hathaway.

The nun goes on to describe the scene at the cemetery where there's another prayer for Willie and how the

# An Eye for an Eye
*William T. Harper*

appearance there of Willie's often-incarcerated father brings her to tears. The words pour forth – all 508 of them. No where, however, in either of the nun's two books is there a single word about Faith Hathaway's funeral, about Dennis Hemby's, nor Sergeant Louis Wagner's, nor any of the victims of the killers she champions. Theirs' were truly *The Death of Innocents*.

\* \* \*

The revisionists publicly, very publicly, anguish about the mental cruelty death row inmates go through during the appeals process; the psychological highs and lows, the hopes raised and dashed by judicial reviews and denials, awaiting that last-minute reprieve via a governor's phone call to a warden. At least *they* can hope. The death penalty opponents very rarely mention families of those murdered who have absolutely no hope for a reprieve from their anguish.

Pity the killers…Forget the victims.

And what rights do death penalty opponents have to weep and wail about the length of the appeals process? They're the ones who encourage and often financially sponsor them. They're the ones who string out the process of delay and delay and delay even though the odds of overturning death penalty sentences are extremely remote. They're the ones who give false hopes to the condemned, causing them to hang on to the bitter end, waiting for that call from the governor that rarely ever comes. They and their lawyers are the ones who "get the capital" – be it financial or notoriety – while their clients "get the punishment," in a direct reversal of the mocking way Sister Prejean put it.

You never hear of public servant district attorneys and public prosecutors getting rich on the job. But we're all aware of Johnny Cochran, Mark Geragos, and other superstar attorneys who join the gliteratti's Rich and Famous as they got TV face time trying to keep the high-profile O. J. Simpsons and the Scott Petersons off death row. Geragos'

# An Eye for an Eye
*William T. Harper*

client list included former Congressman Gary Condit and his involvement with Chandra Levy's murder, former first brother Roger Clinton; Whitewater former business partner of President Bill Clinton, Susan McDougal; Academy award-winning actress Winona Ryder, the now-deceased pop star Michael Jackson, hip hop star Nate Dogg, international arms dealer Sarkis Soghanalian, and Peterson. The late Johnnie Cochran, another of Michael Jackson's super-star lawyers, became a celebrity across America after the Simpson trial, receiving a million-dollar advance to write his memoirs and a hefty fee for personal appearances.

When sorrowful death penalty opponents sob for the poor death row murderer because of his/her agony of living under the cloud of years of litigation during the appeals process, they need to be reminded of one thing. It is neither the State nor the People that bring on those oft-times phony appeals claims that only prolong the agony.

In addition to deploring the self-induced appeals process, abolitionists also bemoan how tough those killers have it while in prison. They cry that Elmo Patrick Sonnier's "life is lived 23 out of 24 hours a day in a space six feet wide and eight feet long."[298] They don't mention that his victims are in their space 24 out of 24 hours a day in a "cell" three feet wide and six feet long and six feet deep in the ground. There's little or no weeping for victims in anti-death penalty circles.

"On one wall," goes the lament about Sonnier's cell, "is a bunk, on the back wall a stainless steel toilet and washbasin, a stainless steel plate above the washbowl instead of the mirror."[299] One has to ask if his victims had a washbasin to remove the bloody gore that was once their brains the Sonniers blew out. They surely wouldn't want a mirror – stainless steel or otherwise.

Sonnier "is allowed out of his cell for one hour a day..." the wailing continues. How many hours, minutes, seconds a day are Loretta Bourque and David LeBlanc allowed out of their graves? What about the parents? How

# An Eye for an Eye
*William T. Harper*

much time are they allowed for relief from their monumental, unending pain? Lloyd LeBlanc cries "the Sonniers exterminated the LeBlanc name" with the murder of his only son. Meanwhile, Sonnier complains "that the grits for breakfast [in prison] had been hard that morning..." and how he was hoping to be served some "scrambled eggs soon."[300] As the old song goes, "Life gets tedious, don't it."

We're alerted to the fact that poor Eddie Sonnier, Elmo Patrick's partner/brother in that killing field, is also suffering while incarcerated. "He's pale," the nun writes consolingly, but he is "holding up okay, except for his 'tore-up' stomach" and his sleeping difficulties.[301] One would have to imagine that the Bourque and LeBlanc families are tossing and turning at night, that their stomachs are pretty "tore up" too, but we're not told about that.

Pity the killers...Forget the victims.

\* \* \*

Yes, it is "hell on earth" for those "poor souls" ensconced on death row. Danny Robbie Hembree, Jr. was found guilty of murdering 17-year-old Heather Catterton in 2009 and was sentenced to death on Nov. 18, 2011. He has also been accused of killing two other women. Here's Hembree's view on just how hellish it is living on death row at Central Prison in Raleigh, N.C.:[302]

> "Is the public aware that I am a gentleman of leisure, watching color TV in the A.C., reading, taking naps at will, eating three well balanced hot meals a day," Hembree asked in the letter. "I'm housed in a building that connects to the new 55 million dollar hospital with round the clock free medical care 24/7.... I laugh at you self righteous clowns and I spit in the face of your so called justice system. The state of North Carolina has sentenced me to death but it's not real," he wrote.

# An Eye for an Eye
*William T. Harper*

Hembree also asks if the public knows that the chances of his "lawful murder" taking place in the next 20 years, if ever, are "very slim."

Yes, life (both literally and figuratively) sometimes is not all bad in a lot of prisons today even when you're not on death row. Some killers who may get that Life-Without-Parole sentence revisionists are advocating, end up imprisoned in a place like "Camp Cupcake." That's the name assigned to Alderson Federal Prison Camp, a campus-like collection of cottages tucked up in the picturesque mountains of West Virginia. Jean Harris, who in 1980 murdered Herman Tarnower, her paramour of many years and author of the *Scarsdale Diet*, served her time there. And in those cozy confines, Ms. Harris wrote and had published three books. Obviously, she had plenty of time and the means to concentrate on her literary endeavors instead of her punishment. What about the Tarnower family?

Pity the Killers...Forget the victims.

One penitentiary this writer visited might be typical of the norm. Just about every one of the 1,900 inmates there had an eight-hour job to do — whether it was making cloth in the textile factory for bed linens; cooking or cleaning or serving food in mess halls; repairing state vehicles in the automotive maintenance center, or cleaning up the prison chapel. It keeps them busy (i.e. again, "Idle hands are the Devil's workshop."). This writer once did a one-on-one interview with a murderer doing a life sentence in the pen and the only ambient difference between that interview and one done with the prison's warden was the color of their uniforms.

In a lot of places, racial segregation exists within the walls. It has to in order to control some of the gang violence which often breaks out. But overall, things aren't much different for those serving Life-Without-Parole than they are for residents in communities surrounding prisons. The inmates get to "shoot hoops" in the exercise yard, lift

# An Eye for an Eye
*William T. Harper*

weights, shadow box, play shuffleboard, or toss quoits. They play chess or checkers, watch television or listen to the radio – sometimes in a Day Room and sometimes in their cells. They have movies and occasionally, even live entertainers come in from the outside. (Unlike their neighbors outside the walls, some convicts even get visits from Hollywood glitterati like Susan Sarandon.) They eat three square meals a day; have clean clothes and shoes and socks; fresh bed linens, and all kinds of counseling and medical care. They have their own chapel services, libraries, and some go to school within the walls and get a GED or a college degree – whether they are short- or long-timers. It sounds a lot like "boot camp" in the army.

    Yes, life is tough inside the gray walls. Sometimes it even brings tears to the eyes of the inmates – like those participating in a Playwriting Program at Northpoint Prison in Kentucky. By so-doing, it was reported on a glowing video production, some inmates get to "express their inner voices." As one of those inmates gushed about the prison program – funded in part by the National Endowment for the Arts – put it, "I'm blessed to be at this prison." That's understandable – when you consider that six of the Arthur Millers-to-be were taken to New York City to perform their work Baruch Performing Arts Center in the heart of Manhattan in May of 2011. Receiving thunderous applause from the socialites attending was inmate #236216, a registered sex offender, Calvin Sturgill's play entitled (you guessed it), "The Innocent Man."[303]

    For anyone who is in any way artistically or mechanically inclined, there are "piddling shops" in prisons in which inmates can ply their crafts. Some penitentiaries have therapy classes and band rooms where they get to jam on guitars, keyboards and drums. They get visits with friends and family. And yes, some prisons do allow conjugal visits for inmates in the general population – for both gay and straight prisoners. In other prisons, "girlfriends" – who never met their "boyfriends" outside the prison walls, are invited in for

# An Eye for an Eye
*William T. Harper*

chats. Some even end up getting married. Ted Bundy did. It really isn't tough duty. Some prisons actually have lakeside homes on prison grounds – homes that many economically unfortunate, tax-paying citizens on the outside would give their eye-teeth for – inhabited strictly by unsupervised convicted felons. Those minimum security inmates even get to cook their own meals using vegetables they grow in their own gardens. In California, if you pony up a fee, you can upgrade your prison accommodations to those nearly rivaling first-class hotels.

For most institutions, prison life is nothing like the truly hard-core penitentiaries that are sensationalized on TV or in movies and books – places like California's San Quentin and Corcoran penitentiaries and the "Castle on the Cumberland," Kentucky's State Penitentiary. Conversely, most prisons today are also nothing like the old Georgia chain-gangs and the horrendous agricultural farms where inmates would seriously abuse their bodies (i.e., cutting their Achilles tendon with an "Aggie-hoe") and even commit suicide to get off "ag-lines." Some maximum-security prisons even have a community day-room in their death houses where those awaiting execution get to come and go from their unlocked cells and gather together, visit, play games, lift weights, etc.[304]

The stereotypical impressions the public has about prisons being places where inmates do "hard time" are those which the sympathetic anti-death penalty cabal gleefully promotes. The movies and TV spectaculars we see on prison life are, for the most part, made by liberal film-makers located where? In California, in Hollywood. And it is no mere coincidence that many of those "hard time" penitentiaries are where? In California – Corcoran, San Quentin, Folsom, et al. Conversely and in the real, non-Hollywood world, in some prisons today, the clientele – including the murderers – are not even called "inmates" anymore; they're deferentially referred to as "clients" or "offenders" or other mild-sounding euphemisms! "Cool Hand Luke," as portrayed by Hollywood

# An Eye for an Eye
*William T. Harper*

actor and death penalty opponent Paul Newman, doesn't live here anymore.

One would be hard-pressed today to find gangs of convicts "making little ones out of big ones," except perhaps in Alabama. The days of staged "gladiator" fights among inmates with prison guards making bets on who will be the last man standing are not totally gone, but they're not as common as they used to be. And unfortunately, inmates raping inmates still exists in all too many prisons but most sex is consensual. Yes, and many Correctional Officers are sometimes a little too eager to "kick inmates' butts," feces-thrown-in-their-face notwithstanding.

Today, conversely, thousands of inmates access the Internet indirectly using inmate telephone and mail privileges and a network of family, friends or activists. Once on the Web they enlist celebrities to plead their case, pillory the prosecutors who imprisoned them, or simply find pen pals. The Canadian Coalition Against the Death Penalty "publishes web sites for about 500 U. S. death row inmates, and pen pal solicitations for about 700 more, said co-founder Tracy Lamourie.... [She] and her partner pay for envelopes, stationery and postage out-of-pocket or with donations that trickle in. The server space for the Web is donated by a European death penalty opponent...."[305]

Among the things Life-Without-Parole prisoners cannot do is jump in the old SUV and run down to the supermarket for a six-pack. They can't just pack up and go off on a vacation to the Blue Ridge Mountains of Virginia (or anywhere else, for that matter). And, for the most part, they can't make decisions about most things that affect their lives. But then again, what decisions can now be made by the victims of those killers whose heinous crimes put them behind bars in the first place?

How about "doing time" at the Great Plains Correctional Facility in Oklahoma? Joseph T. Hallinan describes it as:

# An Eye for an Eye
*William T. Harper*

"…a private prison, its cells are spacious measuring eleven feet by five feet. Outside each cell is a dayroom, where prisoners gather during idle hours. The dayroom has one TV and three phones, which inmates can use until 11 P.M. on weeknights and until 1 A.M. on weekends. The TV has cable and gets twenty-three stations.

"Nearby," Hallinan continues, "there is another room with eighteen new desktop computers. Each is equipped with software for word processing and desktop publishing so an inmate, if he wishes, can learn these skills. He can also study at the prison's law library or go to the 'multipurpose room' and take a class in drawing or leatherwork. He can even fire some pottery in a ceramic kiln or play the organ or strum a guitar.

"If the weather is nice, there are picnic tables and benches outside for the inmates to enjoy, along with a full-size basketball court, a handball court, a running track, and a ten-station weight machine. There's even something," Hallinan said, "I've never seen before: small vertical posts that look like futuristic police call boxes, but that are, in fact, permanent cigarette lighters, installed because inmates are not allowed to have matches."[306]

Why do you think we hear of so many cases where a newly-released inmate commits some second-rate burglary and waits for the police to come catch him so he can go back "home" to the joint? Lifers don't have to worry about revamping Social Security, HMO's, four-dollars-a-gallon gasoline prices, rising medical costs and the price of prescription drugs. They don't have to worry about escalating or crashing real estate taxes and voting on school bonds. They don't have to worry about their 401-K pension plans failing.

For some inmates, life in the Big House can get

# An Eye for an Eye
*William T. Harper*

downright cozy. One account talks about an "inmate whose job in the clothing issue office provided him with a comfortable existence: The officers were congenial, the inmates were friendly, they could cook food there for their lunch and avoid the mess hall, and the work was not difficult...."[307]

And through it all, the anti-death penalty crowd would have us *reward* the Jeffrey Dahmers, the Kenneth McDuffs, the Charles Mansons, etc., by putting them in a "Camp Cupcake" prison for the rest of their lives, sometimes giving them "cushy" jobs, and relieving them of all these concerns that good, law-abiding citizens sit up nights worrying about. That's the "punishment" for Dahmer, killer of 17 young men who kept some of his victims' body parts in his refrigerator. That would be it for McDuff, "The Bad Boy from Rosebud" who "didn't just kill his victims; he savaged them in unspeakable ways." That would also be it for Charles Manson and members of his "family" which – at his direction – brutally and viciously murdered seven people in 1969. Oh yes. Everybody knows about poor Charlie Manson and his "family." But, does anyone know any of the names of the victims' families?

Pity the killers…Forget the Victims?

\* \* \*

Life on *death row* is admittedly harsh - sometimes. It should be harsh. The killers are there in most cases because of the brutality of their actions and because they pose a continuing threat to society – in and out of prison. They are in those cubicles with the limitations on their freedom because they deserve to be there. But, abolitionists are begging for the killers' release from death row and their integration back into the general prison population via their lie-filled advocacy of life-without-parole.

Consider this: As of the spring of 2012, there were 3,170 inmates sitting on death row in America's prisons [vis-

# An Eye for an Eye
*William T. Harper*

à-vis the 558 residing there in 1972 as noted in Chapter Three herein].[308] In effect, dismantling the death penalty sends all 3,170 back into the prisons' general population. Even more frighteningly, it gives all 3,170 another chance to do what Kenneth Allen McDuff did after he too was released from death row in via the Supreme Court's *Furman v. Georgia* decision in 1972 and paroled in October of 1989. All 3,170 death row inmates could then somehow get out of prison – because Life-Without-Parole *does NOT mean incarceration forever* – as shown conclusively in Chapter Four.

All 3,170 of them could get out and murder five more innocent people just as McDuff did. Did you read that number correctly? Three-thousand, one-hundred and seventy deliberate murderers. The death penalty opponents would, if they have their way, reward 3,170 killers for their horrific crimes by committing them to a "Camp Cupcake" somewhere. Is that what criminal justice is all about? In the world of Fyodor Dostoevsky's classic *Crime and Punishment*, where's the punishment that fits the crime?

\* \* \*

Who are the good guys and who are the bad guys in the death penalty abolitionists' world? Maybe there aren't any "bad" guys in that world. It's hard to tell when listening to death penalty opponents. While the parents of Faith Hathaway talk lovingly about their raped and ravaged daughter and the savage, "mad dog," "son-of-a-bitch" who killed her, Sister Prejean describes her killer as "the young man I have just visited with neatly combed hair and the quiet voice..." who politely "exhaled his [cigarette] smoke downward so that it didn't blow into my face."[309] Dare one ask if Willie's hair was "neatly combed" while he was raping Faith Hathaway and was his voice "quiet" as he plunged a knife into her body 17 times? Which way did he blow his cigarette smoke?

While reflecting on Willie and Vaccaro and their trials, Faith Hathaway's mother Elizabeth Harvey said,

# An Eye for an Eye
## William T. Harper

"If they got a life sentence they could talk to their family on the telephone, they could visit with them, they can see 'em at holidays, they can visit with them at Christmas time. Christmas time my chair is still empty at my table. To go visit Faith, I have to go to the grave. She can't come – I can't talk to her. I can't put my arms around her."[310] Who are the victims?

Ah, but death penalty revisionists have a solution for Ms. Harvey and others. "Surely American politicians must know," they suggest while presenting the anti-death penalty cabal's solution for the grieving families,

"...that the *real* way to help murder victims' families is to make available victims' support groups and compensation funds. At the state level, victims' assistance for medical care, counseling, lost wages, and funeral expenses is almost always underfunded."[311]

There we have it. "The *real* way to help" grieving families of those slaughtered by killers such as Robert Lee Willie, Elmo Patrick Sonnier, Dobie Gillis Williams, and Joseph Roger O'Dell (plus hundreds of others like Kenneth Allen McDuff) is to just throw a few bucks their way. Tell us, Mr. and Mrs. Harvey, would a few bucks for "medical care, counseling, lost wages, and funeral expenses" be the *real* way to relieve *you* of *your* 25-year, 24/7 anguish over *your* daughter Faith Hathaway's brutal rape and murder?

\* \* \*

According to a newspaper headline, "Murderer [Robert Lee] Willie [Went] to Chair a Proud Man."[312] So reported a New Orleans *Time-Picayune* reporter who was "sensitive to issues of

# An Eye for an Eye
*William T. Harper*

social justice."[313] What does Willie, fortified by his own sense of "uncompromised manhood," have to be proud of? His three savage murders? His repeated rapes of 16-year-old Debbie Cuevas and his attempted murder and ultimate, lifetime paralyzation of Mark Brewster? His desires to be a terrorist? His membership in the Aryan Brotherhood? His comments about "niggers, spics, and chinks?" Yet, when one reads reports from death penalty opponents about Robert Lee Willie's execution, the feeling for some remains that he belongs right up there with Joseph O'Dell who's "life and death resembles that of Jesus" (see Chapter Two).

"At the 1995 Academy Awards," wrote Detective Mike Varnado in his all-too-graphic account of Faith Hathaway's murder at the hands of Robert Lee Willie and Joseph Jesse Vaccaro...

> "Susan Sarandon in her acceptance speech for Best Actress praised Sister Helen Prejean and her work in the fight against the death penalty in America, and the crowd applauded for the nun who was now a celebrity.
>
> "No word was spoken about the victims of murder. No word was spoken about Faith Hathaway who was then more than 15 years in her grave. No word was spoken of the lives of her parents who were decimated by the crimes committed by Robert Lee Willie. No one remembered or seemed to care about a poor young girl named Faith Colleen Hathaway. Although innocent of any crime, she had been slaughtered like an animal in the woods and now her death had become mere fodder for those with a political agenda to abolish the death penalty."[314] Via the movie and the book that inspired it, "Robert Willie...has attained the status of a victim."[315]

Faith Hathaway, the true victim, has as a result, attained the status of a footnote.

# An Eye for an Eye
*William T. Harper*

Pity the killer…Forget the Victim.

\* \* \*

That said, who is the victim in the following case? A 25-year-old University of Minnesota student was called on the telephone by a co-worker who asked him if he could fill in on the midnight-to-eight shift in a 24/7 convenience store. The student said yes. Four hours later, the student was dead, shot through the head with a Saturday-Night Special derringer by a drug-addict who got about $23 from the till in the holdup/killing. The shooter fled the scene, was ironically picked up by local police and given a ride home because officers saw him reeling along the sidewalk and feared for his safety. Shortly thereafter, the murder was discovered and by the time the accommodating police realized the possibility their reeling rider may have been the shooter, he had fled the scene to the East St. Louis, Illinois area.

Some months later the killer was arrested, extradited back to St. Paul, Minnesota where he stood trial and was convicted of the store clerk's murder. The killer was sentenced to *seven years* in a penitentiary – with, of course, time off for good behavior. Imagine the agony of the student's family with a sentence as lenient as that. But the worst was yet to come.

While incarcerated, the murderer developed a form of leukemia and, as reported by Dan Rather on the CBS Evening News on March 11, 1986, the Minnesota Department of Corrections petitioned the courts to have the killer released so he could receive a new type of bone-marrow transplant (which the prison system said it could not afford).

Once again, the anguished family of the victim faced the prospect that their son's killer was not only going to get out of prison long before the end of his measly *seven-year* sentence, but those same family members were, in effect, going to have their tax dollars spent for the indigent murderer's operation and recuperation.

# An Eye for an Eye
*William T. Harper*

Letters to the Editor in some local newspapers even chastised the dead student's family for its "heartless opposition" to the transplant. But others around the state also raised a public outcry that delayed action on the state's request and divine intervention solved the dilemma by giving the killer the ultimate sentence he so richly deserved before he could get out of prison.

Pity the killer. Forget the victims.

\* \* \*

Both of Sister Prejean's two books are not about *The Death of Innocents* such as Faith Hathaway, Loretta Bourque, David LeBlanc, Sergeant Louis Wagner III, and other helpless souls such as Dennis Hemby, Sonja Knippers, and Helen Schartner. The real *Innocents* seem merely to be "extras" on the stage and screen, put there to serve only as props for "the cause," for those who abolitionists zealously want everyone to believe are the actual "victims" – Robert Lee Willie, Elmo Patrick Sonnier, and others whose despicable crimes are discussed throughout these pages.

Where are the death penalty revisionists when the killers are killing? We know where they are when the killers are being killed. They're out there in front of prisons with their candles and their signs, with their burning American flags, with their chants and their bullhorns, and screaming insults from behind the barricades, with their Joan Baez, Arlo Guthrie, and Bob Dylan protest songs, with their crocodile tear-stained tissues and hankies, with their Bibles and beads, with their appearances on those sympathetic Phil Donahue and Larry King television programs, with their verbal (and sometimes physical) attacks on the people who are doing their job in ridding the world of the vermin the protesters are praying for. Who are the victims?

Where was the ACLU when Faith Hathaway was being raped and murdered by Robert Lee Willie and Joseph Jesse Vaccaro? Where was Amnesty International when

# An Eye for an Eye

*William T. Harper*

Loretta Bourque and David LeBlanc lay face down in the dirt as Elmo Patrick Sonnier and his little brother Eddie were pumping those bullets into the backs of their skulls? Where were the editors at the Death Penalty Information Center when Jeffrey Dahmer was cannibalizing those kids in Milwaukee? Where was the Illinois Coalition against the Death Penalty when John Wayne Gacy was murdering all those young boys in Chicago? Where were the Students Against the Death Penalty when he were savagely murdered eight nurses in Chicago?

In a 700-word article about the execution of Robert E. Williams appearing on December 3, 1997 in the University of Nebraska's "Daily Nebraskan.com" (an electronic version of the school's student newspaper), there were a lot of words including even a quote from a *seven*-year-old (?) little girl who reportedly asked, "how many men had to die before people realized killing was wrong?" Some protesters at the state's capital in Lincoln "celebrated Williams' entrance into a better place," and some "regretted the loss of Williams." One demonstrator, Marylyn Felion, Williams' spiritual advisor, cried, saying "I am ashamed to be in the state of Nebraska." One might guess a lot of Cornhuskers reciprocate her shame.

No where, not once in all those 700 words does the writer mention, or even vaguely hint at the crimes for which Robert E. Williams was put to death. No where in that story would a reader know Williams was tried and convicted for the murders of Catherine Brook, Patricia McGarry and Virginia Rowe and the rape and brutalization of two other women in 1977. Nowhere in the story did the writer mention Williams had spent 20 years on death row while filing appeal after appeal, many of which were labeled "frivolous" by the courts hearing them. Brad Davis, author of the Williams story, must have graduated *magna cum laude* along with others such as *New York Times* reporter Jayson Blair; Janet Cooke of the *Washington Post*, the *New Republic*'s Stephen Glass, the *Boston Globe*'s Patricia Smith, and Jay Forman in *Slate* as journalists

# An Eye for an Eye
*William T. Harper*

who got caught embellishing, exaggerating, and even outright lying in print.

\* \* \*

Stretching the limits of absurdity to the nth degree, death penalty opponents carry their plea even into the state motor vehicle department – a place where victims of killers are never going to visit again. Never missing an avenue of attack no matter how far they have to stretch, legal and social theorists are deeply concerned about wording on death certificates for executed killers. Currently in some states, the Cause of Death on certificates for executed inmates is entered as "Legal Homicide." When some states tried to have that designation changed to "Judicial Order," abolitionists demanded to know if advocates of the change wanted to *punish the killers* further with such language. There seems to be no end to the abolitionists' effort to provide aid and comfort to killers – at the expense of the victims and their families.

"How," a death penalty opponent demanded to know, "do you think the inmate families would feel if they have to take a death certificate to settle the estate of a person who was just executed to such as a car dealership or a bank and it says 'Judicial Order'?" (One might wonder how many of these shiftless killers have "estates" that need settling.) But, it matters not to revisionists. This is just another bullet in their clip, another arrow in their quiver. Having faced such frivolous demands, Andy Kahan, Crime Victims Advocate for the City of Houston, and a supporter of the language change, responded to the questioner:

> "With all due respect, sir, I really wasn't concerned about the visits to a car dealership." [316]

Teenaged murder victims Elizabeth Peña and Jennifer Ertman (see Chapter Eight) will never have cause to be concerned about a car dealership either. Their killers never

# An Eye for an Eye
*William T. Harper*

gave them a chance to grow old enough to get a driver's license. Who are the victims?

In the Index to *Dead Man Walking*, Sister Prejean gives four mentions to 18-year-old Loretta Bourque. To her convicted co-killer, Elmo Patrick Sonnier, the sympathetic nun gives almost *an entire column* of the Index in agate-size type listings. Robert Lee Willie, the co-killer of yet another 18-year-old, Faith Hathaway, got 29 carefully-annotated listings. Miss Hathaway got four. Even the prison warden who officiated at Sonnier's execution got more Index listings than did the two kids who were murdered by Elmo Patrick Sonnier and his brother Eddie. This is yet another example of how abolitionists turn killers into "victims" and let the innocent dead – along with Civil War-era abolitionist John Brown's body – go a-moldering in their graves.

John Walsh, who became a nationally recognized leader in the push for victims' rights after his six-year-old son Adam was ghastly murdered, says:

> "Each year 40 million Americans become victims of crimes. Behind each of these numbers is a terrible trauma, a story of unimaginable personal suffering and loss. Yet the needs of victims are an afterthought in our criminal justice system. We protect the rights of criminals; we must take equal care to protect the rights of victims.
>
> Here's a typical experience," he continued, "in the words of one victim: 'They explained the defendant's constitutional right to the nth degree. They couldn't do this and they couldn't do that because of his constitutional rights. And I wondered what mine were. And they told me, I hadn't got any.' Too often, our system treats victims as irrelevant bystanders and they feel as though they're being victimized for a second time."[317]

# An Eye for an Eye

*William T. Harper*

Faith Hathaway's mother and step-father would surely say "Amen" to that.

And John Walsh knows all too well from heart-rendering experience whereof he speaks. Here's how this story was told about John Walsh's kidnapped son, Adam.

> HOLLYWOOD, Fla. — A serial killer who died more than a decade ago is the person who decapitated the 6-year-old son of "America's Most Wanted" host John Walsh in 1981, Florida police said Tuesday.... "Who could take a 6-year-old and murder and decapitate him? Who?" John Walsh asked. "... The not knowing has been a torture, but that journey's over...."

Yes, "that journey's over" but imagine the 31 years of unrelenting torment John and his wife Reve have had to endure.

> A suspect, Otis O'Toole, the MSNBC News story continued, "had twice confessed to killing the child, but later recanted. He claimed responsibility for hundreds of murders, but police determined most of the confessions were lies.
>
> O'Toole's niece told John Walsh, her uncle confessed on his deathbed in prison that he killed Adam.... O'Toole was serving five life sentences for murder when he died of liver failure at the age of 49....
>
> Adam disappeared on July 27, 1981. His mother left him playing in the toy department at a Sears store at a Hollywood mall, but didn't find him when she returned. Over the loudspeaker, the plea sounded: "Adam Walsh, please come to customer service."
>
> Two hours after the disappearance, police were called. His mother and grandmother searched the

# An Eye for an Eye
*William T. Harper*

mall in a growing panic and John Walsh tried to work with uniformed officers to find his son.

Two weeks passed before the boy's fate was learned. Fishermen discovered his severed head in a canal 120 miles away near Vero Beach; his body never was found.[318]

Another parent sharing those feelings is Sharron Mankins. Her son Michael Baker and his friend John Mayeski, both 16, were brutally murdered in July of 1978 by 25-year-old *paroled murderer* Robert Alton Harris. Along with his brother, Daniel, 18, Robert Harris kidnapped the two teenagers from a San Diego fast-food restaurant parking lot and drove them to a remote area. According to court testimony by Daniel Harris, Robert Harris shot Mayeski in the head and back, killing him. Baker bolted, trying to find cover in the bushes, but Robert Harris chased him. Baker pleaded for his life, but Harris shot him in the back and abdomen, killing him. Then Robert Harris ate the boys' hamburgers, laughing at the blood gushing from Mayeski's fatal head wound.[319] The Harris brothers were arrested hours later and in 1979, a jury sentenced Robert Harris to die.

Re-married Sharron Mankins said the pain of Michael Baker's death was compounded by the decade of litigation and appeals that kept Harris alive. "It's frustrating," Sharron Mankins said.

> "We'll be doing fine, and then there's the footage of Harris on TV with that smirk he always has on his face. And it just opens up all the wounds, and we hope maybe, just maybe, the judicial system is going to prevail. And then we take two steps back."
> 
> "This is a political game now," Ms. Mankins said of pleas coming from celebrities such as Mother Teresa and Hollywood television stars to spare Harris' life. "The politicians are making a name for themselves off my loss.... Mother Teresa is telling

# An Eye for an Eye
*William T. Harper*

the governor [Pete Wilson] to pray for these men (on death row) and make the right decision by granting clemency," she said. "Well, how about praying and giving the victims' [families] inner strength?"[320]

Despite further intervention by such as Amnesty International, the death sentence was finally carried out on April 21, 1992 – 14 years after teenagers Michael Baker and John Mayeski were murdered. That's a long time to wait for "thy will" to be done. That's a long time to wait for mushy-headed jurists, conniving defense attorneys, and death penalty revisionists to deny that "will" from being done.

\* \* \*

Meanwhile, the Hollywood elite keeps polluting motion picture theaters with its anti-death penalty propaganda, foisting it on an unsuspecting public that thinks it's merely being entertained. In 1999 alone, three full-length feature pictures hit the nation's movie theaters – all of them with the revisionists' death penalty views paramount in the story lines:

- "The Green Mile," starring Tom Hanks, about the lives of prison guards on death row leading up to the execution of a *wrongly accused* man.
- "The Hurricane," starring Denzel Washington, about a boxer allegedly *wrongly imprisoned* for murder.
- "True Crime," starring Clint Eastwood, about a journalist investigating the case of an *innocent man* on death row.[321] [*emphases* added]

Does the name Tony Pope ring a bell? Probably not. But it does to some people in Chattanooga, Tennessee. In 1995, Pope pleaded guilty to killing Susan Yarbrough by beating her in the head, ribs and throat so hard he shattered

# An Eye for an Eye
*William T. Harper*

an 18-inch frying pan. He was sentenced to 15 years in prison. Pretty cheap price to pay for a life, especially when you consider the parole board voted 4-0 in 2001 that he could be released after serving only five years of that sentence. Four years later, Pope was charged with killing his wife with a hammer; strangling his 13-year-old stepdaughter; and fatally dropping and punching his five-week-old son. Investigators said Pope told them his wife was leaving him and taking the children. Oh yes, one of the parole board members said, "I'd give my right arm to change that vote." [322]

Looking at it from an even broader landscape are death penalty advocates like Michael Paranzino, president of death penalty support group "Throw Away the Key." Noting some November 2005 plans by dissenters to memorialize the 1,000th execution following repeal of the ban on capital punishment in 1976, Paranzino said, "Since 1999 we've had 100,000 innocent people murdered in the U.S., but nobody is planning on commemorating all those people killed."

Pity the Killers…Forget the Victims.

\* \* \*

Another poster child for the death penalty abolitionists was Karla Fay Tucker. Here is how Ms. Tucker's trip to death row started in June of 1983:

> "A wild-eyed, 23-year-old prostitute – after a weekend orgy of methadone, heroin, Dilaudid, Valium, Placidyls, Somas, Wygesics, Percodan, Mandrax, marijuana, rum and tequila – smiles maniacally at 27-year-old Jerry Lynn Dean. It ticked her off that he once parked his oil-leaking motorcycle in her living room. She takes her first swing with a pickax. Flesh tears. Blood spurts. Bones crack as the 3-foot-long tool thuds first against Dean and later against his companion, 32-year-old Deborah Thornton. By the time the

# An Eye for an Eye
*William T. Harper*

screams end, Tucker and her accomplice [Daniel Ryan Garrent] will have hacked their victims more than 20 times." [323]

Even grislier descriptions of these murders abound in the nation's media files.

Once again, the list of "the usual suspects" lined up to plead for the clemency for Ms. Tucker that she didn't grant her victims. Jerry Falwell, Bianca Jagger, and Pat Robertson pleaded for Karla Fay. "Religious leaders from all over the world – not just the pope" came to her defense. [324] Sister Prejean's argument in favor of clemency for Karla Faye Tucker went like this:

"Yes, she's guilty of a horrible crime—she killed two helpless people with a pick ax—but she seems genuinely remorseful for her crime; she seems to have under gone genuine life-changing religious conversion. Even the warden and corrections officers attest that for 14 years she's been a model prisoner. Couldn't she spend the rest of her life helping other prisoners to change their lives?" [325]

One might answer: "Yes, if Jerry Lynn Dean and Deborah Thornton could remove the pick ax from their bodies and "spend the rest of [their] life" just simply living. Is the argument by abolitionists that all murderers have to do is kill, repent and be "genuinely remorseful" and then they can spend their rest of their lives living off the state's largess while their victims, again, lie a-molding in their graves? The answer to all these questions is an unqualified, "NO!" It reminds one of the often heard of cliché:

"I'm sorry. But what I'm really sorry for is I got caught."

Joe Freeman Britt, a former North Carolina prosecutor, is unfazed by arguments convicted killers should not be executed because of their Christianity – long-term or

# An Eye for an Eye
*William T. Harper*

jail-house induced. He says, "I probably brought more people to the Lord than Billy Graham. I mean when they go to prison, they all find the Lord." [326]

Britt's sentiments were echoed by Jerry Cox, a former officer in the Texas Department of Criminal Justice. "When those inmates hit the [back door of the prison], the only thing 90 percent of them wanted was a Gideon Bible," said the 17-year veteran of service in Texas prisons.

> "They found God. They wanted to go to Chapel. And then, when they would leave the prison (one way or another) and we would go in and clean out the cells, guess what we found? The Bibles. Those inmates tore the pages out of the Bibles and used the paper to make cigarettes." [327]

Now there's a real religious conversion – from Bible pages to cigarette papers.

Or, as former Texas Department of Criminal Justice warden Jim Willett put it after his 30 years in prison work:

> "It's ironic that some of the men who died on the [death house] gurney and professed to being believers in Jesus Christ as their savior, might not have done so if they hadn't been condemned to die." [328]

Converts are not rare in prison yards – especially after that back gate clangs shut behind you. Apparently, God (however you define Him/Her) is pretty easy to find within the cold, gray walls of a penitentiary – especially when you're on death row.

\* \* \*

# An Eye for an Eye
*William T. Harper*

# Chapter Seven

## Wrongly Sentenced Doesn't Mean... Wrongly Convicted

*On July 29, 1994, Megan Kanka — an innocent seven-year-old girl with a candid smile and pudgy cheeks — picked up her bicycle and went for a ride around her quiet neighborhood outside of Trenton, New Jersey. As the second-grader pedaled less than a hundred feet from her front door, she noticed her awkward, 33-year-old neighbor from across the street, Jesse Timmendequas, cleaning his boat in the driveway. Megan stopped by in hopes of seeing the boat, but Timmendequas, a paroled sex offender who was sharing the home with two other convicted child molesters, had other plans.*

*He instead asked Megan if she wanted to come inside and see his puppy....*

**Megan Kanka**

*Once inside, Timmendequas, who was twice convicted on child molestation charges, closed the bedroom door, touched Megan and tried to kiss her. When Megan tried to run away,*

# An Eye for an Eye
*William T. Harper*

*Timmendequas put a belt around her neck -- strangling her as he sexually assaulted her. He then tied two plastic bags over her head, placed her body in a toy box and drove his pickup truck to a nearby park. There, he molested the body one more time and dumped Megan in a patch of high weeds....*

*In the hours following Megan's disappearance, the family held impromptu news conferences on its front porch, anchored by a tearful Maureen [Kanka] who pleaded for her daughter's safe return. While the Kankas were holding out hope that Megan was still alive, police were instantly drawn to Timmendequas -- the peculiar neighbor with the oversized eyeglasses and pie-shaped face -- after learning that he and his roommates were convicted sex offenders. Timmendequas' two roommates were quickly dismissed as suspects [and] all eyes were now on Jesse.... By the next day, he had confessed to investigators and led police to the body.*

*Timmendequas "looked up and said to a hushed room, 'She's in the park'," former Deputy First Assistant Mercer County Prosecutor Kathryn Flicker said at his trial, describing the end of the interrogation. With a final glimmer of hope, investigators then asked if Megan might still be alive. "No, she's dead. I put a plastic bag over her head," Timmendequas allegedly told police.*[329]

\* \* \*

Megan Nicole Kanka is the unfortunate Megan of "Megan's Law," known as the Sexual Offender (Jacob Wetterling) Act of 1994. The law requires persons convicted of sex crimes against children to notify local law enforcement of any change of address or employment after release from custody (prison or psychiatric facility). The law, in a number of states, also requires law enforcement authorities to identify sex offenders and alert their surrounding public to their whereabouts.

On May 30, 1997, a jury returned a verdict of guilty against Jesse Timmendequas on all counts including capital murder, kidnapping and aggravated sexual assault. He was sentenced to death. His sentence was twice confirmed by the

# An Eye for an Eye
*William T. Harper*

New Jersey Supreme Court. There is absolutely no doubt of Timmendequas' guilt in this ghastly crime – nor of two similar though not deadly previous assaults on little girls. However, that sentence was never enacted because, as noted above, the New Jersey Legislature and the State's then-governor, Jon Corzine, collapsed under pressure from the abolitionists and disallowed the death penalty in the Garden (of Evil?) State on December 17, 2007.

That action reduced Timmendequas' sentence to the good, old "Life-Without-Parole" panacea the abolitionists like to console themselves with. And there he sits, with death penalty abolitionists from just about all points of the globe citing a killer's "dignity" and probably congratulating each other because another heinous killer didn't get the ultimate penalty for his ultimate crime. There is even a chance that one day Timmendequas will be labeled among the grossly misnamed "117 wrongly convicted" inmates noted herein and he – as an inmate previous to his Megan Kanka savagery was labeled as a possible threat to society should he be released – may get out of prison for a *third* time to do who knows what!

\* \* \*

One of the salient points made by Adolph Hitler when he wrote *Mein Kampf* – his 1923 thesis for his ultimate ascension to power and for world war – was his claim the bigger the lie and the more often it's told, the more apt people are to believe it. The death penalty abolitionists have taken that page out of *Der Fuhrer's* book and labeled it the "117 wrongly convicted."

Again and again and again, abolitionists talk about "117 wrongfully convicted persons [who] have been released from death row" Starting right off on the very first page of the Preface of her second book, Sister Prejean claims:

> "As of September 2004, 117 wrongly convicted persons have been released from death

# An Eye for an Eye
*William T. Harper*

row."

On page 17, she writes:

> "Recently, we have been witness to astounding admissions of error by state and federal courts forced to free 117 wrongly convicted people from death row since 1973, and the number keeps growing."

Again, on page 61, she claims "over a hundred wrongly convicted death row inmates [were] vindicated in the last thirty years...." The inference, the implication is obvious. But insinuations inherent in words like "forced to free" and "released from death row" and the blatant claim those 117 death row inmates were "vindicated" is patently misleading at its best – if not dishonest at its worst.

It is a devious way to get readers and listeners – especially among young, impressionable student groups – to believe 117 wrongly convicted inmates have been absolved and the state and justice have been denied the full measure of the law. It must be said, right here and right now, "released," "freed" and "vindicated" do not mean – as abolitionists shamefully imply – "exonerated." Exonerate means "to free from blame." Though these are, in many cases, merely releases from death row back into the prison's general population, they are by far in no way shape or form releases from prison or clearances from blame – no matter how hard the anti-death penalty cabal tries to spin them in that direction.

Furthermore, we are left to wonder why death penalty resisters didn't make an even further preposterous claim that every death row inmate in the nation was "exonerated" when the U. S. Supreme Court put a hiatus on the death penalty in its *Furman v. Georgia* decision in 1972. Had *Furman* been issued in 2012, 3,170 prisoners being held in State and Federal prisons under sentence of death, would have been "exonerated," according to abolitionists' falsehoods.

# An Eye for an Eye
*William T. Harper*

The most egregious false impression seems purposely put forth by death penalty opponents with the sweeping claim "...the system cannot even be relied upon to convict the right people."[330] Does this mean David "the Son of Sam" Berkowitz, Albert "the Boston Strangler" De Salvo, Jeffrey Dahmer, Ted Bundy, John Wayne Gacy, Richard Speck, Charles Manson, Richard "The Iceman" Kuklinski, Elmo Patrick Sonnier, Robert Lee "the Marlboro Man" Willie and thousands of other wanton killers were not duly convicted?

If the system, as death penalty abolitionists claim, cannot "convict the right people," it must be convicting the wrong people, right? Are all of those listed above the wrong people? That's what abolitionists would have you believe. That impression is stamped by the following statement: "Since reinstatement [of the death penalty] in 1976, for every 8 persons executed, 1 wrongfully convicted person has been released from death row."[331] Notice the numbers are the same when presented as a mathematical equation (1,000 executions since 1976 ÷ 117 = 8.5). This is not to say the system has never made a mistake; that an innocent person has never been convicted of a crime or even of a murder. But it is to say the system *has yet to execute anyone certifiably innocent* since reinstatement of the death penalty in 1976.

Getting back to the death penalty opponents' dishonest argument implying 117 wrongly convicted inmates were "released from death row," there are, as we have seen, many ways in which a convict can be released from death row while still being as guilty as they were the day they first entered it. Their victims are still dead. If 117 persons have been "released," why isn't the entire list of names given? It surely would help the abolitionist cause. "Released from death row" does not necessarily mean "freed," but that is what is implied. Nor does "released" necessarily mean "permanently," again which is what is suggested. In refutation of the patently bogus claim about the infamous "wrongly convicted," the *Kansas v. Marsh* case before the U. S. Supreme Court is cited and extracted herewith:

# An Eye for an Eye
*William T. Harper*

"Instead of identifying and discussing any particular case or cases of mistaken execution, the dissent simply cites a handful of studies that bemoan the alleged prevalence of wrongful death sentences. One study (by Lanier and Acker) is quoted by the dissent as claiming that 'more than 110' death row prisoners have been released since 1973 upon findings that they were innocent of the crimes charged, and 'hundreds of additional wrongful convictions in potentially capital cases have been documented over the past century....' For the first point, Lanier and Acker cite the work of the Death Penalty Information Center...and an article in a law review jointly authored by Radelet, Lofquist, and Bedau....

"For the second point, they cite only a 1987 article by Bedau and Radelet [also referred to by Lanier and Acker as] ... 'hav[ing] identified 23 individuals who, in their judgment, were convicted and executed in this country during the 20th century notwithstanding their innocence....' This 1987 article has been highly influential in the abolitionist world. Hundreds of academic articles...have cited it. It also makes its appearance in judicial decisions [i.e.] 'the system is allowing some innocent defendants to be executed.' The article therefore warrants some further observations.

"The 1987 article's obsolescence began at the moment of publication. The most recent executions it considered were in 1984, 1964, and 1951; the rest predate the Allied victory in World War II.... But their current relevance aside, this study's conclusions are unverified. And if the support for its most significant conclusion – the execution of 23 innocents in the 20th century – is any indication of its accuracy, neither it, nor any

# An Eye for an Eye
*William T. Harper*

study so careless as to rely upon it, is worthy of credence." [332]

So said Supreme Court Associate Justice Antonin Scalia.

The absolute tragedy of "unverified" studies and surveys such as Bedau and Radelet's is their adoption as gospel by capital punishment abolitionists without verification nor confirmation, as shown in a 1988 "Capital Punishment: Arguments for Life and Death" study in which those authors "...studied capital convictions from 1900 to 1986 and identified 350 cases in which defendants were erroneously convicted of capital crimes. Twenty four of these people were executed for crimes that they did not commit." [333]

Noted conservative journalist and talk-show regular Ann Coulter also did some research on that outrageous claim. "Newspapers," she wrote, "rushed to trumpet the astonishing results: '25 Wrongfully Executed in U.S., Study Finds' (*New York Times*); '25 Wrongfully Executed Since 1900, ACLU Says' (*Chicago Tribune*); 'Innocents Executed, ACLU Claims; 25 Said to Have Died Since 1900 for Crimes They Did Not Commit' (*The Washington Post*); 'Study Says 25 Innocent People Were Executed in This Century' (*Los Angeles Times*); 'Report Says 25 Innocent People Executed' (United Press International); and so on. (The later corrections did not receive such prominent coverage.)" [334]

*"Twenty-four people were executed for crimes that they did not commit."* That claim comes from an article in the *Canadian Journal of Behavioral Science* by Jennifer Honeyman and James Ogloff. [335] They are herewith challenged to prove the statement they so blithely pass on as Chapter and Verse. Where did that number come from? Was it part of the "117 wrongly convicted" fairy tale? Who are the 24? Surely they can come up with ONE name of ONE person who was "executed for a crime they did not commit" without going back to the Antiquities.

# An Eye for an Eye

*William T. Harper*

It is outrageous that respected (?) authors and researchers would write and accept such a damning statement without confirming it. Just because, for whatever reasons that won't be speculated upon here, Messrs Bedau and Radelet and Lanier and Acker said it is so doesn't necessarily make it so – not by a long shot.

Again, as the Supreme Court affirmed above, if those who may have been released from death row, as is claimed, were wrongfully convicted, it does not mean – as the anti-death penalty lobby implies – those people were innocent and got out of jail free. It means, for instance, as in 1977, the Supreme Court declared in *Coker v. Georgia*, 433 U.S. 584 (1977) that applying the death penalty in rape cases was unconstitutional because the sentence was disproportionate to the crime. *Coker* resulted in removal of 20 inmates – three whites and 17 blacks – awaiting execution on rape convictions from death rows around the country.[336]

What this shows is 20 inmates had their sentence changed from death to something less. It does not at all show they were "wrongly convicted." It does not in any way shape or form show they were innocent. They may have been wrongly sentenced because, as in this case, laws were retroactively changed. But those 20 inmates are – each and every one of them – still as guilty of their crime on this day as they were the day they were convicted.

To imply innocence by claiming they were "wrongly convicted" is dishonest reporting at its worst. This is a deliberate attempt to deceive people. Not once are readers told that though those "117 wrongly convicted people" were released from death row, most if not all, were released because of governmental conscience, judicial edict, questionable evidence, and technicalities in lower court proceedings. Other factors were changes in laws that put them there in the first place (i.e., new definitions of rape disproportionality, juvenile and mentally-retarded exemptions). It was not because they were – as abolitionists so unfairly try to make us believe – innocent.

# An Eye for an Eye
*William T. Harper*

\* \* \*

Amnesty International, as with many others, has naturally jumped on the 117 figure saying, "Since 1973, 117 people have been released from U. S. death rows after evidence of their innocence emerged."[337] Again, that is simply not true. The infamous 117 may have been released from U. S. prison death rows but not simply because "evidence of their *innocence* emerged." It is dishonorable that anyone would present such a false impression in a legitimate debate, especially on such an important subject as life or death in a penitentiary.

Without further review, reading these repetitious statements over and over, one is led to believe gross injustices have been committed and at least 117 innocent, falsely-convicted, God-loving, upstanding citizens have been exonerated for their murderous crimes, thereby proving the frailty of America's criminal justice system. Stating (purposefully?) over and over that these "wrongfully convicted persons" were "released" from death row leads an uninformed reader to believe they were all innocent; they were all exonerated; they were all given the requisite $200 and a bus ticket home as they all walked out the front gate of their respective penitentiaries as innocent victims, and they were all returned to their loved ones to live happily ever after. If one of the Big Three auto manufacturers made such a patently false claim, the company would be sued for millions under "Truth in Advertising" laws.

Uninformed and unfair (sometimes both) newspaper reviewers perpetuate The Big Lie(s):

"In her attack on the death penalty in practice, Prejean convincingly recounts appalling injustices. These include prosecutorial and judicial misconduct, reliance on untrustworthy jailhouse informants, unreasonable procedural rules, arbitrariness in sentencing, racial bias, politicized pardons boards and a public defender system frequently so inept that, as residents of housing project put it, 'Capital

# An Eye for an Eye
*William T. Harper*

punishment means them without the capital get the punishment'."[338] If it's in the paper, it must be true, right? Answer: How many newspapers have had to give back Pulitzer Prizes for dishonest reporting? Ask the editors at the *New York Times* about Jason Blair or Walter Duranty. Ask the *Washington Post* about Janet Cooke.

The fact of the matter is, "upon further review," the vast majority of those 117 "innocents" got off death row but did not get out of prison. Most of them were in a class similar to the Illinois' death row inmates who were "released from death row" by Governor George Ryan on his last day in office in 2003. Ryan granted the moratorium because he wanted to "sleep well knowing [he] made the right decision." As a result of that sleeping pill, "the former disgraced Governor's emptying of death row, [resulted in] no person – even when they plead or admit their guilt in open court – will be sentenced to death," wrote Illinois State Senator Edward Petka.[339]

And please note the following from the *Chicago Tribune* on June 10, 2007: "The Illinois moratorium on executions in 2000 [sic] *led to 150 additional homicides* [emphasis added] over four years following, according to a 2006 study by professors at the University of Houston."

Those who were "exonerated" or whose sentences were commuted in Illinois had committed some of the most heinous crimes. For instance, on an MSNBC televised panel debate on the death penalty, Joshua K. Marquis, district attorney in Clatsop County, Oregon, cited one couple who "cut a fetus out of a woman to steal a baby and killed her other two children because they were witnesses to her murder. I just don't see how we can get a graver, more heinous offense than that. And," Marquis continued, "Governor Ryan commuted those folks' sentences, right along with everybody else's. It wasn't his job to determine innocence or guilt."[340]

Also sitting on that panel was Scott Turow, an award-winning author and anti-death penalty lawyer, who had an

# An Eye for an Eye

*William T. Harper*

awakening while serving on a commission earlier empanelled by Governor Ryan to determine what reforms, if any, would ensure the state's death penalty would be meted out with fairness.

> "It didn't really dawn on me that losing a loved one to murder is unlike any other blow in life," he says. "It's one thing if somebody you love gets cancer, or they're washed under by Hurricane Isabel. Those are things beyond human control. But when somebody makes a conscious choice to end the life of somebody you love, it really turns civilization on its head. Much of the victims' anguish is that everything we assume from living with one another has been taken away." [341]

Another panel participant, Kim Ogg, then a Victims' Rights Advocate and now in private law practice in Texas, said...

> "While it was Governor Ryan's legal right, I suppose, to commute these folks' sentences, it was not his moral right to do so. He subverted the will of the people."

Marquis further agreed, saying:

> "The fact of the matter is, in [Governor Ryan's] commutations, he spit on the clemency commission. He spit on thousands of jurors. He spit on hundreds of judges."

\* \* \*

Not only did Governor Ryan "spit on hundreds of judges," he figuratively vomited all over the entire City of Chicago police force because one of those whose sentence he

# An Eye for an Eye
*William T. Harper*

commuted was Kenneth Allen. On the afternoon of March 3, 1979, Kenneth Allen – angry because police officers had conducted an authorized search of his home where they found a cache of seven weapons and a thousand rounds of ammunition – parked his car across the street from Chicago police officers William Bosak and Roger van Schaik as they were conducting a routine traffic stop. With the officer's back to him, Allen opened fire on Bosak with a .45 caliber semiautomatic pistol, emptying the clip. Bosak was hit three times and was killed instantly.

Allen drew a second pistol and exited his car to engage Van Schaik – who was on the opposite side of the unmarked police cruiser from Allen – in a gun battle, the two men circling the officers' car. Both men exhausted their ammunition without scoring a hit. Allen then returned to his car and retrieved a .30 caliber carbine rifle, again opening fire on Van Schaik, wounding but not killing the officer. The rifle jammed after two or three shots. While Van Schaik lay wounded on the ground, Allen retrieved the .38 caliber service revolver from the corpse of Officer Bosak. He returned to the front of the car where the wounded Van Schaik lay, pleading for his life, and executed him with two shots to the face at point blank range.

Allen was quickly captured after an extended police chase during which he attempted to shoot pursuing officers. From his car, officers confiscated several guns, about 250 rounds of ammunition, and a notebook containing names, addresses, license plate numbers and phone numbers of several police officers and the name of the judge who had signed the search warrant authorizing Chicago police to enter Allen's home.[342]

Kenneth Allen was just one of the killers for whom Governor Ryan gratuitously commuted his death sentence. It is certain the Chicago police department did not send any "Thank you, Governor Ryan" messages. (By the way, the late governor who "needed to sleep well" eventually did his

# An Eye for an Eye
*William T. Harper*

sleeping in a Federal penitentiary after being sentenced to six-and-one-half years on racketeering and bribery charges.)

However, as opposed to the abolitionists' inference of release because of innocence, all but three of the Illinois commutations were reduced to Life-Without-Parole; and the remaining three had their sentences reduced to 40-years-to-life to bring theirs' in line with co-defendants. Ryan was also accused by a father whose daughter who died at the hands of one of those with a commuted sentence of arrogantly substituting his own judgment for those of juries and courts that have imposed and upheld the death sentences.[343] And still one more of Governor Ryan's conscience-easers, a murderer serving a Life-Without-Parole sentence, was – after Ryan's gift – sent back to the state of Missouri where he was tried, convicted and sentenced to death for still another murder.

While on the subject of the Ryan commutation, it might be noted that according to a report from the Fayette, Kentucky Commonwealth Attorney's office, the state of Illinois went through a similar and disastrous program in 1980s. In a report quoting Thomas Sowell in *The Washington Times* during January, 1996, "Illinois back in the early 1980s, saved $60 million by releasing prisoners three months earlier than they would normally have been released. However, the people of Illinois lost more than five times as much – an estimated $304 million – in direct and indirect costs of the crimes committed by those released during the 90 days they would have otherwise been behind bars.

"That," according to the Commonwealth Attorney's report of Sowell's story, "was not all of the costs, nor the most important part. Twenty-three persons lost their lives at the hands of those same released prisoners during those same three months. In addition, those turned loose early committed 32 rapes, 262 acts of arson, hundreds of robberies and thousands of burglaries - all during the three months they were originally supposed to be behind bars."[344]

# An Eye for an Eye
William T. Harper

\* \* \*

In football, piling on is illegal and warrants a penalty. No such punishment deters abolitionists. They pile it on higher and deeper (in more ways than one) regarding the "117" syndrome — no matter how much of a stretch in credulity it might take, such as: "At the present time in the United States, with over a hundred wrongly convicted death row inmates vindicated in the last thirty years, we're hearing stories of just how many ways prosecutors make sure their 'version' prevails-even when the accused is innocent."[345] In this latest version of The Big Lie, the desired presumption is all those "wrongly convicted" killers were, indeed, "innocent." Fifteen-yard penalty for piling on.

The following story is about as close as you can come to a base-case scenario and a more truthful example of how one of those "wrongfully convicted persons" [was] "released from death row:" A newspaper story in the *Houston Chronicle* — with a headline proclaiming the prison inmate therein had his conviction "overturned" — is (upon further review) a typical example of how the brain-washed media tries to brain-wash its customers via mis-reporting facts about those who get off death row and how they do.[346]

Martin Draughon, after nearly 20 years on Texas' death row, was freed on mandatory supervision because of a plea agreement he reached with prosecutors after U.S. District Judge Lee Rosenthal in September 2004 overturned his 1987 capital murder *conviction*, the newspaper reported. Not so. Draughon's *conviction* for the 1986 killing of Armando Guerrero during a restaurant robbery was not overturned. His *sentence* was overturned when later evidence showed Guerrero was killed by one of Draughon's ricocheting bullets. Draughon is still guilty of murder — whether it be capital murder or unintended manslaughter. (Never mind asking the question: What difference should it make when one person murders another if the killing is done by a directly aimed bullet or one that ricochets?)

# An Eye for an Eye
*William T. Harper*

Instead of retrying Draughon, then-Harris County (Texas) District Attorney C. A. (Chuck) Rosenthal (no relation to Judge Rosenthal) opted for a plea agreement calling for a 40-year sentence. Draughon already had served enough time to be released under the law requiring mandatory supervision. He also must wear a global positioning satellite (GPS) device that tracks his whereabouts and he also must meet with a parole officer nine times each month. These multi-faceted conditions hardly mean his *conviction* was overturned. His *sentence* was overturned. He still is guilty of murdering Armando Guerrero.

Once again, one of those "wrongly convicted" death row inhabitants may have been released but he surely wasn't ruled innocent. Another among those other "wrongfully convicted" inmates could be one such as George Rodriguez who "was released from prison in October [2004] after retested evidence showed his 1987 conviction for kidnapping and rape may have been based on mistakes by the Houston Police Department's crime lab analysts.... District Attorney Rosenthal is not convinced Rodriguez is innocent. Rodriguez was released, he says, because the jury 'got improper evidence'," and not because he was "wrongfully convicted." Rosenthal said, "There is still a victim that says he did it."[347] Thus, "wrongfully convicted" does not *per se* mean "innocent."

There have been cases where murderers, some even on death row, have been released scot-free. But most of these cases are such anomalies as to border on the ridiculous if not the insane. Jeremy Sheets was convicted of rape and murder in Nebraska. An accomplice, Adam Barnett, confessed to the crimes and implicated Sheets via a secret video tape-recording of the acts. "But, the accomplice later committed suicide in jail, depriving Sheets of the opportunity to cross-examine him. This, the Nebraska Supreme Court held, rendered evidence inadmissible."[348] And Sheets went free.

Take the case of Delbert Tibbs. He was convicted of raping and sodomizing a woman and killing her boyfriend

# An Eye for an Eye
### William T. Harper

along a Florida highway. Tibbs subsequently walked because the woman-victim, obviously the primary witness against Tibbs, "had progressed from a marijuana smoker into a crack user and [the prosecutor said], I could not put her on the stand."[349] In still another case – that can't be verified herewith – a young woman who witnessed the murder of her family was so distraught that she, too, committed suicide, thereby depriving the prosecution of its primary witness – which allowed that killer to "get out of jail free." The "wrongfully convicted" argument put forth by abolitionists is as slick and oily as was Prince William Sound in Alaska after the tanker "Exxon Valdez" ran aground there in 1989.

Elsewhere in these pages pseudo-thanks were extended to Dr. David R. Dow, a death penalty abolitionist law professor at the University of Houston, for obviously inadvertently helping make the case regarding the fallacies of the Life-Without-Parole argument. While thanking Dr. Dow on the one hand, he must be chastised on the other for the outrageousness of yet another typically unverified abolitionist statement. Writing about "the 50 or so death row inmates I have represented," he went on to claim: "In 98 percent of the cases, however, in 49 out of 50, there were appalling violations of legal principles: Prosecutors struck jurors based on their race; the police hid or manufactured evidence; prosecutors reached secret deals with jailhouse snitches; lab analysts misrepresented forensic results."[350]

The good doctor, who exerts developmental influence on perhaps hundreds if not thousands of eager students, did not answer a query from this writer asking for "further evidence for that figure." In "ninety-eight percent" of death row cases there are "appalling violations of legal principles"? The courtrooms of Nazi Germany had a better record than that. Can Dr. Dow be serious? If he's right, where is the American Bar Association? Where are all the other lawyers in the land if this kind of legal atrocity is going on? Where is the Supreme Court of the United States? If Dr. Dow is right, then the nation's entire system of jurisprudence is wrong.

# An Eye for an Eye
*William T. Harper*

Or, is this is just another glaring example of exaggerations, mis-statements, and in some cases down-right lies used by abolitionist zealots in their unrelenting drive to do away with justice in our nation's legal system? It is a tragedy that death penalty opponents will go to any length to present their deceptions, which are later offered as facts by those who knowingly or unknowingly assume them to be the truth.

Wrongly sentenced does not necessarily mean wrongly convicted.

\* \* \*

# An Eye for an Eye
*William T. Harper*

# An Eye for an Eye
*William T. Harper*

## Chapter Eight

### There Are Statistics and ... There Are Damned Lies

*Catching up with friends after a family vacation in Florida, Elizabeth Peña beamed as she showed off the stuff she'd bought with her 16th birthday money: a new pager, some new underclothes. As the summer evening waned, Jennifer Ertman, another high school sophomore, checked her Goofy wristwatch and saw that it was pushing midnight. She and Peña would break their curfews if they didn't get home in a hurry. The girls debated how to get to Peña's Oak Forest home in northwest Houston. One route would take half an hour; a well-known shortcut along the railroad tracks through T.C. Jester Park would save about 10 minutes....*

*On the moonless night of June 24, 1993, members of a little-known gang had gathered near a patch of woods in that park for an initiation ceremony. [When the two girls unknowingly stumbled on to the scene, there were gang members Derrick Sean O'Brien, Peter Anthony Cantu, Jose Medellin and his brother Venacio, Raul Villarreal, and Efrain Perez. The Sandoval brothers, Roman and Frank, were leaving the scene just as the two girls arrived.]*

*The [departing Sandoval] brothers watched as Jose Medellin grabbed Elizabeth and threw her to the ground. She screamed for help. Jennifer broke away but returned and was grabbed by Cantu and O'Brien. The girls cried and struggled while the gang members repeatedly sexually assaulted them. At times, two would assault one girl. Afterward, according to court records, Cantu flatly told Jose Medellin, "We're going to have to kill them." The girls pleaded for their lives, but the gang members took them into a clearing beneath a canopy of trees.*

*O'Brien and Villarreal forced Jennifer to her knees and looped O'Brien's belt around her neck. Jennifer clawed at the belt and struggled*

# An Eye for an Eye
*William T. Harper*

*to breathe. O'Brien grunted as both pulled on the belt so hard it snapped. Jose Medellin, Perez and Cantu killed Elizabeth in a similar manner. They then stomped on the girls' throats to make sure both were dead. Later that night, the gang members divided up money and Jennifer's jewelry. Cantu handed Venacio Medellin her Goofy watch. The girls' clothes, including Elizabeth's new undergarments, were strewn among empty beer cans.*[351]

**Jenny Ertman (left) with friends**

**Elizabeth Pena**

\* \* \*

# An Eye for an Eye
*William T. Harper*

Death penalty abolitionists in their boundless zeal to deny justice to victims and survivors of heinous crimes, via their influence with the liberal-leaning media in shaping public opinion, again want it both ways. First they argue in public forums the death penalty for killers under the age of 18 is cruel and unusual punishment. They claim, and in a five-to-four decision on March 1, 2005 the United States Supreme Court in *Roper v. Simmons* agreed saying: "When a juvenile offender commits a heinous crime, the state can exact forfeiture of some of the most basic liberties, but the state cannot extinguish his life and his potential to attain a mature understanding of his own humanity."[352]

The decision, which overruled the Court's prior ruling upholding such sentences on offenders above or at the age of 16, in *Stanford v. Kentucky*, 492 U.S. 361 (1989), further stated 18 years of age "is the point where society draws the line for many purposes between childhood and adulthood...." When, one might ask, will the Court in its infinite wisdom, again raise the age limit – and to what number? Will it be 20? Twenty-five? At exactly what age does a killer "attain a mature understanding of his own humanity"? At exactly what age will *future* courts/societies "draw the line"?

Paraphrasing from a March 2, 2005 story in the *Washington Times* and from an abstract published in the *American Academy of Psychiatry and the Law Journal*, here is the crime upon which the Court based its opinion in *Roper v. Simmons*, in what even the Court's majority described as a "wantonly vile, horrible, and inhuman" crime:

> "At the age of 17, when he was still a junior in high school, Christopher Simmons committed murder. About nine months later, after he had turned 18, he was tried and sentenced to death. There is little doubt that Simmons was the instigator of the crime. Before its commission Simmons said he wanted to murder someone. In chilling, callous terms he talked about his plan, discussing it for the

# An Eye for an Eye
*William T. Harper*

most part with two friends.... Simmons assured his friends they could 'get away with it' because they were minors.... Simmons and [one of the friends] entered the home of the victim, Shirley Crook, after reaching through an open window and unlocking the back door.... Simmons entered Mrs. Crook's bedroom, where he recognized her from a previous car accident involving them both. Simmons later admitted this confirmed his resolve to murder her.[353]

"Using duct tape to cover her eyes and mouth and bind her hands, the two perpetrators put Mrs. Crook in her minivan and drove to a state park. They reinforced the bindings, covered her head with a towel, and walked her to a railroad trestle spanning the Meramec River. There they tied her hands and feet together with electrical wire, wrapped her whole face in duct tape and threw her from the bridge, drowning her in the waters below.

"...fishermen recovered the victim's body from the river. Simmons, meanwhile, was bragging about the killing, telling friends he had killed a woman 'because the bitch seen my face.' [After his subsequent arrest] Simmons confessed to the murder.... The State charged Simmons with burglary, kidnapping, stealing, and murder in the first degree. As Simmons was 17 at the time of the crime, he was outside the criminal jurisdiction of Missouri's juvenile court system....[and] he was tried as an adult.... The jury having returned a verdict of murder, [and sentenced Simmons to death for the murder of Ms. Crook, which was] outrageously and wantonly vile, horrible, and inhuman...."[354]

"Capital punishment must," the Supreme Court majority said, "be limited to those offenders who commit 'a narrow category of the most serious

# An Eye for an Eye
*William T. Harper*

crimes' and whose extreme culpability makes them 'the most deserving of execution.' ...Three general differences between juveniles under 18 and adults demonstrate that juvenile offenders cannot with reliability be classified among the worst offenders. Juveniles' susceptibility to immature and irresponsible behavior means 'their irresponsible conduct is not as morally reprehensible as that of an adult.' ...Their own vulnerability and comparative lack of control over their immediate surroundings mean juveniles have a greater claim than adults to be forgiven for failing to escape negative influences in their whole environment. ...The reality that juveniles still struggle to define their identity means it is less supportable to conclude that even a heinous crime committed by a juvenile is evidence of irretrievably depraved character."[355]

One could argue some of these points *ad infinitum*. Was Christopher Simmons struggling "to define [his] identity" when he threw Ms. Crook into the river? Was it less "morally reprehensible" for 17-year-old Efrain Perez to join in the gang-rape and murder of Jennifer Ertman and Elizabeth Peña on June 24, 1993 in a Houston park than it was for his 18-year-old buddy Derrick Sean O'Brien? How does passage from 17 years and 364 days to 18 years "draw the line between childhood and adulthood?" Does some sort of an epiphany occur during that nanosecond cross-over from 17 years of age to 18? What is the "age of reason?" What has changed in the 23 years since the Supreme Court ruled 17 was the age of reason?

If anything, have not young people of America become more informed via television and their electronic toys? Are they not now allowed to view motion pictures, videos, DVDs, etc., that are far more mature in content than that which were allowed their parents? Voting ages, drinking ages, ages of consent for sexual interaction have been lowered

# An Eye for an Eye
*William T. Harper*

in many places. Furthermore, what is the rationale behind the decision that you can lock up a "juvenile" for 50, 60, maybe even 70 years for their heinous crimes but you can't execute them? For many people facing such extended incarceration in places like Supermax, execution might well be a welcomed alternative. And if so, this again illustrates the total lack of care the abolitionists have for those they "minister to." It most surely reveals the only thing they care about is the "cause," the elimination of the death penalty.

\* \* \*

Immediately after the March 1, 2005 *Roper v. Simmons* opinion, it should be further noted, 72 "juvenile" killers – including the above-noted Efrain Perez – were released from death row and sent back to their prisons' general population. The decision by the Court also gave death penalty opponents yet another chance to put forth their Big Lie about "innocents" being "exonerated" and "released" from the death house.

On the other hand, some of these same death penalty abolitionists ardently support the right of *14-year-old* girls to have abortion on demand, saying a "'rich body of research' showed that by age 14 or 15 people are mature enough to choose abortions because they have 'abilities similar to adults in reasoning about moral dilemmas'." [356]

Without getting into the abortion rights argument, consider these two points: It seems odd that death penalty opponents claim a boy of 17 is too young to die for the gang-rape, torture and murder of 14-year-old Jennifer Ertman and 16-year-old Elizabeth Peña because he does not have "abilities similar to adults in reasoning about moral dilemmas." Conversely, a girl of 14 is legally mature enough to abort the life of an unborn child.

In another case that stretches the bounds of credulity, consider this case of 17 as being the age at or under which some murderous "children" as ruled by the courts as being exempt from capital punishment. It's written by Lester

# An Eye for an Eye
*William T. Harper*

Jackson, Ph.D., a former college political science teacher. It appeared in the March 14, 2012 edition of "American Thinker" with this headline: "For Whom Their Hearts Bleed: The Odd Sympathies of Liberal Justices."

...Last month, 18-year-old Alyssa Bustamante, protected from capital punishment by five U.S. Supreme Court justices undemocratically imposing their unrepresentative moral values, was sentenced to mislabeled "life in prison" for the October 2009 murder of nine-year-old neighbor Elizabeth Olten....Alyssa wrote in her diary:

> "I just f--king killed someone. I strangled them and slit their throat and stabbed them[;] now they're dead. ... It was ahmazing. As soon as you get over the 'ohmygawd I can't do this' feeling, it's pretty enjoyable. I'm kinda nervous and shaky though[.]"

Alyssa confessed and led police to Elizabeth's body. Her muddy shovels and clothes were found. This crime was premeditated, with "cool deliberation" [and] reflection." Beyond dispute is that Alyssa dug two graves in advance and used her unsuspecting sister to lure Elizabeth to come outside to "play." Alyssa wanted to know how killing felt, and she listed "killing people" as one of her hobbies. Contrary to five "compassionate" justices who assert that anyone under the age of exactly 18 cannot be fully expected to tell right from wrong, Alyssa's "ohmygawd I can't do this" feeling clearly shows that she well knew that the murder was wrong, leaving her "nervous and shaky."

Despite objection, she was sentenced to "life **with** possibility of parole" -- language that surely belongs atop any list of disingenuous oxymoronic legal absurdities....[357]

As does Dr. Jackson, we too have to wonder where does judicial activism end? The death penalty has been eliminated for murderers under the age of 18. Give them

# An Eye for an Eye
*William T. Harper*

Life-Without-Parole, say the abolitionists. OK. The courts have so ruled. And, as might be expected, having won that battle, the death penalty opponents are taking the next step. With the legal system convinced the death penalty is too harsh for those juvenile killers who are deemed different from adults because their judgment is lacking (no kidding!), the Teeny-Bopper killers now pay their penalty through Life-Without-Parole. And in the above "ahmazing" throat-slitting and strangulation verdict, it was handed down as "life in prison" with, naturally the possibility (probability) of parole.

Now, it seems, Life-Without-Parole is believed by some as also being too harsh so let's get rid of that, too. The state of Colorado has already done so. Lifers in the Centennial State are all now *eligible for parole after serving 40 years*. The state of Michigan is considering similar leniency.[358] California's Legislature will also, no doubt, soon pass a bill that allows lifers to seek a sentence of 25-years-to-life with a chance for parole *after serving 15 years*! Again the question: "Where does it all end?" Will the death penalty opponents never be happy until our judges and legislators pass a G. I. Bill for murderers, send them off to Ivy League colleges with a guaranteed 4.0 GPA, and give them interest-free home loans?

\* \* \*

Most, if not all, "statistics" cited by the death penalty abolition cabal must be taken with a grain — if not a whole box full — of salt. For instance, they demand an explanation for the preponderance of executions taking place in "the killing belt," the southern states. Could it be because the southern states are those whose citizens, via the ballot box and their elected representatives, have approved executions for the worst of the worst?

As of this writing, the death penalty is authorized in 33 states. With but four exceptions among the 17 states not authorizing, all are in the socially liberal northeast and upper

# An Eye for an Eye

*William T. Harper*

Midwest (i.e., Iowa, Illinois, Maine, Massachusetts, Michigan, Minnesota, North Dakota, Rhode Island, Vermont, New York, New Jersey, Connecticut and Wisconsin. The exceptions are Alaska, Hawaii, New Mexico and West Virginia). Is it any wonder there's an absence of executions in those "slap-on-the-wrist" states? Abolitionists' rhetoric on death penalty statistics here is like saying most automobile accidents happen in the northeast and Midwest states – because that's where the icy roads are.

It is not the intent of this effort to enter ala Daniel into today's lion's den of racial disparity in administration of the death penalty. But, at the risk of being eaten alive by abolitionists who constantly cite statistics claiming a huge differential in the number of African-Americans executed vs. other races ("Race plays a part," says Sister Prejean in her Presentation High School speech noted here in Chapter One), one can also note fat people generally eat more than thin people. If African-Americans kill people more people than any other race proportionally, then it stands to reason more African-Americans would be executed vs. other races, again proportionately. (Non-proportionately speaking, according to the Bureau of Justice Statistics, there were 1,989 Whites on America's death rows in 2000 and 1,515 African-Americans.) Likewise, let it also be noted here the vast majority of barbaric, sadistic, ruthless killers cited in these pages – Couey, the Sonniers, Willie, Berkowitz, De Salvo, McDuff, Speck, Bundy, Dahmer, Gacy, et al. – are white. So much for charges of racial imbalance.

But again, the abolitionists' "more" claim above is not proven by facts. As of March 29, 2007, according to U. S. Department of Justice figures, 1,069 people have been executed in this country since the death penalty was reinstated in 1976. Of that total, the DOJ reports 57 percent of those executed were White, 34 percent were Black, and nine percent were "Other." Even so, what difference does it make if murderers were White, Black, or "Other"? It makes no difference if it's white-on-white killing; if it is black-on-

# An Eye for an Eye
*William T. Harper*

black killing, if it is black-on-white killing or any other variation thereof? If they committed the ultimate crime, they should pay the ultimate penalty – regardless if they are White, Black, or "Other." This is like citing the fact that more males commit murder than do females; therefore, the abolitionists would charge: more men are executed than women!

\* \* \*

The media is almost as bad with its errors of omission as are abolitionists in their errors of commission. Leonidas Koniaris, of the University of Miami Miller School of Medicine and associates, published an April 2005 study on anesthetic effects of the lethal injection method of state executions – the so-called three-drug "cocktail" (typically a barbiturate, paralytic, and potassium solution that first puts the recipient to sleep, then stops his/her breathing, which then stops his/her heart. See Chapter Six for a more detailed description. Note: this procedure has been replaced in some states by a one-drug method, about which more later).

 The Konaris study concludes lethal injection *may* cause unnecessary suffering because prisoners *may* get too little sedation. The study therefore calls for a halt to lethal injection. That's like saying baseball umpires *may* call too many strikes which *may* diminish home runs therefore let's call a halt to baseball umpires. This too is a bit of a stretch.

 According to one report on the study, it reviewed post-mortem "blood records of inmates from Arizona, Georgia, North Carolina and South Carolina" to determine the content of the lethal injection chemicals in the bodies. "Texas," the report continues, "the national leader in executions, *refused* [emphasis added] to provide data for the study."[359] With an emphatic "However," Andy Kahan, Crime Victims Advocate for the City of Houston, Texas, clarified the situation by saying:

# An Eye for an Eye

*William T. Harper*

"Texas did not REFUSE to provide information. The State simply did not have the kind of information researchers were asking for."[360]

So much for the truth, the *whole* truth, and nothing but the truth.

(Parenthetically it should be noted the above report quoted Dr. Lydia Conlay, who chairs the department of anesthesiology at Baylor College of Medicine, later said the [Koniaris report] is by no means a proven method. "It's an interesting and thought-provoking study. I just don't think we can draw any conclusions from it, one way or the other."[361])

Another who questioned some of the conclusions of the Koniaris report is Dr. William R. Klemm, former Professor of Pharmacology at Texas A&M University. In correspondence with this author, Klemm noted:

> "Dr. Conlay is absolutely correct when it comes to anesthesia. Blood levels of anesthetic," he continued, "do not necessarily indicate the concentration in brain tissue. Anesthetic also sequesters in fat deposits." Concluding, Klemm also noted, "Anesthetics have a preferential affinity for lipids (fats). The amount available in the blood, and therefore accessible to the brain, is influenced by body-fat stores, which of course can vary from person to person."

One more factor that can skew studies such as Koniaris' is, said Klemm:

> "That some people think a very fat person might take more anesthetic than a skinny one. Indeed, anesthetics are given 'to effect.' That is, what is important is not necessarily the dose but the effect. The drug is infused until the desired level of anesthesia is reached. In the case of execution, an

# An Eye for an Eye
*William T. Harper*

over-abundance of the anesthetic is administered so even fat people will become unconscious (the muscle paralysis and lack of breathing will take care of the rest)."

Commenting further on the abolitionists' claim that the three-dose cocktail is in itself "cruel and unusual punishment" for the recipient, Dr. Klemm reported:

> "[A] normal adult with no anesthetic can only last about three minutes without breathing and getting oxygen. In my mid 20s, I took an altitude chamber training test in which when the oxygen was cut off. I went unconscious pleasantly, being oblivious to what was happening."

A recent study in the online journal "PLoS Medicine" also suggested some inmates suffer extreme pain during lethal injections because of insufficient and haphazard doses of the chemicals. Former Oklahoma Medical Examiner Dr. A. Jay Chapman, generally acknowledged as the inventor of the lethal injection method of execution, blames incompetent executioners. "This protocol will work if it's administered as it should be," he said. "If it is competently administered, there will be no question about this business of pain and suffering." If states are looking for a way to quickly and painlessly put someone to death, he has a suggestion.

> "There is absolutely nothing wrong with the guillotine," he said impatiently. "It can be operated by an idiot and it is a very effective instrument." [362]

Another drawing a conclusion about lethal injection was Jim Brazzil, a chaplain with the Texas Department of Criminal Justice. Part of his job was to be in the death chamber at the time of executions. He has been there 114 times. He has, literally, seen it all. He commented about how

# An Eye for an Eye
*William T. Harper*

swift and apparently painless the lethal injection process was – for one inmate, anyhow. "Had one man who wanted to sing 'Silent Night'," Brazzil recalled. "He made his final statement and then after the warden gave the signal he started singing 'Silent Night,' and when he got to 'Round yon virgin mother and child,' that was his last word."[363]

\* \* \*

In a published essay entitled "Why Capital Punishment Should be Abolished," an unnamed author espousing the anti-death penalty line, writes about a study that "spans twenty-five years, from 1957 till 1982, and [it] shows that in the first year the study was conducted, there were 8,060 murders and 6 executions. However, in the last year of the study there were 22,520 murders committed and only 1 execution performed.... This clearly shows that many violent criminals are not afraid of the capital punishment."[364]

It is no wonder the author is unnamed. This is an outstanding though typical example of distortions the anti-death penalty cabal goes to in illustrating its' points. The unnamed author tells his/her audience the murders to execution ratio dropped from 8,060 murders to six executions in 1957 to 22,520 murders and one execution in 1982 – some 25 years later. S/he is being totally deceptive if not dishonest or ignorant of the facts in using these selective numbers. According to the U. S. Department of Justice statistics, 360 persons were executed over the 25-year period, 1957-1882 – with not six as the author said but 65 executions in 1957 alone![365] For the entire 15-year period of 1968-1982, as the nation was going into *Furman v. Georgia* and coming out of *Gregg v. Georgia*, the U. S. Supreme Court-mandated death penalty moratorium, there were only six executions in all! No wonder the ratio went down.

A lengthy, 1,000-word Associated Press story running across news wires on December 15, 2006 announcing death penalty moratoria in Florida and California because of a

# An Eye for an Eye
*William T. Harper*

"botched" execution in the Sunshine State, quite clearly illustrates media bias against capital punishment. The article quotes Dr. J. Kent Garman, an emeritus professor of anesthesia at the Stanford School of Medicine in California. Dr. Garman "said he was ethically opposed to lethal injection."[366] And, David Elliot, spokesman for the National Coalition to Abolish the Death Penalty, was quoted as saying:

> "Florida has certainly deservedly earned a reputation for being a state that conducts botched executions, whether its electrocution or lethal injection."[367]

Joining the chorus was Jonathan Groner, associate professor of surgery at Ohio State University. He said the injection would cause excruciating pain "like your arms are on fire."[368] The AP writer apparently was unable to find anyone in the entire state of Florida who cared to defend the lethal injection process. Or, at least, the story contained no quotes along those lines.

It is hereby noted the Florida's ban on executions was rescinded after a commission appointed by then-governor Jeb Bush subsequently reported the so-called "botched" execution actually was not and the charge the IV needles were not properly applied was refuted. On the other hand, brand-newly elected governor of Maryland, Martin O'Malley almost immediately called for outright repeal of the death penalty, telling his state's lawmakers:

> "Can the death penalty ever be justified when it inherently necessitates the occasional taking of a wrongly convicted, innocent life?"[369]

Someone might want to ask the rookie governor to prove there has been "the occasional taking of a wrongly convicted, innocent life?"

# An Eye for an Eye

*William T. Harper*

In light of the U. S. Supreme Court decision in October of 2007 to review the processes of lethal injection, one still has to ask: Was there nowhere in the entire United States of America writers of articles such as the above AP report could find someone, anyone to explain that accidents (which this proved not to be) do happen, that this so-called "botched" execution was perhaps a freak occurrence, let alone that the executed killer, Angel Nieves Diaz, committed a crime that deserved the punishment? Could not the writers find anyone to explain that during a December 29, 1979 holdup of a bar, Diaz and two companions robbed and killed the manager; that Diaz was convicted of first-degree murder and the defendant's prior record in this instance included an armed robbery, two escapes, assault and battering of correctional officers, and a conviction for murdering the director of a drug rehabilitation center by stabbing him 19 times while he slept?

The answer to all these questions would have to be "No" if you are a media member ingrained with the politically correct belief the death penalty must be abolished. Once again, editorial bias dominates so-called "News" pages. As in virtually all stories dealing negatively with the death penalty, reporters, writers, editors, and publishers totally ignore the pro-death penalty stance while quoting "expert" after so-called expert who are patently anti-death penalty.

One more question: Is it also merely coincidental that whenever writers – be they on news or editorial pages – need a source for their stories, they almost all jump with knee-jerk reaction to the most vehement anti-death penalty site on the Internet, the Death Penalty Information Center?

\* \* \*

As noted earlier herein, abolitionists are constantly carping about "the sleeping lawyer syndrome." They make it sound like the only reason any brutal killer is on death row is because s/he was represented by incompetent, state-

# An Eye for an Eye
*William T. Harper*

appointed defense counsel. Among constant attacks on the country's legal system in *Dead Man Walking* and *The Death of Innocents*, is the following:

> "It is rare indeed that they [the Courts] ever uphold that the constitutional rights of death row petitioners have been violated, especially the claim of ineffectiveness of defense counsel – even when defense lawyers have been shown to sleep during trial." [370]

(The emphasis here is on the plural, "defense lawyers.")

Just as abolitionists "don't give a shit about" the Kevin Scudders on death row, nor do they care about destroying a man's reputation in their encyclopedia of lies used to justify their cause. Defense attorney Joe Cannon is one of those so attacked when they said Texas "had gone too far in allowing [his] abysmal representation" and that Cannon, "in full view of everyone in the courtroom, had slept during his client's trial." [371]

"But now, for the rest of the story." Former Harris County (Texas) District Attorney Chuck Rosenthal is well-acquainted with the lawyer and that oft-repeated charge against him.

"I know Joe Cannon very well," said the DA of his courtroom adversary, "and he's a very thoughtful thinker. He sits back and closes his eyes when he's listening to information – whether in his office or in a courtroom. The man does that so he can blot out all extraneous stimuli with his thought process and concentrate solely on what he's hearing. He leans back with his eyes closed, drums the tips of his fingers against each other, and ponders what he hears. Trial judges recognize his mannerism and

# An Eye for an Eye
*William T. Harper*

out-of-hand they dismiss charges of 'sleeping' against him."[372]

The claim of a "multitude of sleeping lawyers" is plainly bogus and simply is another way abolitionists try to skew arguments to their favor, regardless of whose career they have to destroy to do it.

While speaking of the "sleeping lawyer" charge, Andy Kahan, Crime Victims Advocate for the City of Houston, said:

> "…one guy almost in the entire history of jurisprudence now has been turned into a legend of his own. Henceforth," Kahan said, "every darling of the liberals who gets convicted is because of the 'sleeping lawyer' [syndrome]. The propaganda continues and it takes on a spin of its own."[373]

Bryan Stevenson, New York University law professor and executive director of Equal Justice Initiative of Alabama, piles on unabashedly. In a televised debate about the death penalty, he jumped on that time-worn sleeping lawyer fantasy by charging that:

> "…the 5th Circuit has just reversed a case because a lawyer was asleep during the trial. That man put 23 people on death row."[374]

Unfortunately, no one on that television panel asked Mr. Stevenson to document his charge.

The anti-death penalty lobby's political agenda is obvious. One would be hard-pressed to find snide and disrespectful references to Democratic presidents and governors, but Sister Prejean is unrelenting in her obvious bias against those in the Republican camp. Not only does she show her disdain for Ronald Reagan with her last-name-only first reference to the nation's 40th President as early as page

# An Eye for an Eye
*William T. Harper*

nine of *Dead Man Walking*, but she carries on her sarcastic tirade against number 43 when he was governor of Texas.

> "When," she writes, "Texas governor George W. Bush, who presided over the killing of 152 prisoners, was asked what he thought about the sleeping lawyer, he chuckled. Nor would he later concede that even one convicted prisoner on Texas's death row might have been wrongfully convicted." [375]

Nor might have the former Major League baseball club owner "concede" that any one of Babe Ruth's 714 homers was a foul ball! Why should he? Facts are facts. In all cases.

Is there a reason why so many abolitionists vent their spleen against Republican officials? In the above case, they act as though then-governor George W. Bush invented capital punishment and instituted it himself in Texas. It is the LAW of Texas and it is not the job of the Governor to ignore the law just to placate any single-interest group. The Law of Texas (and by extension the desire of the people of Texas and every other state having the death penalty) is that the most heinous of murderers be put to death.

It isn't very often that members of the anti-death penalty league talk negatively about Democratic officials who might not support their anti-death penalty position. But, sometimes, it happens. For instance, there is the case of Rickey Ray Rector. *Baltimore Sun* columnist Dan Rodricks contends when William J. Clinton was governor of Arkansas, "[he cast] aside for the sake of votes …perhaps his own sense of humanity, civility and morality." Rodricks goes on to say:

> "Clinton is remembered for many things … But his legacy is also marred by Rickey Ray Rector, the brain-damaged killer whose lethal injection Clinton

# An Eye for an Eye
*William T. Harper*

approved as governor of Arkansas in the midst of his first campaign for the White House.

"...To become a death penalty supporter, Clinton had to jettison moral arguments and ignore the intellectual ones and put the likes of Rickey Rector to death. Clinton showed that the 'new Democrat' was capable of just about anything to lock up voters who had been sliding across to the Republican side." [376]

In other words, if you uphold the law, which then-Governor Clinton did, stand by for more arrows shot at you than General Custer saw at the Little Big Horn. For instance.

The Rev. Al Sharpton – Democratic member of Congress from New York City and hardly a staunch political Conservative – also was critical of the former Arkansas governor's handling of Rickey Rector's case when he wrote:

"In 1992 Bill Clinton was running for president. Though many saw him as some kind of liberal savior, in my judgment he was seriously flawed – a member of an all-white segregated country club, a governor who was extremely cozy with big business like Tyson Foods, and a man who could calmly and cold-bloodily order the execution of a retarded and lobotomized black man, Rickey Rector, to preserve his image as tough on crime in the presidential campaign." [377]

And, in another instance of attack via an August 5, 1994 article in the *Houston Chronicle*, columnist Clay Robison bashes another member of the "home" team:

Texas Gov. Ann Richards said (yesterday)... "I do believe that we should carry out the laws of this state in a more timely fashion." Some 388 inmates are awaiting execution in Texas, and the average stay

# An Eye for an Eye
*William T. Harper*

on death row is 10.5 years, the governor said.

Richards proposed legislation to help the Court of Criminal Appeals expedite the first automatic direct appeal of a death sentence that now takes three to four years to decide. She also called for limits on *habeas corpus* petitions filed by death row inmates in state courts.

"The truth is, nothing is gained by keeping condemned inmates, their families and the families of crime victims on a 10- or 11-year death watch," she said. "If someone has been wrongly convicted, we should find out as quickly as possible. If not, we should carry out the sentence imposed by the jury and move on."

Although death penalty abolishers would never tell you, Governor Richards was much in accord with her successor in the Texas governor's mansion in Austin, Texas, as witnessed by the following comment:

> The death penalty, like high school football, is an institution in [Texas] where no politicians in his or her right mind chooses to speak against. Former Governor Ann Richards, who often blasted the draconian social policies of religious conservatives, never took the step of commuting a death sentence during her administration. [378]

In a continuing tirade showing the liberal slant to the viewpoint of the most avid abolitionists, Sister Prejean throws in some gratuitous slams — slams having little or no bearing on the death penalty argument. She writes that one of her counseled killers "ought to take a closer look at Reagan's economic policies - taxing working people while exempting the rich, bankrolling defense contractors while abandoning the cities...." [379]

# An Eye for an Eye
*William T. Harper*

\* \* \*

As it many times is among those with "causes" to promote, their writings, speeches, debates and arguments often read as excerpts from a modern-day version of the *Communist Manifesto*. Sister Prejean constantly rails against her perceived social injustices. In addition to targeting no-first-name-President "Reagan," the nun refers to conservative Associate Supreme Court Justice Antonin Scalia as one who is "profoundly separated from the human family." She avidly supports the American Civil Liberties Union and Amnesty International. Her teachers are Albert Camus, Dorothy Day, Langston Hughes, et al. There are no Barry Goldwaters in her classrooms nor would her syllabus include such radical teachings as a "Contract with America."

Like so many banner-waving, card-carrying, cause-oriented, death penalty opponents, they seem more dedicated to their view of social reform than they are concerned about individuals housed on death row. Coming from Louisiana, it isn't surprising Sister Prejean would subscribe to the "share the wealth" philosophy that catapulted former Pelican State Governor Huey Pierce Long to national prominence in the 1930s. The rich, they both contend, should relinquish their affluence and divide their resources among the dispossessed.

Talking about conditions in her home Parish of St. Thomas, she writes:

> "I am learning about systems and what happens to the people in them, here in a state whose misery statistics are the highest in the nation – where residents bring home an average yearly income of $10,890, where half the adult population has not completed high school, where one in every six persons is a food-stamp recipient, one of every three babies born has an unwed mother, and the violent crime rate is ninth highest in the nation." [380]

# An Eye for an Eye
*William T. Harper*

It is not intended here to argue against the downtrodden, although it makes one wonder what socio-economic factors have to do with debating the death penalty because if you're for the concept or against it, that should be your position – period. Never mind the smokescreen. But, sometimes, many times, things and systems are not socially and economically fair. The Declaration of Independence merely grants us "the pursuit of happiness." It does not *guarantee* us happiness nor does it say someone who has it or whatever passes for it must "relinquish their affluence and divide their resources among the dispossessed."

\* \* \*

It's an old propaganda ploy: use the most inflammatory words possible to make your point. It's also another page out of the Big Book of Lies death penalty abolitionists speak from. That point is glaringly evident in almost every line of prose written by the anti-death penalty cabal. Take, for instance, an extended series appearing in the *Houston Chronicle* – four lengthy articles running at about 8,000 words each and written by reporter Mike Tolson under a screeching headline: "Harris County is a pipeline to death row." [381]

That writer's goal is to show that to commit a murder "within the arbitrarily drawn boundaries that define Harris County, is to risk entering the most productive death row in the Western world." Not content to merely make his point about the county that includes the nation's fourth largest city, Houston (he didn't miss, however, throwing in three or four jibes about "the sleeping lawyer"), and instead of just giving readers "the facts, ma'am," he liberally (figuratively and literally speaking) sprinkles his prose with inflammatory language, such as these few examples – some with *emphasis* added:

> "Harris County's fatal attraction" with the death penalty....

# An Eye for an Eye
*William T. Harper*

The then-District Attorney sees the death penalty as "divine retribution."

The County is "*notorious for* fatal prosecutions...."

Prosecutors have an "*affinity for* the death penalty...."

"There are other prosecutors *in love with* the death penalty...."

Texas has dispatched 242 murderers since the *death house* reopened in 1982."

The County's "death penalty *machine*...."

"Harris County is at the front door of the *slaughterhouse*."

Houston is "a bastion of bloodlust...."

Do all, or the vast majority, or a significant number, etc., of district attorneys and prosecutors have a fatal attraction with, seek divine retribution from, are notorious about, have an affinity for, or are in love with the death penalty? And do they operate a death house, use a death penalty machine or a slaughterhouse in a bastion of bloodlust? Do abolitionists say anything…we can believe?

Most assuredly, Mr. Tolson is not alone in insinuation, innuendo, and explosive language used to bolster the anti-death penalty argument and perpetuate The Big Lie(s). Sister Prejean beats him to the finish line by a wider margin than Secretariat's 31-length win in the 1973 Belmont Stakes. If one wanted to write a text on propaganda to be used by journalists (?) and advocates, all that need be done is to diligently read *Dead Man Walking* and *The Death of Innocents* by Sister Prejean. Her efforts easily surpass those of Mr. Tolson as she uses sweet talk in writing about her killers and vile pictures to describe those who disagree with her cause. Here again, are just a few passages in both categories:

In introducing the first of her spiritually-advised killers, she writes, "I tell Mr. Sonnier a little about myself."[382] (The President of the United States gets only a last-name reference two pages earlier yet this vicious murderer is

# An Eye for an Eye
*William T. Harper*

granted a respectful "Mr. Sonnier" title. The killer is then henceforth referred to almost reverentially by his "Pat" nickname.)

Sonnier's "sheer and essential humanness...is what draws me most of all...." [383]

"I am surprised by how human, even likable, he [Pat] is...." [384]

(When he's not out killing teenagers.)

The lamentation about killer Sonnier's "'tore-up' stomach and that it's been 'hard to get to sleep'" in his death row cell. [385]

(The parents of the kids Sonnier blew into eternity might be having similar problems.)

Another killer, Joseph O'Dell "became a poised and veteran warrior in his own defense, determined to reveal the truth." [386]

"...there's a child sitting inside this tough, macho dude [Robert Lee Willie]." [29]

(The child-like macho dude violently raped, tortured and murdered Faith Hathaway.)

Patrick Sonnier would be electrocuted in Louisiana's "killing chamber...." [387]

Prosecutors are "so geared for death that even a sentence of Life-Without-Parole seems unsatisfying." [388]

(The implication here is prosecutors are not seeking justice; they're merely out for satisfaction.

Every prosecutor Sister Prejean writes about no doubt has or had a Mother. But every killer she counsels has a loving "Mama." Defense and prosecuting attorneys get no slack either. They are repeatedly referred to as "shamelessly

# An Eye for an Eye
*William T. Harper*

inadequate" resorting to "bargain basement" justice wielded by "abysmally inept" lawyers. And while we're at it, notice the affectionate use of first- and nick-names of killers throughout, "Pat" and Robert and Dobie and Joseph – as the author invariably puts it when she refers to all those who she seems to classify as victims of legal conspiracies rivaling those claimed in the assassinations of Abraham Lincoln and John F. Kennedy.

The vitriolic propaganda isn't limited to Sister Prejean and Mr. Tolson and within United States' boundaries. It would take forever to list the many negative comments coming from elitists in Europe. But, closing this segment is one that comes from our northern neighbor: The *Canadian Coalition Against the Death Penalty* posts on its website its "frothing hatred for George W. Bush, whom they call 'The Texecutioner' and 'America's Biggest Serial Killer'." [389]

Are these killers the abolitionists are so fervent in protecting actually so human, likeable, poised, determined, child-like, tough, macho, and do they really not belong in a killing chamber? Do none of the prosecution and defense counsels have a "Mama"? Is the 43$^{rd}$ President of the United States a "Texecutioner" and "America's biggest serial killer?" There are Lies…and There are Damned Lies.

On the other hand, again as Ohio death-row inmate Kevin Scudder put it regarding anti-death-penalty advocates, "They don't give a shit about me personally." And Sister Prejean's words might give some credence to Scudder's point. "I don't believe," she writes, "that the government should be put in charge of killing anybody, *even those proved guilty of terrible crimes* [author's emphasis]." [390] Degree of guilt, ferocity of the killing(s), number and age of victim(s) seems to matter not to abolitionists. All they really seem to care about is abolition of the death penalty. That is their banner, their crusade, their *raison d'etre*.

\* \* \*

# An Eye for an Eye
*William T. Harper*

That's it in a nutshell. All the death penalty opponents really care about is "the cause;" that those perpetrators who are "guilty of terrible crimes" do not receive their just retribution for their slaughter of innocent victims. If abolitionists and their most prominent spokespersons really cared about *The Death of Innocents*, they should spend as much time bemoaning the fate of victims and victims' families – the really innocent – and not those that judges and juries all the way up to the Supreme Court of the United States have – time and time again – deemed guilty of horrendous murder.

Sister Prejean in *The Death of Innocents* spends 271 pages going to great lengths to play Perry Mason and try to prove Dobie Gillis Williams and Joseph Roger O'Dell were not guilty of the murders for which they convicted. The book's subtitle – An Eyewitness Account of Wrongful Executions – ain't, as composer George Gershwin so eloquently wrote for "Porgy and Bess," necessarily so. Although she did in fact witness the executions of Dobie Gillis Williams and Joseph Roger O'Dell, multiple courts up to and including the United State Supreme Court, ruled they weren't "wrongful." Why bother, one might ask, if you don't give "a hoot" whether or not they were "proved guilty of terrible crimes"? Isn't it just 271 pages of anti-death penalty propaganda? If Dobie Gillis Williams and Joseph Roger O'Dell had received life sentences instead of the death penalty, it's a safe bet *The Death of Innocents* would never have been written and their guilt never contested. Do death penalty abolitionists really care about innocents or innocence?

*The Death of Innocents* goes to great lengths to try to prove, among other things, that confessed murderer Dobie Gillis Williams was wrongfully executed for the stabbing death of Sonja Knippers on July 8, 1984 in Many, Louisiana. The author is adamant in her attacks on prosecuting district attorney, Don Burkett, as well as Williams' defense counsel at trial. Burkett comes under withering attack, both personally and professionally for his "outrageously contrived scenario" in the case as well as at least one innuendo that he was being

# An Eye for an Eye
*William T. Harper*

petty when he allowed Williams a stay of execution for a DNA test. (Imagine the vitriol if Burkett had denied that test!) The claim is also made that "so much of the interpretation of the forensic evidence that the prosecution presented to the jury was erroneous or contrived."[391] And the suggestion is made that for the District Attorney, "Finding Dobie guilty of murder wasn't enough." He had to go for the death penalty.

Burkett struck back at the charges, as reported by Vickie Welborn in the *Shreveport Times* on January 24, 2005:

> "'Court records dispute many of Prejean's claims,' Burkett said, 'specifically her assertion that Williams was mentally handicapped and had a low IQ of 65.' For Burkett, one of the more blatant errors in Prejean's book is her claim that Williams was mentally retarded. Though Prejean doesn't dwell on it, she states he had an IQ of 65, 'well below the score of 70 that indicates mental retardation....'
>
> "Burkett said Prejean relies on the results of only one of the many intelligence tests that were administered to Williams over several years. 'The one she is using says he is retarded ... but the bottom line is that test is only an estimate. She doesn't mention the other tests that were much more comprehensive that says he was of borderline intelligence, but not retarded.'
>
> "Williams scored an IQ of 65 on a Slosson Intelligence Test, a 10- to 20-minute test that serves as a quick estimate of general verbal ability. A 60- to 90-minute Wechsler Adult Intelligence Scale-Revised Test, administered to Williams by the same doctor who did the Slosson test, indicates that Williams had a verbal IQ of 79, a performance IQ of 75 and a full scale IQ of 76. He had a reading and spelling level in excess of the 12th grade and a math level in the sixth grade. 'All of these scores are in the

# An Eye for an Eye
*William T. Harper*

borderline range of intelligence,' wrote Mark Zinnerman, clinical psychologist, in report that was part of Williams' post conviction hearing in August 1988."[392]

There is no mention of the Slosson test nor of the Wechsler test in *The Death of Innocents*. Likewise, just about each and every claim of "erroneous or contrived" evidence in the book never found any credence through 14 years in the appeals process during which, apparently, no expense was spared. That's despite abolitionists constant claims that just about everyone now sitting or ever sitting on death row was there because of their indigence. For some, the Dobie Gillis Williams and the Joseph Roger O'Dell cases as defended in *The Death of Innocents* belong in the "Believe it or Not" comic strip in the Sunday funny papers.

Another favorite tactic of death penalty abolitionists is to exaggerate almost to the point of laughability. For instance, in a speech delivered at the 10th Anniversary of the United Nations Convention on the Rights of the Child where the anti-death penalty screed was certain to be enthusiastically received, the inflammatory speaker – perhaps even with tears in her eyes – told the story of "George Stinney, a 14-year-old black boy who was so small they had trouble strapping his tiny legs to the electric chair" in 1944 in that *barbarous* state of South Carolina. Better yet, the speaker said, "When the colony of Massachusetts executed 16-year-old Thomas Graunger in 1642 for the crime of bestiality, the tradition of executing children in this country was born." 1944 and 1642. The speaker had to dredge back 55 years in one case and 357 years in the other to try to make her point. One wonders why the speaker didn't go back to Biblical days and relate the Stoning of Stephen (Acts 7:54) and imply such treatment is part of this country's "tradition of executing children."[393]

\* \* \*

# An Eye for an Eye
*William T. Harper*

## Chapter Nine

### In Football, Interference...Gets Penalized

*Robert Glen Coe gave two confessions to agents of the Tennessee Bureau of Investigation in September 1979 - one taped, one handwritten - admitting to the kidnapping, rape and murder of eight-year-old Cary Ann Medlin in Greenfield, Tenn. Here is* [an extract from] *the graphic handwritten confession. Though it is disturbing,* The [Memphis] Commercial Appeal *feels it is important that readers see it as Coe moves closer to becoming the first person to be executed in Tennessee in 40 years:*

*COE'S CONFESSION* [Editor: As written by Coe, misspelling, etc.]
"*On Saturday September 1, 1979 ... I drove around in Greenfield trying to find someone to flash at when I pulled into the parking lot of the church and parked and...saw the little girl and boy on the bicycles.... I pulled up and stopped beside them and talked to the little girl. I ask her where her daddy was and she said at home. I ask her to show me where he lived....* "*I told her I had not seen her daddy for awhile and that is when I ask her to show me where he lived.... (S)he got into my car* (and) *told the little boy to watch the bicycles.*

"*I drove around some streets and I drove up a gravel road...and turned around and stopped. The little girl did not say anything. (Coe then describes in graphic detail how he raped Cary.)*

"*I told her to shut up as I finish my sex act. She told me that Jesus loves me and that is when I got so upset and I decided to kill her. When I finished the sex act I pulled up my pants and I got out of the car and I walked around the car and I opened the door on her side of the car and I caught her around the neck and jerked her out of the car and I tryed to choke her to death with my hands. She turned blue in the face,*

# An Eye for an Eye
*William T. Harper*

*but she woud not die so I choked her and made her walk down the road into the weeds away from the car. She walked backward down the lane and I pushed her and choked her.*

*"I stopped and I told her to shut her eyes and I took out my pocket knife and opened the blade and I caught her by the hair on her head and I pulled her head back and I stabbed her in the neck once and pushed her down on the ground.*

*"After she fell to the ground she ask me if I was going to kill her. She started jerking and grabbing at her shirt at the neck. I stood there and watched the blood come out of her neck like turning on a water hose. She struggled and jerked. I don't remember her shoes but I may have placed them by her body I don't know. I got some blood on my hands and I pulled some leaves off the bushes and wiped the blood on them. I then ran and tried to get away from there.... The above statement is true and correct. I am giving this statement of my own free will.*

*"(Signed) Robert Glen Coe 9-7-79"*[394]

### Robert Glen Coe

Coe goes on to describe how he left the murder scene, how he tried to avoid detection by throwing away his knife and some of his blood-stained clothes, changing his hair color, and selling the car in which he kidnapped Cary Ann Medlin. In February 1981, Coe was convicted of kidnapping, raping and murdering eight-year-old Cary Ann. On April 19, 2000, his ninth execution date, 21

# An Eye for an Eye
*William T. Harper*

years after the little girl's brutal death and six months before what would have been her 30<sup>th</sup> birthday, Robert Glen Coe was finally executed by lethal injection. Justice finally came for Cary Ann Medlin, her family and, thankfully, to Robert Glen Coe. It took 19 years of appeals of his two life sentences and his death penalty via death penalty abolitionist supporters, with re-hearings during which Cary Ann's family had to relive the horrific details which are only touched on above. But justice finally came.

\* \* \*

When asked by the Gallup polling organization, "Are you in favor of the death penalty for a person convicted of murder?" in May of 2006, 65 percent of the responders said they were. Compare that to the same organization polling result a dozen years earlier (September 1994) when the answer to the same question was *80 percent*. One of the primary reasons death penalty abolitionists are winning the war against capital punishment is plain, pure and simply because they have the main stream media, the glitterati, the literati, the ultra-liberal legislators, the so-called intelligentsia, the racial caucuses, and the international *hoi polloi* espousing their cause.

How long do you think a pro-death penalty advocate would last at a well-covered soiree at Barbra Streisand's Hollywood mansion before being driven from the premises? How often do you ever see Laci Peterson's parents on Sunday morning TV talk shows while her killer waits years for his execution? Has C-Span ever covered a firebrand speaking *for* the death penalty in the Congress of the United States? Has one black, brown, or yellow national leader ever spoken *for* the death penalty? That's not to say they're not out there. It is to say they haven't been heard proportionately. Those in the anti-death penalty cabal have. It only goes to show that the pro-death penalty cabal needs a louder trumpet.

In 1981, Pulitzer Prize-winning author and literary gadfly Norman Mailer (*The Naked and the Dead*) and many

# An Eye for an Eye
*William T. Harper*

others of New York City's literati embraced convicted killer and fledgling writer, Jack Henry Abbott. The mutual attraction was the genre of both writers: anti-establishment views and rants against perceived oppression – as it is with many of those in the world of the arts and artists. Abbott was a political "revolutionary" who compared America to Russia's gulags. It was exactly that kind of rabble-rousing writing that initially caught Mailer's eye for he too held similar views of his homeland.

Abbott was 37 when Mailer interfered with the justice system and helped get him sprung from a penitentiary in Utah where he was serving time for various crimes including forgery, escape, bank robbery, and murder of a fellow inmate. By encouraging Abbott with his book, *The Belly of the Beast*, Mailer helped him get an early release from prison via his connections and with a promise of hiring Abbott as a research assistant. "This guy isn't a murderer, He's an artist," Mailer said. "Culture is worth a little risk," he continued.[395] As it turned out, Mailer was a better judge of characters when he was writing about them than when he was "reading" them.

Via Mailer's media influence in The Big Apple, Abbott immediately became the toast of the town, gaining support from glitterati actress Susan Sarandon (who named a son after the killer), appearing on the banquet circuit and television's early morning broadcasts. Even though a first-time author, he received a $12,500 advance for his book, not bad for 1981 – and for an ex-con who had spent nearly 25 of his previous 37 years behind bars.

Abbott was, however, probably nothing more than liquid clay, a box of putty, a package of Legos that Mailer and the Park Avenue literary set toyed with in trying to make an image illustrating their own beliefs. They seemed to be play-acting in the role of Mary Wollstonecraft Shelley's *Dr. Frankenstein*. They too ended up with a monster. Even while Mailer was wining and dining him around Manhattan, the inmate-killer quickly reverted to form.

# An Eye for an Eye
*William T. Harper*

Just six weeks after his prison release, Abbott got angry with Richard Aden, the 22-year-old son of a restaurant owner, over the use of the employees' men's room in the eatery. So, in another fit of rage, Abbott stabbed Aden to death. The two-time killer fled, was later captured, and was returned to prison where he committed suicide in 2002.

At least Mailer was man enough to say his Abbott ("He's an artist") episode was nothing he took pride in. Yet, even through all of this, Mailer remained an outspoken and highly visible opponent of the death penalty until his demise, November 10, 2007. He seemed to collect killers like philatelists collect stamps – having also joined the "causes" of Caryl Chessman (see below) and Gary Gilmore, the first convict executed after the death penalty was reinstated by the Supreme Court in 1976. Despite the magnitude of the Abbott folly, Mailer practically had a standing invitation to speak anytime, anywhere against the justice of capital punishment.

\* \* \*

On March 5, 1957, the body of 15-year-old schoolgirl Victoria Zielinski, her brains splattered about, was found along the bank of a sandpit in Mahwah, New Jersey.[396] Within three months, Edgar Smith was charged, tried, found guilty and sentenced to death for her murder. For years, via some semi-eloquent writing – both commercial and in 19 court room appeals processes – Smith staved off his date with the Garden State's electric chair. Some of his commercial writing which included his book *Brief Against Death* caught the attention of ultra-conservative publisher, author, talk-show host, and commentator, William F. Buckley, Jr.

Like Mailer/Abbott, Smith became a Buckley "project." The "National Review" publisher called the killer "a most extraordinary man who may not succeed in triumphing over the chair, but who has clearly triumphed over himself."[397] Once again, the glitterati prevailed over

# An Eye for an Eye
*William T. Harper*

common sense. Buckley "ran interference" for Smith and helped him overturn his conviction and negotiate a plea bargain instead of a second trial and he was released in December 1971.[398]

And, of course, "the rest of the story" was almost as tragic as its beginning. After living the high life as a best-selling author for his death house book, his fame hit the skids and so did he. He ended up in California and there he ended up in prison – again. In 1976, he was arrested in San Diego for attempted murder of a seamstress during an abduction and robbery. To Buckley's credit this time, he called the F.B.I. when Smith phoned him while hiding out from California authorities.

It is not unheard of for vicious killers to become prison celebrities. For instance, George L. Jackson was founder of the notorious Black Panthers at San Quentin State Prison in California in 1966. "The gang has a strong political ideology that promotes Black revolution and the overthrow of the government."[399] Jackson, who died from multiple bullet wounds at San Quentin during an escape attempt on August 21, 1971, was author of *Soledad Brother* and *Blood in My Eye*. On January 16, 1970, guard John Mills was killed and Jackson and two other inmates were accused of the murder. The three became known as the "Soledad Brothers." Noted protest song-writer and singer Bob Dylan wrote and sang a reverential song about him: "They Cut George Jackson Down." Jackson himself said authorities labeled him as a brigand, thief, burglar, gambler, hobo, drug addict, gunman, escape artist, Communist revolutionary, and murderer. Meanwhile, prison guard John Mills is murdered and his murderer, George L. Jackson has songs written about him. Who is the victim here?

And do you ever wonder why, just because you happen to be among The Rich and Famous – like Mailer, Buckley, Streisand, et al – you're so able to insert your show-biz talent into the courts of law? Because you can sing, write books, and newspaper columns, your words are the

# An Eye for an Eye
*William T. Harper*

instruments that can and do subvert justice? When Bob Dylan writes and sings protest songs, does that make him a candidate for a seat on the Supreme Court?

\* \* \*

"The new Death Row *cause celebre*," writes columnist Michelle Malkin, "is Kevin Cooper, convicted in California of hacking, stabbing, and slashing three children and two parents – all but one of them to death – 21 years ago." Without a zebra-striped referee to call an "interference" penalty against them, "actors Ted Danson, Richard Dreyfuss, Mike Farrell, Janeane Garofalo, Danny Glover, Anjelica Huston, and Mary Steenburgen all signed their names to a *New York Times* ad *demanding* Cooper's execution be halted. And what gives this crowd of Hollywoodians the right to "demand" anything in a court of law?

No Hollywood celebrity is speaking out on behalf of Cooper's victims: Doug and Peggy Ryen; their 10-year-old daughter Jessica; and their 11-year-old houseguest, Chris Hughes. Or for the sole survivor, Josh Ryen, who was stabbed with a screwdriver, hit with an ax, and slashed across the throat."[400]

Some wonder what really drives abolitionists to such dead-end, point-of-view extremes. For most, it's an abiding belief that for *anyone* to take a life is wrong – whether it's an individual, a serial killer; or a government exacting the ultimate penalty on that serial killer. Sister Helen Prejean, C. S. J., has been nominated for the Nobel Peace Prize four times by her fellow believers. What a coup that would be for their cause, even though she modestly dismisses the effort. For some, there's surely political gain (outside perhaps the states of Texas, Louisiana, Florida and Georgia, that is). Others have careers in the world of show business that would be enhanced by their advocacy. The age-old theory is: Any publicity is good for my career as long as you spell my name right.

# An Eye for an Eye
*William T. Harper*

Don't these people ever learn? One has to wonder why they support these murderers? Why do they take on so many of these "causes" and "projects?" Is it because they're too rich and too famous? Is it because these members of the glitterati are (in most cases) so phony themselves that they can't spot a fellow phony? Is it because "it takes one to know one?" Are they so gullible that they fall for every sob story they hear – whether it's in a motion picture script, a new book proposal, or bawling words they hear coming from a killer's tear-streaming face? Are they as dependent on public attention and acclaim as a drug addict is for a needle or a pipe?

Cannot the bleeding hearts of the world of art spot an actor when they see and hear one? Was Jack Henry Abbott a Pulitzer Prize for Norman Mailer? Was Edgar Smith a Peabody Award for Bill Buckley? Was James Vernon Allridge one more "Oscar" for Susan Sarandon? As another character actor in some old-time Gene Autry western films, Lester Alvin "Smiley" Burnett, used to say, he's been "hornswoggled." Trouble is, old Smiley's hornswogglers were fictional.

Don't they have anything better to do with their time – when they're not posing properly coiffed and meticulously made-up before movie and television cameras making millions of dollars – other than standing outside court houses and prisons across the land proclaiming innocence for legally convicted killers? Or when they're not lighting hand-held candles, waving placards and shedding buckets full of crocodile tears? Or when they're not out preaching from their bully pulpits in churches, at universities, or editorial rooms? What, other than their gushing fan-inspired notoriety, gives them credence to spout opposition to justice as they read their lines as they would with any movie script?

\* \* \*

# An Eye for an Eye
*William T. Harper*

The liberal media bias against the death penalty, which is almost unanimous and never-ending among the cultural elite, is so pervasive — with the following extract from an article in *The Boston Globe* as witness. The premise of the story as shown in its headline said the state of Massachusetts was having a capital punishment debate. So, "We [the article's author] went to Texas to see what we could learn from a land that embraces capital punishment."[401] The writer, Karen Olsson, apparently didn't learn much that differed from her obviously preconceived ideas as she dutifully regurgitated every bit of claptrap ever put forth by those in the anti-death penalty "cause."

In her 4,200-word diatribe against the death penalty, Ms. Olsson leaps to the attack almost immediately with the prerequisite inflammatory rhetoric.

"On October 6," she writes in her opening sentence, "it was Ronald Ray Howard's turn." Here we go again. The government, it is implied, willy-nilly takes turns executing murderers.

"The execution chamber [is a] stark box of a room...." What did she expect — Leonardo de Vinci paintings of Mona Lisa with Glenn Miller recordings of "In the Mood" and "Moonlight Serenade" playing softly in the background?

Howard admitted to and was convicted of what Jackson County, Texas prosecutor Robert E. Bell characterized as "a cold-blooded execution" of a husband and father just doing his job. That husband and father was State Trooper Bill Davidson who had pulled Howard over for a traffic violation while driving what was later determined to be a stolen vehicle. Ms. Olsson quickly reveals the killer was a "black man from Houston" and the officer was "a white state trooper." Ms. Olsson didn't mention the killer was on probation at the time of the cop-killing, nor that he was a cocaine and marijuana user. Details, details.

She did mention that the killer at the time of his execution was "a big handsome 32-year-old black man." The reader wasn't given any description of the murdered officer —

# An Eye for an Eye
*William T. Harper*

although the author does tell us his widow and their daughter who witnessed Howard's execution were "substantial women in heavy makeup...." But, the writer continues with much condescension:

> "This is the way it goes in Texas...." Y'all know how those Texans are, right?

It doesn't take long for any *objective* writer to ask the prerequisite questions: "How does the death penalty help? What purpose has it served? And given the *egregious* [emphasis added] flaws in existing death penalty systems, could the death penalty ever be made 'fair'?" Then of course, she jumps to the front seat of the abolitionists' bandwagon to write about "the number of exonerations from death row – 122 have been released since 1973...." If you've read this far in this book, those words and numbers must sound familiar. "There's little evidence," she continues with the party line, "that the death penalty serves as a deterrent to crime." It is humbly suggested that Ms. Olsson review the chart in Chapter Three. And without a doubt, she had to use the usual throw-away line about "the risk of convicting and killing an innocent person (an act that has almost certainly happened)...." At least she threw in the caveat, "almost".

It's *de rigueur*, of course, for all death penalty opponents now to mention "the sleeping lawyer" and Ms. Olsson doesn't miss that opportunity; she too pluralizes it. And of course, she takes up the cudgel against the death penalty for 18-year-olds and/or those who murder "impulsively" – even when they use a nine millimeter pistol and hollow-point bullets to kill a cop. Who knows what impulses may have driven the litany of killers mentioned in these pages? And, she doesn't miss the usual attack on defense attorneys when she quotes the aforementioned capital punishment opponent Dr. David Dow who, not surprisingly asks, "How many on death row get executed because of a failure of their lawyer?"

# An Eye for an Eye
*William T. Harper*

She also repeated the fallacy that court-appointed defense attorneys don't do a good job because they're not paid enough. The defense attorney in the Howard trial was Allen Tanner. If you go back to Chapter Five herein, you'll find that Allen Tanner said the courts "give me as much money as I need" when representing an indigent client. It's hard to imagine Mr. Tanner is the only court-appointed defense attorney who ever got "as much money as [he] needed" to represent his client. Although, maybe that is hard for the abolitionists to imagine.

Naturally – as the anti-death penalty propaganda blitz continues – the killer, who defended his action by saying he was motivated by rap music lyrics – is characterized familiarly by Ms. Olsson as "soft-spoken" but he was driven to murdering the police officer by soaking up music that "advocated violence against cops."

So, just like Boston's Ted Williams after hitting a home run in Beantown's Fenway Park, *Boston Globe* writer Karen Olsson touched all the mandatory bases in her discourse about the death penalty. Next thing you know, they'll be making a movie and writing reverential songs about Ronald Ray Howard, too.

\* \* \*

Another horrific case in point is another cop-killer story. Danny Faulkner was a Philadelphia cop. The man who killed him, Black Panther Party member Mumia Abu-Jamal, is a fanatical leftist who has become, writes Steve Lopez, "an international celebrity and a symbol of everything that's wrong with the American judicial system." Abu-Jamal is just one of the current poster boys for death penalty abolitionists like (again and as usual) Susan Sarandon and her husband Tim Robbins, the late Paul Newman and Ossie Davis, Ed Asner, Alec Baldwin, et al.[402]

# An Eye for an Eye
*William T. Harper*

On December 9, 1981, Officer Faulkner made a traffic stop on Abu-Jamal's brother William Cook for a traffic violation. A fight ensued during which Abu-Jamal showed up and put five .38 caliber bullets into the officer – the last one coming execution style to the wounded officer's head. Convicted by the evidence (the gun's registration, shell casings, bullet markings) and testimony of four witnesses, the killer got the death penalty. Suddenly, Hollywood is again back on the scene, klieg lights and all.

"An international crusade to free Mumia," Lopez wrote, "fueled by endorsements from Hollywood celebrities including Susan Sarandon, Paul Newman, Ossie Davis, Ed Asner, Tim Robbins and Alec Baldwin – has had people marching in the streets from Africa to Asia and beyond" claiming "Abu-Jamal is a political prisoner who was framed, scapegoated and railroaded by a racist police force and a hanging judge." Lopez was not alone in his observation. "Before you know it," wrote Jonah Goldberg in the *National Review*, "Alec Baldwin, Molly Ivins, Oliver Stone, Salman Rushdie, E. L. Doctorow, and over a hundred others are signing a full-page ad in the *New York Times* calling for Mumia's release." [403]

As did Jack Henry Abbott (Norman Mailer's "Culture is worth a little risk" friend above) who got a $12,500 advance for his literary effort, Abu-Jamal was given a $30,000 advance by Addison-Wesley (a division of London-based media giant Pearson PLC) to publish his *Live from Death Row*, which came out in 1995. Incensed by the publisher's largess, Daniel Faulkner's widow Maureen chartered an airplane to fly over the company's headquarters trailing a banner reading: "Addison-Wesley Supports a Cop Killer." Still, her understandable outrage, shared by the Fraternal Order of

# An Eye for an Eye
*William T. Harper*

Police, was not enough to prevent the ruthless killer from eventually getting the book published. [404]

Not too surprisingly, the World Socialist Web Site had nothing but raves for Abu-Jamal's work, saying:

> "*Live from Death Row* [is] the work of a talented journalist who documents, from his 16 years of experience behind bars, the brutality as well as the social consequences of capitalist 'justice' in America. [His] books stand as an indictment of the profit system and should be read by all those concerned with the defense of democratic rights." [405]

One has to wonder what "the cause" is here?)

Everybody (well, almost everybody) knows of the sneak attack on Pearl Harbor on December 7, 1941 – "a date which will live in infamy."

Another dastardly attack brought us a new "date which will live in (judicial and social) infamy," on December 7, 2011, exactly 70 years later.

As reported on that date:

> Mumia Abu-Jamal is a former Black Panther who was convicted in 1981 of killing a white Philadelphia police officer and sentenced to death. In December 2011, prosecutors in Philadelphia brought the three-decade long legal battle that followed to an end, announcing that they would no longer seek the execution of Mr. Abu-Jamal.
>
> Instead, he will serve the rest of his life in prison. [406]

As it must have been in the headquarters of Japan's Imperial Army on that Sunday that launched America into World War II so many years ago, so too must have jubilation reigned in the homes and hearts of every death penalty abolitionist throughout this country. They were most

# An Eye for an Eye
*William T. Harper*

probably dancing, singing and shouting, "We Won! We Won!! We Won!!!" The partying may even get more raucous via speculation that the convicted cop-killer could even be sprung from more prison time under "time-served" provisions!

\* \* \*

In one of the most publicized cases, Caryl Chessman, the notorious "Red Light Bandit," spent almost 12 years on California's death row before going to the gas chamber in 1960 for kidnapping and rape. During his incarceration, he published three books (from which he was paid hundreds of thousands of dollars in royalties) and thereby caught the attention of the Hollywood and the international communities and their publicity machines. Appeals for clemency poured in from noted authors and intellectuals from around the world, including Robert Frost, Aldous Huxley, Ray Bradbury, the ubiquitous Norman Mailer, and "the usual suspects" from the Humphrey Bogart-Claude Rains conversation in the film, "Casablanca."

Phyllis Kirk, who once starred in movies with Frank Sinatra and Jerry Lewis, turned to political activism (i.e., "interference") after her acting career was over. She joined others of the glitterati in railing out against the death penalty for Chessman.[407] And, like the Susan Sarandons of later decades, she too made pilgrimages to visit Chessman in prison (from whence he suggested he had also committed a murder for which he was never indicted). She brought her stardom and notoriety to his benefit, enabling his then well-publicized efforts to gain appeal hearing after appeal hearing and seven different stays of execution.

As happened elsewhere in these pages, these appeals and stays resulted in the bogus claim of "cruel and unusual punishment." However, not even the ultra liberal Ninth Circuit Court of Appeals in California could buy that argument. It ruled the Chessman case

# An Eye for an Eye
*William T. Harper*

"...may show a basic weakness in our government system that a case like this takes so long, but I do not see how we can offer life (under a death sentence) as a prize for one who can stall the processes for a given number of years, especially when in the end it appears the prisoner never really had any good points."[408]

Supreme Court Justice William O. Douglas echoed the charge saying, "The conclusion is irresistible that Chessman is playing a game with the courts."[409]

Chessman was convicted of 17 felonies and sentenced to death for two of those crimes. "In itself," reported "Time" magazine, "the man, his crime and his punishment would scarcely cause a ripple of interest beyond the California state line. Yet, in days preceding the reprieve, concern for Caryl Chessman's fate had swept itself into a passionate whirlwind that whipped around the globe, gathered up pleas for clemency and dumped them in an overwhelming cascade on [California Governor] Pat Brown's shoulders.

"From Brazil," the "Time" article continued, "came petitions signed by 2,000,000. The Vatican newspaper, *L'Osservatore Romano,* called for mercy. In France, where dialectical discussion is served with each bottle of wine, the arguments raged as if the Dreyfus case had come alive again...."[410]

The U. S. State Department was so concerned in 1960 as Chessman's execution date loomed, it warned Governor Brown of "anticipated hostile demonstrations of student elements and others to Chessman's execution when our President [Eisenhower] visits Uruguay on March 2." Brown, placating the mobs, quickly granted the killer another stay of execution.

# An Eye for an Eye
*William T. Harper*

Obviously, Chessman won another round in the "game" Justice Douglas concluded he was playing.

\* \* \*

Mike Farrell, who made his fame and fortune through the highly successful television series about a medical evacuation team in the Korean War, M*A*S*H, is another of those misguided — and misinformed — Hollywood types who continues to seek publicity via the anti-death penalty union by defending the likes of Oklahoma City bomber Timothy McVeigh and multi-killer Robert Massie. In arguing against the death penalty and for Life-Without-Parole, Farrell said:

> "Since 1992, 435 people were convicted of capital crimes, only to be found innocent later." [411]

There have been a lot of outrageous statements made by death penalty opponents and cited in this book, but this one tops them all! Does Mr. Farrell even know definition of a "capital crime?" Just in case, it's "a crime for which the punishment is death." Is Mr. Farrell trying to tell us that 435 persons sentenced to capital punishment since 1992 have been found "innocent?" Once again, the challenge goes out:

> If 435 people convicted of capital crimes were later found innocent, prove it, Mr. Farrell. **Name those 435 innocent people!**

Massie, by the way, viciously and wantonly murdered Mildred Weiss during a January 7, 1965 California robbery. He was caught, tried, convicted and sentenced to die for that killing. However, thanks again to the 1972 Supreme Court ruling in *Furman v. Georgia,* his sentence was converted to life imprisonment and, just like the infamous Kenneth Allen McDuff in Texas, Massie was ultimately paroled. Then, on January 3, 1979, Massie murdered San Francisco liquor store

# An Eye for an Eye
*William T. Harper*

owner Boris G. Naumoff during another holdup. Again, he was caught, tried, convicted, and sentenced to the death penalty. A subsequent re-trial *convicted him for a third time*, gave him a third death sentence, and he was finally executed on March 27, 2001 – Mike Farrell and other death penalty protestors notwithstanding.

\* \* \*

Another area having inordinate bearing on the death penalty debate is international interference in our system of jurisprudence. In arguing against capital punishment, death penalty opponents gleefully cite examples of laws, mores, and legal practices from other "enlightened" countries around the world. They constantly demand the United States follow the lead of this country or that country in abolishing the death penalty. But not once do they reveal that this country or that country – such as Pakistan, Iran, Afghanistan, the Grenadines, Sudan, and the United Arab Emirates – permits stoning execution of miscreants. Not once do they mention Algeria, with its abdomen-splitting with machetes for enemies of its government (see Chapter Two).

In China in the Year of our Lord, 2007, a businessman was executed for *fraud*! In some other countries, fathers and brothers are allowed by their country's laws to murder their daughters and sisters if the women reveal they've been raped – in many cases, by those same fathers and brothers. When the death penalty opponents cite "enlightened" countries whose lead America should follow when it comes to abolishing capital punishment, they never tell us about countries such as those above.

If the United States is to be, as abolitionists would have it, a world-follower rather than a world-leader, does it not then naturally follow that we should have public stoning pens for miscreants (i.e., infidels, heretics, the depraved and villainous)? In today's geopolitical world, who are the infidels and heretics? Sister Prejean writes, "Nigeria, for example,

# An Eye for an Eye
## William T. Harper

demands that a woman convicted of the crime of adultery be stoned to death. If a child is born as a result of her unlawful act, she is allowed one year to wean her infant before she is taken away to be stoned."[412] If the U. S. is to be a world-follower – as the abolitionists would have it – shall we follow the lead of Nigeria?

Indeed, should the United States really follow the lead of the international community when it comes to exercising the death penalty? Should America emulate Iran, for instance? In July of 2005, that paragon of legal world leadership executed two teenage boys for engaging in homosexual activities. Furthermore, one of those boys executed was 16 years of age. Should the United States Supreme Court reverse its *Roper v. Simmons* decision (see Chapter Eight) and follow the international lead of the benevolent Iranian government? The "No!" answers are resounding.

Should America adopt the abolitionists' stance and follow the legal lead set by Saudi Arabia? You know the Saudis. They're the ones who supply all the imported fuel for the U. S. so the abolitionists can travel all over the nation in their private jets and gas-guzzling SUVs staging their candle-lit protests outside prisons on execution night. Well, the Saudis have a legal precedent for us, too. In March of 2007, one of their female citizens who had been raped, was sentenced to 90 lashing with a whip for "being alone with a man," her rapist. Should the United States follow the Saudis' lead, as the enlightened abolitionists would have us do, and conduct its lashing its women with a whip in the heart of Times Square in New York City? Where do the abolitionists draw the line when it comes to following the internationalists' lead?

To those who lament the United States is one of only four nations in the world today using the death penalty, death penalty proponents say, in effect: "So what?!" Are we to base our policies on what the rest of the world does? Some of those nations chop the hands off petty thieves. Are we supposed to follow their lead? Some foreign countries mass-

# An Eye for an Eye
*William T. Harper*

murder their citizens at the whim of the ruler and bury those victims in common trenches. Are we supposed to do that because they do? Again, the "No!" answers are resounding.

The anti-death penalty people say we – the unwashed; the supporters of the death penalty – should follow the examples set for us by the international community; as long as, of course, those examples agree with the anti-death penalty position. If they don't, abolitionists are, naturally, against them. They again want it both ways; they get to pick and choose. When abolitionists demand the United States should jump on the international bandwagon in doing away with the death penalty, their opponents ask why when many of those same nations don't even have trial by jury.

What or who gives abolitionists the right to crown these other foreign governments with the aura of righteousness when it comes to saying their abandonment of capital punishment is "the way," the Tao. A number of studies have shown it is the political elitists in some of those foreign countries that are opposed to capital punishment and not the people they govern. "Seen through American eyes, Canada seems almost totally nonviolent. And it's true that Ottawa administered its last execution in 1962 and formally abolished capital punishment for civilians in the mid-'70s (a ban on military executions came in 1998). But public support for the death penalty runs only slightly lower in Canada than in the United States: polls consistently show between 60 percent and 70 percent of Canadians want it reinstated."[413] Whatever happened to the will of the majority?

The European Union (the EU) takes an active stance against the death penalty. Is it any wonder the anti-death penalty movement constantly cites the fact that "all of Europe is against the death penalty?" The EU, established in 1992, is comprised of 27 European countries. It is the largest economic entity with a common trade policy and a single currency, the Euro. Abolition of the death penalty is a *prerequisite* to membership in or accession to the EU. If your country has the death penalty, it cannot join the EU. And

# An Eye for an Eye
## William T. Harper

despite the fact polls show the majority of citizens of some European countries actually favor the death penalty, their governments cannot possibly renew capital punishment because they would become economic outcasts. In some circles, that's called "blackmail."

Crass commercialism rears its ugly head in even more publicly intrusive ways. The internationally-known, high-fashion clothes manufacturer, Benetton, launched an advertising campaign in 2000 featuring, "We, On Death Row." It highlighted the issue of capital punishment with intimate photographs of 26 convicted killers awaiting execution. With text that never revealed the nature of the inmates' crimes nor anything about their victims, the $20 million campaign, stirred up a critical and legal tempest.

"Sears, Roebuck & Co., Benetton's longtime client, stopped selling its products. The California Assembly called for a boycott against the Treviso, Italy company. Victims' rights groups, such as Parents of Murdered Children (POMC), are appalled that the murderers...are remembered in the catalog, rather than the victims. 'They make victims out of the murderers,' said Greater Portland, Oregon, POMC member Mary Elledge...."[414]

Unfortunately, in today's world with its death penalty opponents, making victims out of murderers is not surprising.

\* \* \*

The international outcry is echoed in other death row cases reported herein. In the socialist land of Lafayette, a French boulevard was named for cop-killer Mumia Abu-Jamal. Joseph Roger O'Dell, one of Sister Prejean's "causes" was made an Honorary Citizen of Palermo, Italy and "the Italian parliament [shouldered] all of Joe's funeral expenses as well as

# An Eye for an Eye
*William T. Harper*

the cost of flying his body to Palermo," after the murderer was executed in Virginia.[415]

In a number of these cases – such as O'Dell's – death penalty opponents implore intervention by the Vatican. Those efforts usually fail, although in one case, they had a modicum of success. Darrell J. Mease, convicted of murdering an elderly couple and their paraplegic grandson in 1988 in Missouri, was scheduled to be put to death on January 27, 1999. This was the same time as a planned visit to the state by Pope John Paul II, who actively opposed the death penalty. After this embarrassing coincidence of events became known, the state Supreme Court rescheduled the execution for February 10th.

However, at a meeting with Governor Mel Carnahan on January 27th, the Pope made a personal plea that Mease be granted clemency. The next day, Governor Carnahan commuted the death sentence to life in prison: "I continue to support capital punishment, but after careful consideration of his direct and personal appeal and because of a deep and abiding respect for the pontiff and all he represents, I decided last night to grant his request."[416]

Isn't this a hallmark of dictatorship wherein the ruler (Governor Carnahan) blithely inserts his will (i.e., "I decided…") over that of the people?

The active Pope was less successful in Roger Keith Coleman's case (see Chapter Two for the killer whose baby-face was splashed across the cover of "Time" magazine in 1992). The Pontiff tried unsuccessfully to block Coleman's execution. Mother Teresa personally added her international opposition from Calcutta, India – also to no avail. Could it be that Mark Warner, the governor of Virginia at that time, was not a practicing dictator?

\* \* \*

Interference in the legal process by members of the glitterati and the so-called intelligentsia with their "causes" brings no

# An Eye for an Eye
*William T. Harper*

end to the pain and suffering of subsequent victims. Clinton Brewer, a musician with big dance bands of the 1930s and 1940s, spent 19 years in a New Jersey prison for the murder of his wife. Famed writer Richard Wright, author of the best-selling book *Native Son*, discovered Brewer's plight in 1940. Using his fame and influence, Wright finagled a pardon for Brewer, got him a new gig with Count Basie's world-famous band, and even brought the killer home to live with him. Within months, Brewer was back in the penitentiary because "his lady love, Wilhelmina Washington, was found dead, all cut up with stab wounds." [417]

Jon Wayne Nobles was executed in 1998, having admitted to the murders of Kelley Farquar and Mitzi Nalley. He stabbed them to death in 1986. His cause was taken up by noted country-western singer Steve Earle (nominated 14 times for the music industry's prestigious Grammy award). When one goes to the Google online search engine to look up Nobles, the convicted killer has 37 listings (as of this writing). Of those listings, 34 are in English and 21 of them are stories about Earle's involvement in the killer's cause. Without the intervention of this former drug-addict-turned-country-western-singer and member of the glitterati, Jon Wayne Nobles would be almost unheard of for researchers. By the way, nowhere in any of those 21 websites is one able to find anything about the two girls who were murdered; the stories are all about the singer's commitment to the murderer. [418]

Then there's "the life of Riley" behind prison bars. That's where the glitterati and the abolitionists would have abominable killers such as Richard Speck and serial killer Richard (The Night-stalker) Ramirez serve their Life-Without-Parole sentences. It's hard to find any hue and cry from the anti-death penalty crowd over the money many of those fiends are making while they're locked up. It's through a flourishing business that Andy Kahan, Crime Victims Advocate for the City of Houston, has labeled, "Murderabelia." [419] Kahan reports that...

# An Eye for an Eye
*William T. Harper*

"...manufactured auction and sale items include serial killer dolls, snow-globes, clocks, t-shirts, calendars, and psycho-killer comic trivia. Items produced by the killers themselves include artwork, handprints, autographs, hair samples, autographed socks, and fingernail clippings. Clumps of hair," Kahan continues, "have been sold by a veritable serial killer Who's Who – New York cannibal Arthur Shawcross; Florida's highway killer Glen Rogers; railway killer Angel Rasendiz Ramirez; and California serial killers Lawrence (Pliers) Bittaker, Roy Norris, William Suff, Douglas Clark, and Charles Manson. Even dirt from John Wayne Gacy's crawl space was auctioned." [420]

Paintings by James Earl Ray, convicted assassin of Martin Luther King Jr., and Gacy are in demand and are available for a price through the Internet and other sources. In one particular case, an art gallery sponsors a one-man annual show of the works of a reprehensible killer. In another, a "collector" said a Manson autograph is "kind of like baseball cards. Once you start collecting, you have to get the whole set." Also available are such things as more dirt from the grave of Ed Gein, the "inspiration" for the movie "Psycho." [421] Talk about your psychos.

One newspaper article described a "work of art" offered to the public. "The sketch," the newspaper reported, "traces the shapely backside of a nude female as she glances over one shoulder. It appeared on a Web site peddling art 'from the hand' of Elmer Wayne Henley, who is serving six life sentences for his involvement in a sex-torture ring that killed 26 boys in the Houston, Texas area. The victims, many of them runaways, were shackled, sexually abused, tortured and killed, authorities said....

"The issue remains," the story continues, "far from settled after Andy Kahan first raised concerns over death row

# An Eye for an Eye

### William T. Harper

inmate James Allridge III [see above] selling his art to actress Susan Sarandon and other celebrities.... His greeting cards sold for as much as $10 a box, and a large print went for $465.... Henley paints with acrylics. Besides the nude woman shown on the Web site, he has other works such as handprints in red paint listed for $50, a floral bouquet for $125, a woman's face for $475 and a painted ostrich egg for $175." [422]

    Just imagine: Kill as many people as you can, get caught and be sentenced to abolitionist-sanctioned Life-Without-Parole, and become a darling of the glitterati with your "art" becoming maybe even more desirable than an easel-mounted Picasso. Your work might well hang in Susan Sarandon's mansion. While you're at it, think also of the horror experienced by some victim's family members should they go surfing the Internet and come across some of these items for sale by their loved ones killer. It has already happened.

    The above described "weakness in our government system" is that it allows celebrities to unduly interfere with due process. Through their celebrity status, they influence the public via their supporting media and bring the wheels of justice to a grinding halt. And the irony of it all is in almost all of these cases, the "projects" and the "causes" the glitterati are literally and figuratively adopting end up in the death house right where they belong after all. But once more, the Rich and Famous, as Kevin Scudder, that Ohio death-row inmate so succinctly said about death penalty abolitionists, "They don't give a shit about me personally."

\* \* \*

# An Eye for an Eye
*William T. Harper*

# Chapter Ten

### The Bible, the Baby and...What If?

One thing about the Bible, it seems, is anyone can make almost anything they want out of it. Sister Prejean avails herself of that option time and again in her writings. For instance, when responding to such Biblical teachings as "an eye for an eye," she writes, "I cannot believe in a God who metes out hurt for hurt, pain for pain, torture for torture." [423] Her extension of the meaning of "an eye for an eye" seems to be a typical tactic employed by death penalty protesters: absurd exaggeration. It's hard to believe the Bible is advocating "torture for torture." Or is it only Sister Prejean?

A further ploy of abolitionists is to claim Government "can't be trusted to control its own bureaucrats or collect taxes equitably, or fill a pothole, much less decide which of its citizens to kill." [424] Once again, that view seems at odds with the Bible that says:

> "Everyone must submit himself to the governing authorities, for there is no authority except that which God has established. The authorities that exist have been established by God. Consequently, he who rebels against the authority is rebelling against what God has instituted, and those who do so will bring judgment on themselves" (Romans 13:1-2).

In this country today, as it has been since the signing of the Constitution in 1789, Federal, State and Local governments are the "governing authorities."

# An Eye for an Eye
*William T. Harper*

One thing you can be sure of is this writer is definitely not going to engage in any religious debates on the death penalty (nor anything Biblical, for that matter; not when an adversary might well be a Sister of the Church). This author believes in the words of Louisiana prison Captain John Rabelais as he was about to be engaged in a Biblical debate with Sister Prejean. He smiled, put up his hand and said, "I ain't gonna get into all this Bible quotin' with no nun, 'cuz I'm gonna lose." [425] Precisely. We'll leave that kind of arguing to theologians like Greg Koukl of the evangelical study group Stand to Reason. That organization feels the death penalty is warranted and religiously permissible according to passages of both the Old and New testaments – particularly the "eye for an eye" teaching espoused in Deuteronomy. The idea of punishment "fitting" the crime is not just about vengeance, they say, but fostering a basic sense of justice. [426]

But, death penalty abolitionists are quick to point out almost all those things in the Old Testament starting with Genesis about "Thou Shalt Not Kill," etc., have been superseded by words of the New Testament. Then we quickly hear from proponents of the death penalty that even the New Testament upholds the "eye for an eye" proclamations of the Old Testament. They point again to Paul's statements in the Book of Romans (13:3), "Do you want to be free from fear of the one in authority? Then do what is right, and he will commend you, for he is God's servant to do you good. But if you do wrong, be afraid, for he does not bear the sword for nothing. He is God's servant, an agent of wrath to bring punishment on the wrongdoer." Or, as Supreme Court Associate Justice Antonin Scalia put it,

> "...government, however you want to limit that concept, derives its moral authority from God. It is the minister of God with powers to revenge, to execute wrath, including even wrath by the sword, which is unmistakably a reference to the death penalty." [427]

# An Eye for an Eye
*William T. Harper*

Both sides of the death penalty argument seem to be in agreement that the moral aspects of our governments are based on the beliefs of the Framers of the Constitution, in the religion of the age. Thus, anti-death penalty believers are double-quick to point out that "Thou shalt not kill" means "thou" is both the Individual and the State. "That's what the Bible says," they pontificate. However, the original writing in the Bible says in Exodus 20:13, "You shall not *murder*" (emphasis added).

Despite abolitionists' vehement denial of the fact, there is a significant difference in the verbs to "kill" and to "murder." According to one dictionary (Webster's Ninth New Collegiate), murder means "to kill a human being unlawfully and with premeditated malice." Its definition of to "kill" is to "deprive of life." Ted Bundy acted "unlawfully and with premeditated malice" when he murdered 30 (or more than 100) women, for which the State deprived him of his life. When the State executes a killer, it does not do it unlawfully; on the contrary, it is lawfully mandated to do so.

The Bible's intent was "You shall not murder." In a state-directed execution, it is not "one person" killing/murdering another. It is not the prison warden, nor the "strap-down" team, nor the Governor, nor the Pardons Board. It is the State doing the killing – at the will of the people. The people will the government to levy taxes, build Interstate highways systems, send men and women into outer space, and punish malefactors by means of penalties commensurate with the gravity of the crime.

Beyond such nebulous religious arguments centered on "Thou shalt not Kill" and "Thou shalt not Murder" and "Vengeance is mine," sayeth the Lord and what He/She really meant by that, the abolitionists' anti-death penalty stance is concentrated on the "cruel and unusual" aspects. First off, with a reported more than 15,000 legal executions in this country since the 17th century, how can anyone argue that death in the electric chair or by hanging or in a gas chamber

# An Eye for an Eye
*William T. Harper*

or by lethal injection is "unusual"? What is cruel and unusual is how Jessica Lunsford died at the dirty hands of John Evander Couey.

Commencing on page 115 of *The Death of Innocents*, Sister Prejean puts forth an extensive history of the death penalty, the Church's involvement therein pro and con, of her intervention with the Pope, etc., etc. We're told of the change in the Catholic Catechism after Pope John Paul II read her 1,500-plus word letter of January 1, 1997 which was delivered to the Vatican on January 22. Proudly it seems, she writes, "on Jan. 29 Cardinal Joseph Ratzinger, Prefect of the Congregation of the Doctrine of the Faith [and who would on April 19, 2005 become Pope Benedict XVI], announced that a change would be made in the Catechism to reflect recent 'progress in doctrine' about the death penalty."[428] (Cause and effect?)

And what was the "most substantive change in church teaching about the death penalty in 1,600 years" that "...perhaps [her] unique contribution to the dialogue" brought about? The previous wording in the 1992 Catechism read:

> "...for this reason the traditional teaching of the Church has acknowledged as well-founded the right and duty of legitimate public authority to punish malefactors by means of penalties commensurate with the gravity of the crime, **not excluding, in cases of extreme gravity, the death penalty.**"

That reads quite plainly that the Catholic Church approved use of the death penalty. But, in the September 8, 1997 version of the Catechism, the above bold-faced words Sister Prejean enthusiastically wrote "have been removed."[429] To some readers, however, there seems to be no great significant difference in the old wording vs. the new. Both say there is "the right and duty of legitimate public authority to

# An Eye for an Eye
*William T. Harper*

punish malefactors by means of **penalties commensurate with the gravity of the crime**."

It does not say, as the nun goes on to proclaim, "no matter how grave (terrible, outrageous, heinous, cruel) the crime, the death penalty is not to be imposed." It merely eliminates a reference to the death penalty. To some readers, the change in Section 2266 of the revised Catechism is merely pacification for the abolitionists. It still says the penalties to be imposed for "grave" crimes are to be "commensurate with the gravity of the crime." If a crime is "grave," then the penalty for committing the crime should be "grave" too. And that "grave" can be either a noun or an adjective or an adverb.

Furthermore, abolitionists now tell us "modern societies must refrain from killing criminals because incarceration gives [those societies] a way to incapacitate violent offenders" thereby eliminating the need for the death penalty.[430] If only that were true. As shown minimally but repeatedly on these pages, incarceration **does not** always incapacitate violent offenders. Kenneth Allen McDuff was incarcerated many times – twice for murders.

The war of words over biblical interpretations rages between the diametrically opposed, such as Sister Prejean and Supreme Court Justice Antonin Scalia, vis-à-vis the death penalty. Each side can and does claim, "The Bible says this" and/or "The Bible says that." According to the Bible-interpreter, often those claims contradict each other. But, what about those to whom biblical interpretations are meaningless? What interpretations, if any, are left to those who don't get their guidance from the Bible? Isn't the "real law" the "law of the land" by which we are all judged in this world – regardless of that of the hereafter? Will those who obey the law of the land be acquitted in this world but possibly be condemned in the next? And visa versa?

When biblical law, with its multi-interpretations, conflicts with contemporary law, which law is contemporary man/woman to abide? And where does biblical law leave the

# An Eye for an Eye
*William T. Harper*

man/woman who have no belief in the Bible whatsoever? Surely, contemporary law cannot be written to comply with any one of several interpretations (such as we have now) to the detriment of those who only believe in their own interpretation of the Bible and exclude others' beliefs, be they in or out of the Bible.

If the "law of the land" requires a death sentence for the "Bad Boy from Rosebud," then so be it – at least until the law of the land is changed by the citizens of the land through their elected representatives. Whether or not one believes in the Bible and it's multitude of interpretations, one has to be directed by the law of the land. And the latter applies to everyone in the land as opposed to the Bible which, in many cases, means different things to different people.

Obviously, Sister Prejean's interpretation of the Bible sometimes differs from Justice Scalia's as those two Christians debate the application of the death penalty. But, as Christians argue over interpretation, what about Jews and Muslims and agnostics and atheists? The Law of the Land applies to Christians, Jews, Muslims, agnostics, atheists and everyone else living in the land and under its laws.

Again, this is prolonging a religious debate and one is hard-pressed to find in the history of mankind where anyone comes out a clear winner in religious debates. Another thing one has to wonder about when various chapters and verses of the Bible are invoked by either side of the death penalty argument is – what "law" governs those whose religious beliefs come from a source different from the Good Book? Is it "the law of the land," or "the law of choice"?

\* \* \*

Those against the death penalty are indeed all too quick to say capital punishment is "cruel and unusual." The first established death penalty laws date as far back as the Eighteenth Century B.C. Babylon, which codified the death penalty for 25 different crimes.[431] One database of executions

# An Eye for an Eye
*William T. Harper*

in the United States from 1608 to 1987 lists 14,634 executions.[432] After a four-year hiatus (1972-1976), the death penalty was reinstated by the United States Supreme Court which deemed it not to be cruel and unusual. Starting with Gary Gilmore on January 17, 1977 and running through August 14, 2012 when Michael Hooper paid his price for murdering a mother and her two children aged three and five in 1993, 1,302 men and women have been executed by federal and state governments in this country. Again, these numbers indicate jury-determined death sentences and the carrying out thereof is surely not "unusual." Jeffrey Dahmer's multiple, cannibalistic, barbaric murders were cruel and, to say the least, unusual.

To further say a jury-determined and a state/federal-executed death penalty is "cruel" begs the question: Compared to what? The victims of those upon whom the death penalty is being enacted? We would dare say that almost any murderer ever executed by the State would most willingly accept that fate rather than the one they meted out to their victim(s). Go back to Chapter One and ask John Evander Couey if he would prefer a sedative needle stuck in his alcohol-swabbed arm or would he rather be raped and buried alive in a plastic bag as was his nine-year-old victim, Jessica Lunsford?

Ask Donald Eugene Harding if he would prefer to die in a sterile state prison execution chamber or, as it says here in Chapter Six, would he rather die like Martin Concannon did. Harding shot him in the left chest perforating his spinal cord, shot him again near the temple from about three inches distance, and when he still did not die instantaneously, he was then suffocated to death when Harding stuffed Concannon's stockings stuffed down his throat? Or, how about the villainous Robert Lee (the "electric chair don't scare me") Willie who made the helpless, raped, stabbed teenager Faith Colleen Hathaway beg for her death? Let the death penalty opponents tell Jessica, Martin and Faith about "cruel and unusual." Or better yet, tell it to the families.

# An Eye for an Eye
*William T. Harper*

* * *

The death penalty abolitionists demand a perfect system when it comes to capital punishment – knowing full well perfection is not possible. Their demand for perfection is a ruse. As long as there is a possibility that a certifiably innocent person *could* be executed, objectors demand perfection. Their self-anointed goal is to stop state/federal executions. It is not, as they would have us believe, to prevent execution of a certifiably innocent person. There are those who truly believe some death penalty opponents are actually, silently, and selfishly hoping for the execution someday of a certifiably innocent person. Anything for "the cause."

One of the "tricks" being used by the anti-death penalty bloc is their call for death penalty moratoriums – hoping they will lead to the ultimate goal: Death Penalty Banishment. They enlist the aid of medical associations by demanding adherence to the Hippocratic Oath: *primum non nocere*, that doctors should first, "do no harm," and therefore not assist in administration of lethal injections. (Of course, what they're saying here is lethal injections should be left up to medical amateurs.) But, when they plead "do no harm," it's a little too late for that. The harm has already been done – by the person laying on the death house gurney while singing an abbreviated version of "Silent Night."

Lethal injection, protestors cry, is "cruel and unusual punishment." It's reaching the point where anything short of the keys to the front gate of the penitentiary and a winning ticket in a Power-Ball lottery is "cruel and unusual punishment." It would be helpful to death penalty advocates if they could believe that the tears shed by the death penalty opponents on behalf of the cannibalistic Jeffrey Dahmer were anything but crocodile.

Can you really cry for someone who cannibalizes his victims and then stores their remaining body parts in his freezer for, perhaps, Christmas dinner? It would help if one

# An Eye for an Eye
*William T. Harper*

could believe the abolitionists honestly care about Ted Bundy's journey into that good night of graceful aging. And, as noted elsewhere herein, would any abolitionist care about punishment – let alone the innocence – of Dobie Gillis Williams or Joseph Roger O'Dell (other than their families) if either one or both of them had been sentenced to Life-Without-Parole instead of death? What the death penalty abolitionists are telling us is they really don't care what the magnitude of the crimes these killers commit; they only really care about their self-proclaimed "cause."

Having so far been mildly successful in selfishly foisting their "cause" on the majority of Americans, they now proclaim lethal injection must go. They're afraid the poor killers stretched out "crucifixion-like" on a gurney in a prison's death house might suffer a tad during the lethal injection process. Ignoring medical evidence to the contrary, it seems abolitionists are concerned about the excruciating pain suffered by the victims of these heinous killers. Now, their tears are shed for the killers who have their veins pricked by a needle, much the way millions of people do every year at American Red Cross and other blood banks. Their claim – totally unproven and only surmised at – is the procedures being used *could* cause pain. This has led to an eruption of litigation over lethal injection. Beginning in 2006, 12 states put a moratorium on the death penalty mainly because of justice-delaying challenges and questionable questions regarding the hand-wringing over the lethal injection process.

Some abolitionists have said the third drug (in the three-drug "cocktail") could cause excruciating pain because of insufficient anesthesia from the first drug and the murderer on the gurney would be unable to say anything because he would be paralyzed by the second. It is *possible* this could happen. Almost anything is possible. It is *possible* there was a second shooter on the grassy knoll near the Texas Book Depository in Dallas on November 22, 1963. Some people believe aliens descended on Roswell, New Mexico,

# An Eye for an Eye
*William T. Harper*

and mysterious forces bring down airplanes and swallow up battleships in the Bermuda Triangle. Almost anything is *possible*.

But because there haven't been many who have come back from an "outer-body" experience to tell us, it's also entirely *possible* the three-drug cocktail administered might even cause various states of euphoria and a delightful journey to "the other side." But, in their one-sided view, abolitionists believe that's one of those things that isn't possible. They're absolutely sure the Dennis Raders of the world, the "Bind, Torture and Kill" types, are suffering some bumps in the road to that other side. As songstress Julie London so eloquently put it in her 1957 million-selling recording lament, go ahead and "Cry Me a River."

And just as anti-death penalty proponents have dredged up all kinds of horror stories from past executions – David Lawson, Leandress Riley, and Lewis Williams, Jr., among others mentioned in these pages – now they have a candidate to join the "sleeping lawyer." In one court case, a judge expressed serious reservations because the physician who had been administering the drugs was dyslexic and had difficulty reading numbers. The doctor admitted he had administered only half the normal dosage of sedative in several executions. You can expect to hear and read many stories linking sleeping lawyers with dyslexic physicians (both assuredly in the plural).

As usual, there is "the rest of the story" as illustrated by the following newspaper reader who wrote:

> "As a now-retired certified registered nurse anesthetist for many years, I find the premise that the injection is cruel and inhumane ridiculous. Millions of people in the United States and around the world have received the agents employed in those injections as part of successfully administered anesthetics for more than half a century. The only difference is the rapid administration of potassium

# An Eye for an Eye
*William T. Harper*

chloride, which results in cardiac arrest. The placement of a very good intravenous line would ensure that the process not be interrupted by having the venous route fail. Then, larger doses of the medication which renders the individual unconscious and paralyzed should, perhaps, be administered and then followed by the potassium." [433]

According to retired warden Jim Willet, he was not specifically sure of the dosage used in the "three-drug cocktail" in executions in the Huntsville prison death house but he did recall that "one of our medical people told me that we gave the inmates enough anesthetic to put a horse to sleep."

\* \* \*

Nonetheless, abolitionists continue their attempt to throw the baby out with the bathwater. The judge in the above dyslexia case said lethal injection should never be used in any executions just because, in this one case, the drug-administering doctor was dyslexic. So, instead of instituting procedures that would overcome this possibility, the judge – in yet another case of judicial law-making – threw out the death penalty instead, temporarily anyhow.

Yet another case arose in 2005 in Kentucky where lawyers for two convicted killers – one of whom, Ralph Baze, ambushed and murdered two police officers with an assault rifle in 1992 and the other, Thomas Browling shot and killed a husband and wife and their two-year-old son in 1990 – asked the lethal injection process be halted (*Baze vs. Rees*, No. 07-5439). Baze, by the way, is another one of those death row inmates using the Internet, saying he "would like a relationship with the right lady that could be more than Pen pals. Times get lonely in here." He didn't mention the dead cops' widows and how lonely they might be.)

# An Eye for an Eye
*William T. Harper*

The lawyers claimed autopsy evidence showed a recently executed Kentucky prisoner was still awake when deadly chemicals stopped his heart. (That dodge was overruled by the State's Supreme Court 18 months later. The U. S. Supreme Court, on April 17, 2008 in a 7-2 ruling, also upheld the State of Kentucky.) A drug junkie on Alabama's death row claims the injection of any needle would now cause him excessive pain. (Did that poor man suffer "excessive pain" every time he jabbed a heroin needle in his arm?) For reasons such as these, the American Medical Association has directed its members to not participate in lethal injections. One has to ask what directions the AMA gives its members regarding, for instance, abortions. Could there be a political agenda here?

If sodium pentothal doesn't do the job it is supposed to do in the death house – dull any sense of feeling for the killer on the gurney – then increase the dosage and totally knock out the condemned before the other drugs start to act. How about all those people who commit suicide by sitting in their cars with the motor running in a closed garage? They obviously are not suffering agonizing physical pain.

What about those people that enlisted "Dr. Death," Jack Kevorkian, to help them commit suicide. He did this dozens of times (for which he eventually went to prison for "administering a controlled substance") and there are no stories of his "patients" dying agonizing deaths. Video-taped evidence of a peaceful death was even presented at one of his court trials. In Oregon, a terminally ill person can legally choose to die under the Oregon Death With Dignity Act (1994). That doesn't sound like "excessive pain."

And if all that doesn't work, there are other methods, some already known and others yet to be discovered. For instance, medical science has shown death by oxygen starvation, such as suffered by firefighters in a burning building, is by itself, totally lacking in pain – excessive or otherwise.

# An Eye for an Eye

*William T. Harper*

In writing about the great Hinckley Fire that raged through northern Minnesota in 1894 and officially killed 418 helpless people, author Daniel James Brown said:

> "Carbon monoxide kills the overwhelming majority of fire victims. Because it is tasteless, sleeping victims often never awaken to see, hear, or smell the fire that kills them. Carbon monoxide is subtle. A stealth killer, it sets off no alarms. It silently fills up the lungs and then – bonding to the hemoglobin in the blood 250 times more readily than oxygen to form a compound called carboxyhemoglobin (COHb) – it rapidly displaces the oxygen in the bloodstream. The brain and other vital organs are caught unawares. Suddenly deprived of oxygen, and having no other choice, vital organs such as the brain shut down, rather promptly. By the time the saturation of the COHb reaches 90 percent, death comes in minutes." [434]

Is the carboxyhemoglobin process a possible alternative to the three-drug "cocktail"? Maybe the infamous Gary Gilmore had the right idea when he elected to be shot by a firing squad in Utah in 1977!

\* \* \*

That perfect system abolitionists call for is just as an impossible solution as is finding a perfect person. Abraham Lincoln, acclaimed by many as the perfect person to be in the White House during America's Civil War, was once a postmaster who's township had the worst efficiency rating in the country. Franklin Delano Roosevelt, who led this country out of the Great Depression and on to victory in World War II, flunked out of Columbia University's law school. Five-star general and later President Dwight David Eisenhower, architect of the world's victory over Adolph Hitler's forces in

# An Eye for an Eye
*William T. Harper*

1945, was passed over three times for promotion before being appointed Supreme Allied Commander in Europe in 1942. Harry S Truman, President of the United States who brought World War II to a climatic close with his decision to use atomic-bombs against Japan in August of 1945, failed utterly as a store-keeper in Kansas City at age 35. And this writer failed to be promoted out of Kindergarten through three semesters! No person, nor any system, is perfect.

The abolitionists scream about "The Death of Innocents" (spelling intentional by that book's author and re-iterated here by this one). Let it be said again and again: "No one who has been executed since the death penalty was reinstituted in 1976 has been proved definitively innocent." But should that ever be the case, must the death penalty be abolished because of a "mistake," an "accident?" When a doctor mis-prescribes a medication and the patient dies, do we rule the prescription off the books? When a surgeon cuts the wrong artery, do we do away with all surgeries? Accidents do happen. When the brakes fail on a school bus and a dozen kids are killed in the ensuing accident, do we burn all the buses and make the kids walk five miles to school?

The death penalty opponents cry "jurors in capital trials generally do not understand the judge's instructions about the laws that govern the choice between imposing the death penalty and a life sentence."[435] If that is the case, clarify the instructions.

No system is perfect. The highest lifetime average in all of major league baseball history was Ty Cobb's .366. That means he got 366 base-hits for every 1,000 times he came to bat. It also means he failed 634 times for every 1,000 times he came to bat. In her two books, Sister Prejean might also be batting .366. But even she – or anyone else walking the face of the Earth today – isn't perfect. As a matter of fact, when you're only getting your "facts" right one-third of the time, that too is far from perfect.

Nobody and no system is perfect. Scientists tell us there is even no such thing as a "perfect" vacuum. The goal

# An Eye for an Eye
*William T. Harper*

in all things is to be as close to perfect as humanly possible. But everyone makes mistakes. Pluto is no longer a planet. Preventable medical mistakes and infections are responsible for about 200,000 deaths in the U.S. each year, according to an investigation by the Hearst media corporation.[436]

\* \* \*

From all angles, we are overwhelmed by well-meaning doctors, lawyers, and Indian chiefs about death penalty inequities. As previously noted herein, for instance, the American Medical Association (AMA) has urged its members to refuse to participate in any way in the legal administration of the death penalty. Likewise, the American Bar Association (ABA) created the Death Penalty Representation Project in 1986. The AMA and the ABA should be fixing the problem and not throwing the baby out with the bathwater.

The bar association says its goals are to "raise awareness about the lack of representation available to death row inmates, to address this urgent need by recruiting competent volunteer attorneys and to offer these volunteers training and assistance."

The ABA also cites the need to…

> "work for systemic changes in the criminal justice system that would assure those facing death are represented at all stages of the proceedings from trial through clemency by qualified, adequately compensated counsel."

No one can argue with that noble goal.

In response to the American Bar Association's Death Penalty Representation Project, the "American Lawyer" magazine presents this story:

"Sidney Austin Brown & Wood partner John Gallo, a former federal prosecutor, says he was

# An Eye for an Eye
*William T. Harper*

deeply moved by a presentation that Robin Maher of the American Bar Association's Death Penalty Representation Project gave...about death row inmates who have no lawyers. [He thought,] 'I want to do better than that.' Seventy Sidney lawyers have signed up for death penalty work, and the firm has taken on 12 cases, all in Alabama.... Maher hopes the recent flurry of firm activity will inspire others to a friendly competition to help ensure that people whose lives are on the line have fair access to justice.

[Again, no one can argue with that noble goal.]

"An 'American Lawyer' survey of the nation's 200 highest-grossing firms showed that 45 firms have never taken a death case.... Another 39 firms refused to respond or disclose whether they had taken a death penalty case...." [437]

There are those that talk and those that do. John Gallo and Sidney Austin Brown & Wood should be commended for recognizing a problem and trying to fix it. It is interesting to note, however, that the bar association and death penalty abolitionist generally only see problems on the prosecutorial side of death penalty cases. As the ABA's Stephen Hanlon, chair of the Death Penalty Representation Project implementation committee, sees it, the death penalty system is "rife with irregularities." [438]

However, the many cases cited herein of defense failures (i.e., the defendant didn't get a proper lunch, the defense lawyer reading "Bon Appetit" magazine, the cold full-of-baloney sandwich appeals, etc.) are conveniently brushed aside. So too are statements regarding the ABA's adequate compensation when they are made by death penalty defense lawyers such as **Allen Tanner**, who said in Chapter Five herein, the courts "give me as much money as I need" when representing an indigent client.

# An Eye for an Eye
*William T. Harper*

Also as noted above, the ABA says there is a need to "recruit competent volunteer attorneys." If there is a lack of "competent" attorneys, volunteer or otherwise in death penalty cases or *Neighbor v. Neighbor* nuisance cases, the lawyers' association should be addressing that problem across the board and not simply tying it to the death penalty debate. The ABA should be fixing the root problem and not throwing the baby out with the bathwater.

\* \* \*

Sometimes, because judgments are made by human beings, innocent persons are found guilty and go to prison. And sometimes, because judgments are made by human beings, guilty persons are ruled innocent and go free. Just as "bad things happen to good people," so too do good things happen to bad. Sometimes, science screws up – as do scientists and so-called "scientists."

The Houston (Texas) Police Department's crime lab is a perfect example of that. Based on a four-and-one-half-year investigation and analysis of its personnel and procedures, nine employees were disciplined for errors in analyzing DNA and other evidence, giving false information to state auditors and failures in supervision and record-keeping.

(It should be noted, however, that the Lab "has revised the Standard Operating Procedures for each of its sections, implemented a new quality assurance and quality control program, developed new training programs for analysts, and hired a number of new supervisors and analysts...[439])

The Dallas County (Texas) District Attorney's office, under Henry Wade of the disputed President Kennedy assassination follow-up, was singled out for its perceived win-at-all-costs posture in capital murder and rape trials.

Because mankind has yet to develop a perfect system for determining guilt or innocence, for determining what are

# An Eye for an Eye
*William T. Harper*

truly appropriate sentences for crimes committed – from petty larceny to capital murder –even if mankind hasn't determined what method of carrying out a sentence is absolutely not cruel and is not unusual. We shouldn't *per se* throw the baby out with the bathwater. As renowned Supreme Court Justice Harry Blackmun of "machinery of death" fame wrote, "human error is inevitable, and…our criminal justice system is less than perfect."[440] The same could be said for Harry Blackmun and as it would be for this writer.

And sometimes airplanes fall out of the sky but does that mean we should ground all airplanes? Look at this tragic history of just one type of aircraft, the Lockheed L-188 Electra, a low-wing, four-engine, turboprop-powered plane:

> February 3, 1959 – American Airlines Electra crashes into New York's East River, killing 63 of the 75 people on board.
> September 29, 1959 – Braniff Airlines Electra mysteriously breaks up over Buffalo, Texas, killing all 28 passengers and six crew members.
> March 17, 1960 – Northwest Orient Airlines Electra crashes in Indiana with 63 fatalities.
> October 4, 1960 – Eastern Airlines Electra crashes after hitting a flock of starlings in Boston, killing 62 passengers and crew.
> May 5, 1968 – Braniff Lockheed Electra flight 352 explodes over Dawson, Texas, killing 85 passengers and five crew members.

And these were just those crashes in the United States! All in all, according to the Aviation Safety Network, 47 Lockheed L-188 Electra airplanes crashed with a total of 1,041 fatalities.[441] (That's almost as many as were executed in the U. S. since 1977.) Therefore, according to the death penalty abolitionists' theory, all airplanes should have been banned from the skies. One-thousand-and-forty-one people

# An Eye for an Eye
*William T. Harper*

died due to mechanical error (substitute – misplaced IV leads in an execution chamber) and pilot error (substitute – faulty evidence in a capital murder trial). But, in Lockheed's case, abolition of the Electra didn't happen because of these cited failures. What did happen was the Lockheed Aircraft Company fixed the system. It imposed speed restrictions, uncovered and modified engine mountings, and strengthened the planes' wing structures. After that the Electra proved reliable and popular in service. Unlike death penalty abolitionists, the Lockheed Aircraft Company didn't throw the baby out with the bath water. It fixed the system.

If there are faults in the administration of capital punishment, fix them. Strengthen the rules of evidence; require more than one eye-witness, increase the dosage of sodium pentothal in the "cocktail." Develop a State Public Defenders Fund which will pay for the most competent defense appeals. Change arbitrary timing in state law rulings that prohibit introduction of new evidence more than 30 days after a conviction. If new, <u>legitimate</u> evidence is uncovered, make it admissible in any appeal. If defense attorneys are delinquent in making appeals deadlines, punish the attorneys; in that way, attorneys will be more careful to follow deadlines. Fixing problems is possible – even in Texas – in a *Houston Chronicle* story reporting on the Timothy Cole Advisory Panel to investigate the causes of, and ways to prevent, wrongful convictions:[442]

> ...The good news is that we know what causes wrongful convictions, and we know how to fix it. From improving the quality of legal representation for the poor to improving the reliability of evidence in our courtrooms, there are simple reforms that can prevent these tragedies. By implementing reforms to police departments' eyewitness identification procedures, we could reduce many wrongful convictions. Some 85 percent of wrongful convictions in Texas are due to mistaken eyewitness identifications - the No. 1 cause of wrongful

# An Eye for an Eye
*William T. Harper*

convictions in the state and the rest of the nation. Other reforms include recording interrogations to reduce false confessions and creating a fully functioning Texas Forensic Science Commission to ensure reliable science is being used in our crime labs and courtrooms. We simply have to summon the political will to advance all of these reforms.

Texas took an important first step toward repairing our broken justice system by creating the Timothy Cole Advisory Panel to investigate the causes of, and ways to prevent, wrongful convictions. The panel brought together representatives from various sectors of the criminal justice system to work collaboratively on recommendations to prevent wrongful convictions. Texas took another important step toward improving justice when the panel's report was approved by the Texas Task Force on Indigent Defense.

\* \* \*

In seeking to remedy some real and perceived faults with today's death penalty systems, state and federal governments could also follow the lead of the state of Massachusetts. According to the *Boston Globe*, in 2003 an 11-member commission was appointed to develop recommendations for "a new kind of death penalty," one that would be narrowly applied and require the highest possible standard of evidence.[443] The Governor's Council on Capital Punishment, which included scholars, lawyers, and forensics experts, pledged to set aside their opinions about morality and desirability of the death penalty.

What a capital punishment system would cost and how it would be implemented were also outside the commission's purview, according to Joseph Hoffmann, an Indiana University law school professor and a co-chairman of

# An Eye for an Eye
*William T. Harper*

the commission. Hoffmann said, "It was an opportunity to go places nobody had gone before and put together something better than anything that exists today." The commissioners limited death-eligible crimes to a short list of highly aggravated murders: murder committed as political terrorism or to obstruct justice; murder following prolonged torture; multiple murders; or murder committed by someone who had already been convicted of first-degree murder.

Some of the commission's other recommendations required use of scientific evidence and a "no-doubt" standard of guilt to avoid false convictions. It established a system of capital-case-qualified defense lawyers to represent the accused, and incorporated multiple layers of review which would detect bad cases or wrongful convictions.[444] (Regrettably, the Massachusetts' legislature vetoed the commission's recommendations two years later for what some termed "political reasons." Another case of, perhaps, "We Won!!! We Won!!! We Won!!!")

There are ways to fix the system and overcome abolitionists' objections — even their legitimate ones. We don't need to throw the baby out with the bathwater.

One United States Senate report looked at risk from another angle and stated this position thusly:

> "All that can be expected of... [human authorities] is that they take every reasonable precaution against the danger of error.... If errors are...made, this is the necessary price that must be paid within a society which is made up of human beings.[445]"

Steven D. Stewart, Prosecuting Attorney, Clark County, Indiana, stated the death penalty advocates' position most succinctly when he said,

> "I believe in capital punishment. I believe that there are some defendants who have earned the ultimate punishment our society has to offer by

# An Eye for an Eye
*William T. Harper*

committing murder with aggravating circumstances present. I believe life is sacred. It cheapens the life of an innocent murder victim to say that society has no right to keep the murderer from ever killing again. In my view, society has not only the right, but the duty to act in self defense to protect the innocent."[446]

The death penalty isn't the only institution containing risks in exchange for social benefits. We, in fact, mindlessly use far more dangerous institutions that take the lives of innocents by the hundreds every day, like the two or three tons of lethal metal we call automobiles. According to the National Highway Traffic Safety Administration, an estimated 7,630 people died in motor vehicle traffic crashes for the first quarter of 2012.[447] Projecting that number over a full year would mean 30,520 deaths. That comes to almost 3,100 deaths per week! Does that mean we should abolish those killer cars? How can we accept the fact that there were 9,337 alcohol-related deaths in car crashes in 2010?[448] Should we revert back to Prohibition?

How can we accept an average of almost 120 automobile-related fatalities a day – with almost 30-a-day being killed in drunk-driving car wrecks – when the very slim risk of wrongful executions is so *unbearable*? To lose just one innocent person would, indeed, be a tragedy. But, compared with other disasters, that one sickening loss should not be enough to require demolishing the entire capital punishment system – something you can be sure death penalty abolitionists will be demanding with increased and unrelenting vehemence.

Society is getting closer to the noble goal of precluding an innocent's execution. Almost monthly it seems, we read of another case of an inmate being released from prison because great strides in DNA testing have retroactively proven innocence. Science in all fields is improving dramatically. Thirty-five years ago, when the death penalty

# An Eye for an Eye

*William T. Harper*

was reinstated by the Supreme Court, there were no Barry Schecks of the Innocence Project and O. J. Simpson-trial fame making DNA-testing a household word. It then was a new and emerging technique in the field of criminal justice. Consequently, mistakes were made in its early use. But through the decades since 1977, forensic science has made great strides – which have caused some inmates to get out of prison and others to go in.

DNA's predecessor in the field of jurisprudence was fingerprinting. It first came into use about 135 years ago. It was the DNA of its time and at one point was the official method of criminal identification. There are no records of how many innocent people went to prison because of foul-ups – accidental and intentional – in the fingerprinting system. Fingerprinting, just like DNA, had to go through a developmental stage and today, it has reached a point where, according to the U.S. Department of Homeland Security, it has more than 120 million persons' fingerprints on file.[449]

The use of fingerprint identification was one of the principle investigative tools that sent infamous Chicago nurse-killer Richard Speck to Illinois' death row in 1968. Not only are we now using it as identification for our school children, it is also being used today in hospitals for infant identification. Thankfully, during its early mistake-filled history, finger-printing was not thrown out with the bath water.

The goal in all things is to be *as close to perfect* as humanly possible. But everyone makes mistakes. Sometimes, because judgments are made by human beings, patients needlessly die on operating tables. Sometimes, because judgments are made by human beings, people try to beat the railroad train to the crossing and people die. And some day, because judgments are made by human beings, an innocent person *may* tragically die in a prison execution chamber.

Just as wrong as that would be, it would be even more wrong to provide an escape hatch for heinous killers, those at the top of Dr. Michael Stone's "scale of evil," those that have

# An Eye for an Eye
*William T. Harper*

murdered – sometimes again and again – to escape the punishment that fits their crime(s).

\* \* \*

The WHAT IF factor, however, is still out there. Human nature, human frailty being what it is, it seems almost inevitable that someday this nation's perfect record in the execution chamber since 1976 is going to be broken. As Thomas Hill, an attorney for a death row inmate in Ohio who recently won a second stay of execution, put it:

> "We have a criminal system that makes mistakes. If you accept that proposition, it means you have to be prepared for the inevitability that some are sentenced to death for crimes they didn't commit."[450]

We do have a criminal system that makes mistakes. We have federal, state and local governmental systems that makes mistakes. We have an educational system that makes mistakes. We have a commercial-industrial system that makes mistakes. And sometimes those mistakes do cost innocent people their lives. Why? Because all these systems are run by people and people do make mistakes. But that doesn't mean we should abandon our governmental system, our educational system, or our commercial-industrial system. And it surely doesn't mean that because people make mistakes we should abandon our criminal justice system.

The last thing intended by this book is to make an outrageous, abolitionist-like claim the nation's judicial system is without fault; that it is perfect. Not so. As an example, the case of Warren Summerlin in Tempe, Arizona is cited. Summerlin was convicted of the 1981 killing of Brenna Bailey, a 36-year-old finance company administrator. In one of the most bazaar episodes in American jurisprudence, it later developed the defendant's public defender was having

# An Eye for an Eye

*William T. Harper*

"an affair" with the prosecutor, her successor presented an "incompetent" defense, and the judge who handed down the death penalty sentence, was later disbarred for marijuana use while sitting on the bench.[451] Meanwhile, Summerlin got a pass out of the death house due to a Supreme Court case known as the Ring Decision (i.e., the death penalty must be handed down by juries and not judges).

The plusses and minuses of our system of jurisprudence are also illustrated in the case of Coral Eugene Watts. In 1992, it was discovered that Watts, following a plea bargain with the state, would be released under a mandatory release law on April 8, 2006, despite having admitted he killed 13 Texas women in 1981 and 1982. Fortunately, before that release could be affected, Watts was transferred to a prison in Michigan where he was charged with a new first-degree murder in the Wolverine state, convicted, and sentenced to Life-Without-Parole. The system isn't perfect. But most of the time, it works.

\* \* \*

Several times in these pages we have turned to Joshua K. Marquis, district attorney in Clatsop County, Oregon, an official with the National District Attorneys Association, and we do so again:

> "Justice is a work in progress.... Will an innocent person ever be executed? Yes, it's possible. The other question nobody has addressed is: how many innocent people will die if we don't have the death penalty?"[452]

To that end, consider this: As previously noted herein, 1,302 murderers have been executed in the United States since the death penalty moratorium was reversed in 1976. Regardless of how the death penalty abolitionists want to argue, that means *at least* 1,302 men, women and children

# An Eye for an Eye
*William T. Harper*

have suffered unspeakable deaths at the hands of *at least* 1,302 killers. With the abolitionists' advocated life-without-parole as the "panacea," how many of those 1,302 may have ultimately been or will be paroled? How many of them may have killed another inmate or a guard? How many of them may have escaped, perhaps to kill again?

The Death Penalty, which is rightly known as "legal execution"…

>…Is Not "Vengeance" – Reprisal inflicted in retaliation for an injury or an offense.
>
>It Is Not "Revenge" – Retaliating in kind.

And even though it may not be perfect (still, NO ONE executed since the death penalty was reinstituted in the 1976 ruling has been proved definitively innocent)…

>The Death Penalty is Justice.
>It is…
>An Eye for An Eye.

**The End**

# An Eye for an Eye
*William T. Harper*

# Epilogue

### Is There No End?

As noted on page 15 of this effort, this book had its genesis on Thursday, December 2, 2004, at Sam Houston State University in Huntsville, Texas, when this writer listened to Sister Helen Prejean tell an auditorium full of impressionable college students her one-sided story of why the death penalty should be abolished. On March 21, 2007 late at night, I finally wrote what I thought was "The End" that you see closing Chapter 10 above with the manuscript subject only to some last-minute inserts and some subsequent editing of the initial manuscript for *An Eye for An Eye*.

On the late night/early morning of March 23-24, about 72 hours after breathing that huge sigh of relief, I sat in my family room, mindlessly surfing the television set therein, hoping to banish the recurring nightmares of Jessica Lunsford, Megan Kanka, David LeBlanc and Loretta Ann Bourque, Faith Hathaway, Elizabeth Peña and Jennifer Ertman and all those other brutalized victims in these pages who were gruesomely murdered by monstrous killers. The remote control unit brought me to a CSPAN2 program already in progress. It was entitled: "Death Penalty, Race and *McCleskey v. Kemp*, 20th Anniversary." The program had been videotaped on March 19, 2007 at – here we go again, *déjà vu* – the University of Miami's law school in Coral Gables, Florida.

This time it was not Sister Prejean putting on her one-woman stand against the death penalty. It was FOUR college professors and one member of the NAACP Legal Defense and Education Fund all spouting the same party line: Abolish the Death Penalty. Once again, there was absolutely no

# An Eye for an Eye
*William T. Harper*

counterpoint, no defense, no one to refute the arguments made by the learned-types in this classroom setting with a similarly impressionable audience of young people as the very same lines that outraged me some 26 months earlier at Sam Houston State University were iterated and reiterated.

I could very easily write another chapter for this book on the misstatements, the blatant subterfuge, the exaggerations, the innuendoes, etc., presented in that law school classroom. For instance, Stephen Bright, visiting professor at Yale and Harvard universities and President, Southern Center for Human Rights, flatly proclaimed Life-Without-Parole is the unassailable answer to the death penalty. It was the same old lock-them-up-forever-and-they'll-never-kill-again fallacy.

Bright further charged...

> "If you're facing the death penalty in Houston, you're going to get some terrible lawyer. Almost by definition, you're going to get some walking violation of the Sixth Amendment to represent you. Every member of the bench there, maybe save one, was a prosecutor in district attorney Johnny Holmes' office."

Once again, death penalty opponents "take no prisoners" as they lambaste and insult everyone who doesn't agree with their position. Also, nobody on the Miami University panel bothered to remind Professor Bright that Johnny Holmes retired as Harris County, Texas district attorney almost seven years prior to Bright's slanderous statement.

Panelist Christina Swarns, with the NAACP Legal Defense and Education Fund, replicated Sister Prejean's device of dredging up old news and making it sound current. The nun did that with her report about some racial slurs in a Dallas district attorneys' training manual written more than 40 years previously and which had been revised and re-

# An Eye for an Eye
*William T. Harper*

written several times since. Ms. Swarns duplicated the innuendo while boasting of having a video tape-recording of a Philadelphia prosecutor "teaching" new prosecutors how to stack a jury.

What Ms. Swarns didn't tell the student audience in this latest instance of a "Kangaroo Trial" against the death penalty, was the video tape she was presenting as "Exhibit A" was more than 20 years old. She left the impression that such distasteful activities are going on at that very moment. Her charge was a 21$^{st}$ Century version of "McCarthyism."

In the first place, as no one on the panel nor in the audience challenged, neither the defense nor the prosecution has to "stack a jury" anymore. Both sides have plenty of access to a plethora of "jury consultants" who will legally do all the "stacking" necessary for either side. She further compounded her subterfuge by implying this one case in Philadelphia was universal throughout the judicial system. Professor David Baldus from Iowa University reinforced the deception by chiming in: *"This* is what's going on in Philly."

It is? Now?

Getting back to the usual switch game of who really is the "victim" in these barbaric murder cases, Ms. Swarns talked about "a gentleman" named Angel Riaz whose case she handled post-sentencing. Riaz came home from work one night, picked up his five-year-old daughter, put her in his car, drove to a bridge and dropped her into the river below where she drowned. In an effort to get his death sentence reduced by "reason of insanity," she went to his former home in Puerto Rico and interviewed his family about his early years.

She found out he was raised in poverty, had no shoes as a child and little clothes. He was abused by his brutal father. With this usual attempt to elicit sympathy for the killer by going on at great length about his impoverished youth, one is again tempted to scream, "So What!!!" How many thousands if not millions of other kids were raised under similar if not worse conditions and didn't go dropping five-year-old babies into the river?

# An Eye for an Eye

*William T. Harper*

We could go on and on. Almost every day there are new outrages to add to this story – such as this one:

Steven J. Hayes and Joshua A. Komisarjevsky were found guilty of capital felony killing, kidnapping, arson and sexual assault in the home invasion murders of Jennifer Hawke-Petit, age 48, and her daughters Hayley, 17, and Michaela, 11. The three victims were tied up, raped, doused in gasoline and left to die in a fire that consumed their Cheshire, Connecticut home.

The husband/father in this ghastly savagery, Dr. William Petit, survived a brutal beating and an attempted arson murder. He has not yet returned to his medical practice. On January 27, 2012, Komisarjevsky was sentenced to death by lethal execution. Hayes was also given an execution date, May 22, 2012. However, the State of Connecticut has since outlawed its death penalty on a retroactive basis. How long will it be before it's total....

Yes, we could go on and on. But you, like me, might be asking....

Is there no end?

\* \* \*

# An Eye for an Eye
*William T. Harper*

# Post Script

As non-fiction writers, we're constantly told, "You have to have a platform" to get your work in book stores, etc. Generally speaking, that means you have to practically guarantee a built-in audience eager to read your "deathless prose."

Another question put to us by literary agents and kindly publishers is: "What makes you the 'authority' to write about this subject?"

I can't say that I have any kind of a platform – even though this is my fifth book, two of which were prize-winners.

But, I *sure as Hell am* an authority of the subject of the death penalty and why it needs to be enforced. One of my sons is the Brian Patrick, the University of Minnesota student mentioned in the Dedication at the outset of this book and on Page 210.

# An Eye for an Eye

*William T. Harper*

# An Eye for an Eye
*William T. Harper*

# INDEX

117 wrongly convicted, **223-25, 227-28**
23rd Psalm, **20**
25 Innocent People Executed, **227**
401-K pension plans, **205**
*54-40 or Fight!* **44**
9/11, 21, **46**
*a political game,* **145, 216**
Abbott, Jack Henry, **269-271, 274, 278**
Abdel-Rahman, Omar, **115**
abolition lobby, **18**
Abraham, Lynne, **75**
Abu Ghraib prison, **15**
Abu-Jamal, Mumia, **277-279, 286**
*abysmally inept,* **151, 263**
Academy Award, **15, 23, 182-3, 198, 209**
Acts 7:54, **266**
Adams, James, **19, 65-67**
Addison-Wesley, **278**
Aden, Richard, **270-71**
Administrative Segregation (ad-seg), **116**
African-Americans, **113, 247**
Aggie-hoe, **203**
Aimee, Laura, **86**
Ake, Glen Burton, **184**
Al Qaeda, **15**
Alaskans Against the Death Penalty, **27**

Alberi, Albert, **59**
Alcatraz of the Rockies, **114**
Alcatraz, **42**
Alderson Federal Prison Camp, **201**
Alexander, Herb, **121**
Alford, Jr., William, **129, 175-76**
Alger, Horatio, **172**
Algerians, **40-41**
All is fair in love and war, **151, 163**
Allen, Clarence Ray, **117-118, 154**
Allen, George, **39**
Allen, Kenneth, **231-32**
Allridge, James Vernon, **181-83, 274, 289**
Allridge, Ronald, **183**
America's Biggest Serial Killer, **263**
*American Academy of Psychiatry and the Law Journal,* **241**
American Airlines Flight #11, **21, 46**
American Airlines, **308**
American Bar Association (ABA), **305-07**
American Civil Liberties Union (ACLU), **29, 50, 81, 211, 227, 259**

# An Eye for an Eye
*William T. Harper*

American Correctional Association (ACA), **189**
American Lawyer magazine, **305-06**
American Medical Association (AMA), **32, 302, 305**
American Red Cross, **299**
Amnesty International, **27, 29, 43, 211, 217, 229, 259**
Angelucci, Joseph, **129**
Angola Prison, **37, 111-12, 129, 174, 176, 190, 192**
anti-abolitionists, **30**
*Anything for Billy*, **173**
*Anything Goes*, **147**
Arapahoe County court house, **127**
Arizona Supreme Court, **139-41**
*Arizona v. James Darrell Johnson*, **26**
*Arizona v. Willie Lee Richmond*, **26**
Arlington Circuit Court, **127**
Aryan Brotherhood, **94, 191, 209**
Aryan Nation, **113**
*Asbury Park* (N. J.) *Press*, **106, 109**
Asner, Ed, **277-78**
Associated Press, **158, 179, 251**
atomic-bombs, **304**
Atta, Mohammed, **21, 46**
Attila the Hun, **174**

Atwood, David, **164-67**
Auschwitz, **22**
Aviation Safety Network, **308**
*Ayers v. Belmontes*, **125**
Babylon, **296**
*Bad Boy from Rosebud*, **69, 89, 206, 296**
Baez, Joan, **211**
Bailey, Brenna, **314**
Baird, Charlie, **112**
Baird, Nancy, **86**
Baker, B.R., **135**
Baker, Brenda, **86**
Baker, Michael, **216-17**
Baldus, David, **163, 319**
Baldwin, Alec, **277-78**
Baldwin, Tim, **104**
Ball, Brenda, **86**
*Baltimore Sun*, **256**
Barlieb, Joanne, **106-07, 109**
Barnes, Valerie, **127**
Barnett, Adam, **235**
Baruch Performing Arts Center, **202**
Basie, William (Count), **288**
Baylor College of Medicine, **249**
*Baze vs. Rees*, **301**
Baze, Ralph, **301**
Beamer, Todd, **20**
Beardslee, Donald, **142**
Becker, Gary, **77**
Bedau, Hugo A., **18, 81, 226, 228**

324

# An Eye for an Eye
*William T. Harper*

Bedau-Radelet study, **18, 226-27**
Beeks, Ricky, **120**
*Believe it or Not*, **266**
Bell, Robert E., **275**
*Belly of the Beast, The*, **270**
Belmont Stakes, **261**
Benallal, Nordin, **91**
Benetton, **286**
Benjamin, Stacey, **142**
Bennett, Alex, **112**
Bennett, William, **129-30**
Berkowitz, David, **23, 225, 247**
Bermuda Triangle, **300**
Beto, George. J., **27, 44**
beyond a shadow of a doubt, **25**
Bidinotto, Robert James, **95**
Biegenwald, Richard, **97**
Big Apple, The, **151, 270**
Big Lie, The, **50, 229, 234, 244, 261**
Billy the Kid, **173**
bin Laden, Osama, **174**
Bird, Rose, **56**
Bittaker, Lawrence Sigmund, **157, 289**
Black Panthers, **272**
Blackmun, Harry A., **44, 46, 78, 308**
Blagojevich, Rod, **77**
Blair, Jayson, **212, 230**
Blanton, Stanton Winston, **135-36**
*Blood in My Eye*, **272**
Blue Ridge Mountains, **204**
Bogart, Humphrey, **280**
*Bon Appetit* magazine, **142, 150, 306**
Bonaparte, Napoleon, **80**
bone-marrow transplant, **210**
Bonin, William, **76, 103**
Bonney, William H., **173**
Bonnie (Parker) and Clyde (Barrow), **173**
Bosak, William, **232**
*Boston Globe*, **212, 273, 277, 310**
Bourque, Loretta Ann, **37-38, 48, 73, 118, 178-81, 185, 197, 199-200, 211, 213, 317**
Bowman, Margaret, **86, 88**
Brace, Michele J., 59
Bradbury, Ray, **280**
Bradeholt, Joseph, **121**
Brand, Robert, **70-71**, 73
Braniff Airlines, **308**
Brazzil, Jim, **250-51**
Brewer, Clinton, **287-88**
Brewster, Mark, **180, 196, 209**
Bridge, Warren, **95**
*Brief Against Death*, **271**
Bright, Stephen, **128, 318**
Brisbon, Jr., Henry, **34-35, 161**
Britt, Joe Freeman, **219**
*Broken System, A*, **49**
Brook, Catherine, **212**
Broomstick Murderer, **70**

Browling, Thomas, **301**
Brown, Andrea, **149**
Brown, Daniel James, **303**
Brown, Edgar, **66**
Brown, John, **214**
Brown, Pat, **281**
Brown, Reg, **50, 54**
Bryan, William Jennings, **172**
Buchenwald, **22**
Buckley, Jr., William F., **271-72, 274**
Bundy, Theodore (Ted) Robert, **23, 38, 42, 76, 85, 87-88, 91, 202, 225, 247, 293, 299**
Bureau of Criminal Justice, **83**
Bureau of Justice, **42. 118, 159, 247**
Burger, Warren, **118**
Burkett, Don, 47, **264-65**
Burnett, Lester A. (Smiley), **274**
burning at the stake, **46, 162**
Bush, George W., **256, 263**
Bush, Jeb, **252**
Busken, Jewell (Juli), **79**
Buss, Phillip, **135**
Bustamante, Alyssa, **245**
Butcher of Baghdad, **80**
California Assembly, **286**
California's death penalty law, **125**
*Callins v. Collins*, **44**

Camp Cupcake, **201, 206-207**
Campaign to End the Death Penalty, **27**
Campbell, Caryn, **86**
Camus, Albert, **259**
Canadian Coalition Against the Death Penalty, **204, 263**
*Canadian Journal of Behavioral Science*, **227**
Canfield, Susan, **82**
Cannon, Joe, **254**
Cantu, Peter Anthony, **239-40**
Cantu, Ruben, **165-67**
capital punishment, **8-9, 16-18, 25, 33, 51, 70-71, 73, 78, 82-83, 96-97, 128, 144-45, 156, 179, 218, 227, 229, 242, 244-45, 251-52, 256, 269, 271, 275-76, 282-83, 285-87, 296, 298, 309-12**
Capital Punishment: Arguments for Life and Death, **227**
Capone, Al, **167**
Capote, Truman, **177**
carboxyhemoglobin (COHb), **303**
Carnahan, Mel, **287**
*Casablanca*, **280**
Cassell, Paul G., **52, 54**
Catechism, 1992 version, **294**

# An Eye for an Eye
*William T. Harper*

Catechism, 1997 version, **294-95**
Cauthen, James, **51-52, 54**
CBS Evening News, **210**
Center for Public Policy Survey Research Institute, **18**
Cernak, Anton, **150**
*Certiorari*, **139-40**
Chaffin, Benny Lee, **99**
chain-gangs, **203**
Chapman, A. Jay, **250**
Chesimard, JoAnne, **123-124**
Chessman, Caryl, **271, 280-81**
Chi Omega sorority, **88**
*Chicago Tribune*, **76-77, 227, 230**
Chmielewski, Leoma, **188**
Cimo, Tony, **94**
Clark County prosecutor's office, **166**
Clark, Douglas, **289**
Clark, Jason, **131-32**
Clements, Diane, **29**
Clendennen, Brian, **182-83**
Clendennen, Shane, **183**
Clinton Correctional Institution for Women, **124**
Clinton, Roger, **198**
Clinton, William, J., **105, 198, 256-57**

Coalition of Arizonians to Abolish the Death Penalty, **28**
Cobb, Ty, **304**
Cochran, Johnny, **198-99**
Coe, Robert Glen, **267-69**
*Coker v. Georgia*, **228**
*cold sandwiches*, **150**
Cole, Timothy, **309-310**
*Coleman v. Thompson*, **45**
Coleman, Roger Keith, **45-46, 164, 167, 282**
collateral damage, **20**
Coloradans Against the Death Penalty, **28, 31**
Connecticut Network to Abolish the Death Penalty, **28**
Columbia Correctional Institute, **121**
Columbia University law school, **303**
Columbia University, **24**
*Communist Manifesto*, **259**
Community Of St. Egidio, **28**
Concannon, Martin, **133-136, 296**
Condit, Gary, **198**
Congressional Record, **102**
Conlay, Lydia, **249**
Constitution of the State of Louisiana, **121, 147**
Constitution of the United States, **162, 291, 293**
Contract with America, **259**

# An Eye for an Eye
*William T. Harper*

Cook County public defender's office, **161**
Cook, Patrick, **33**
Cook, William, **277**
Cooke, Janet, **212, 230**
*Cool Hand Luke*, **203**
Cooley, Melanie, **86**
Cooper, Dan, **137-38, 141-142, 146, 148-149, 151**
**Cooper, Kevin, 273**
copyright laws, **160**
Corcoran penitentiary, **203**
Corner Pack Store, **178**
Cornett, Michael, **112**
Corzine, Jon, **109, 223**
cost of incarceration, **155-156**
Costan, James, **123**
Couey, John Evander, **11-15, 185, 294, 297**
Coulter, Ann, **227**
County Line Lounge, **61**
court-appointed attorney, **22, 55, 137, 147, 166, 276**
Cox, Jerry, **219**
crack cocaine, **95, 102, 275**
Creech, Thomas Eugene, **99**
*Crime and Punishment*, **207**
Criminal Justice Legal Foundation, **29, 109**
Criminology Research Institute, **69**
Critical Resistance, **130-31**
Cronkite, Walter, **162**
Crook, Shirley, **242-43**
Crouch, Ben M., **24**
cruel and unusual punishment, **15, 43, 51, 136, 143, 145, 157, 162, 176, 184, 241, 250, 280, 294, 298**
*Cry Me a River*, **300**
C-Span, 157, **269**
Cuevas, Debbie Lynn (*nee* Morris), **175, 180, 196, 208**
Culver, Lynette, **86**
Cunningham, Julie, **86**
Curtis, Susan, **86**
Dachau, **22**
Dade, Arthur, **113**
Dahmer, Jeffrey, **23, 85, 120-21, 174, 206, 212, 225, 247, 297-98**
Daily Nebraskan.com, **212**
Danson, Ted, **273**
*Dante's Inferno*, **20**
Dardis, Fred, **137**
Darrow, Clarence, **171**
Davidson, Bill, **275**
Davis, Brad, **212**
Davis, John Lee, **101**
Davis, Ossie, **277-78**
Day, Dorothy, **259**
Dayroom, **201**
De Salvo, Albert, **23, 225, 247**
*Dead Man Walking* movie, **182**
*Dead Man Walking* opera, **30**

# An Eye for an Eye
*William T. Harper*

*Dead Man Walking* stage play, 30
*Dead Man Walking*, 8, 15, 18-19, 21, 30, 47-48, 65, 67, 104, 188, 190, 192, 195, 213, 254, 256, 261
Dean, Jerry Lynn, 218-19
Dean, Kenneth, 189
*Death of Innocents, The*, 8, 11, 21, 27, 40, 43-44, 47-48, 55, 57, 61-62, 64, 73, 166, 181, 197-98, 211, 254, 261, 264, 266, 294, 304
Death Penalty Focus of California, 28
Death Penalty Information Center, 211, 226, 253
Death Penalty Representation Project, 305-06
death penalty revisionists, 90, 172-73, 180, 184, 194, 198, 201, 208, 211, 213, 217
Death Penalty Study Commission, 106
Death Penalty Web Page, 29
Declaration of Independence, 260
Del Papa, Frankie Sue, 50, 54
DeSherlia, Thomas, 110
desktop computers, 205
desktop publishing, 205
Deuteronomy, 292
Devine, Kathy, 85
Diaz, Angel Nieves, 253
Dickerson, Charles, 135-136
Dilaudid, 218
Dillbeck, Donald, 98
Dillinger, John, 173
Dirty Dozen killers, 75
DNA, 25, 50, 45, 58, 61-62, 90, 127, 164, 166, 265, 307, 312-13
do no harm, 298
Doctorow, E. L., 278
Doe, Jane, 86
Dogg, Nate, 199
Dogg, Snoop, 30
Doom, Nancy, 120
Dostoevsky, Fyodor, 207
Douglas, William O., 281
Douglass, Brooks, 184
Douglass, Leslie, 184
Douglass, Marilyn, 184
Douglass, Richard, 184
Dow, David R., 79-80, 125, 236, 276
Doxtator, Jamie, 120
*Dr. Frankenstein*, 173, 270
*Dragnet*, 39
Draughon, Martin, 234-35
Dreyfus, Alfred, 281
Dreyfuss, Richard, 273
Druce, Joseph L., 92
Dunman, Mark, 70-71
Durante, Jimmy, 32
Duranty, Walter, 230
Dylan, Bob, 211, 272
Earle, Steve, 288
Eastern Airlines, 308

# An Eye for an Eye
*William T. Harper*

Eastwood, Clint, **217**
editorial bias, **253**
Edwards, Edwin, **104, 122**
Edwards, Nolan, **122**
Efrain Perez, **239, 243-44**
Eighth Amendment, **143**
Eilender, Jeffrey M., **59**
Einstein, Albert, **7**
Eisenhower, Dwight D., **281, 303**
Elledge, Mary, **286**
Elliot, David, **252**
Elmore, Phillip E., **148**
Emory University, **77**
Enron, **160**
Equal Justice Initiative of Alabama, **255**
Ertman, Jennifer, **78, 213, 239-40, 243-44, 217**
Ertman, Randy, **78**
Estelle, Jr., W. J., **71**
European Union, **285**
Exodus 20:13, **293**
*Exxon Valdez*, **236**
Falk, John, **82**
Falwell, Jerry, **219**
Farmer, Millard, **47**
Farquar, Kelley, **288**
Farrell, Mike, **30, 273, 281-282**
Faulkner, Danny, **277-78**
Faulkner, Maureen, **278**
feces-thrown-in-their-face, **204**
Federal Bureau of Investigation (FBI), **100, 118**
Felde, Wayne Robert, **98**
Felion, Marylyn, **212**
Fenway Park, **277**
Ferguson, James E., **103-104**
figures don't lie but liars figure, **49**
Findings of Fact and Conclusions of Law, **139-140**
Fitzgerald, Charles, **97**
Flicker, Kathryn, **222**
Florida State University, **88**
Floridians for Alternatives to the Death Penalty, **28**
Floyd, Charles (Pretty Boy), **173**
Foerster, Werner, **123**
Forman, Jay, **212**
Fortenberry, Thomas J., **76**
Fraternal Order of Police, **278**
Free, James, **146**
*Freed to Kill*, **95**
Friday, Sergeant Joe, **39**
frivolous suits, **141-42, 145, 149, 151-52, 157, 172, 213**
Frost, Robert, **280**
Ft. Knox, Kentucky, **146**
*Furman v. Georgia*, **34, 71-72, 84, 90, 101, 207, 224. 251, 282**
G. I. Bill, **246**

# An Eye for an Eye
*William T. Harper*

Gacy, John Wayne, **23, 38, 76, 85, 174, 185, 212, 225, 247, 289**
Gage, Allan, **136**
Gallo, John, **305-06**
Gallup poll, **7, 29, 269**
Gandhi, Mohandas K., **8**
Garcia, Jesse, **93**
Garcia, Michael, **93**
Garman, J. Kent, **252**
Garofalo, Janeane, **273**
Garrent, Daniel Ryan, **218**
Garrett, Dina, **17**
gas-chamber, **134**
Gaskins, Donald, **94**
Gates, Bill, **24**
Geddling, Patty, **142**
Gein, Ed, **289**
Gekas, George W., **51**
Genao, Divina, **95**
Genesis, **292**
Geoghan, John J., **92-93**
Geragos, Mark, **198**
Gershwin, George, **264**
*get out of jail free*, **105, 236**
Gideon Bible, **220**
Gillis, Lester, (Baby Face Nelson), **173**
Gilmore, Gary, **271, 297, 303**
gladiator fights, **204**
Glass, Stephen, **212**
glitterati, **15, 30, 182, 202, 269-271, 280, 287-88, 290**
Glover, Danny, **273**
Godwin, Glen Stewart, **95-96**
Goebbels, Joseph, **30**
*Going Up the River*, **100**
Goldberg, Jonah, **278**
Goldwater, Barry, **259**
Gomez, Pedro, **166-67**
Gonzalez, Jose Alfredo Ramirez, **149**
*Good Morning America*, **45**
Google, **27, 288**
Governor's Council on Capital Punishment, **310**
Graham, Billy, **219**
Graham, Bob, **66**
Grammy award, **288**
Grant, Ulysses S., **16**
grassy knoll, **299**
Graunger, Thomas, **266**
Gray, Jimmy Lee, **98**
Great Depression, **303**
Great Plains Correctional Facility, **204**
*Green Mile, The*, **217**
Green, Roy Dale, **70-71**
Green, Terry, **189**
Greensville Correctional Center, **127**
*Gregg v. Georgia*, **251**
Griffin, Laura, **142**
Groner, Jonathan, **252**
Ground Zero, **21**
Guerrero, Armando, **234-235**
Guerrero, Richard, **120**
Gulags, **22**
Guthrie, Arlo, **211**
*habeas corpus*, **49, 59, 140-141, 143, 258**

# An Eye for an Eye
*William T. Harper*

Hacking, Lori, **190**
Hacking, Mark, **190**
Hall, Clayton, **135**
Hallinan, Joseph T., **100, 204-05**
Hallinan, Terence, **105-06**
Hamilton, Billy Ray, **117**
Hampton, Marilyn, **104**
Hampton, Steve, **149**
hanging, **41, 162, 182, 278, 293**
Hanks, Tom, **217**
Hanlon, Stephen, **306**
Hardin, Rusty, **128**
Harding, Donald Eugene, **111, 133-142, 297**
*Hardy Boys, The*, **172**
Hargrove Sr., Frank D., **130**
Harlan, John Marshall, **24**
Harper, Bob, **97, 100**
Harper, James, **123**
Harris County Jail, **128**
Harris County, Texas, **7, 260**
Harris, Daniel, **216**
Harris, Jean, **201**
Harris, Robert Alton, **216**
Harvard University, **318**
Harvey, Elizabeth, **42, 170, 176, 186, 193-94, 207-08**
Harvey, Paul, **11, 35**
Harvey, Vernon, **41-42, 186, 207-08**
Hatch, Steven Keith, **184**
Hathaway, Faith Colleen, **41, 73, 121, 129, 151-52, 169-70, 175, 177-78, 180-186, 188, 190-95, 207-09, 211, 214, 262, 297, 317**
Hawke-Petit, Jennifer, **320**
Hawkins, Aubrey, **186-87**
Hawkins, Georgeann, **86**
Hayes, Steven J., **320**
Headley, David, **168**
Healy, Lynda Ann, **85**
Heinous Hall of Fame, **173**
Hemby, Dennis, **73, 181, 198, 211**
Henley, Elmer Wayne, **289**
Hess, Rudolph, **125**
Hiatt, Victor, **120**
Hicks, Stephen, **120**
Hill, Thomas, **314**
Hillman, Harold, **43**
Hills, Walter, **188**
Hinckley Fire, **303**
Hipperson, Marjorie, **89-90**
Hippocratic Oath, **298**
Hitler, Adolph, **22-23, 30, 87, 125, 223, 303**
HMO's, **205**
Hodge, Cory, **113-15**
Hoffmann, Joseph, **310**
*hoi polloi*, **269**
Holmes, Angela, **149**
Holmes, Johnny, **128, 318**
Holocaust, **22, 87**
Holy Grail, **45**
homosexual murders, **63, 157, 284**
Honeyman, Jennifer, **227**

# An Eye for an Eye
*William T. Harper*

Honorary Citizen of Palermo, Italy, **40, 286**
Horswell, Cindy, **183**
*Houston Chronicle*, **18, 78, 114, 131, 183, 234, 257, 260, 309**
Houston Peace and Justice Center, **164**
Houston Police Department crime lab, **235**
*Houston Press*, **29**
Howard, Ric, **12**
Howard, Ronald Ray, **178, 275-77**
Hubbard, James B., **153**
Hughes, Chris, **273**
Hughes, Langston, **259**
Hughes, Tony, **121**
Humphreys, Robert J., **40**
Hunton & Williams, **59**
Hurricane Isabel, **231**
Hurricane Katrina, **124**
Hurricane Rita, **124**
Hussein, Saddam, **23, 79-80, 174**
Huston, Anjelica, **273**
Huth, Gerald, **136**
Huxley, Aldous, **280**
I don't know and I don't care, **7**
I-57 murders, **34**
Illinois Coalition against the Death Penalty, **28, 212**
*In Cold Blood*, **177**
Indiana University law school, **310**
*ineffectiveness of counsel*, **152, 254**
inmates raping inmates, **204**
Innocence Project, **45, 313**
intelligentsia, **269, 287**
*International Herald Tribune*, **77**
International Youth for a Moratorium, **28**
Internet, **27, 32, 105, 204, 253, 289-90, 301**
*Investigative Reports*, **101-02**
Iowa University, **319**
Iowans Against the Death Penalty, **28**
Isaacs, Carl Junior, **76**
Isaiah, **197**
Isle of Elba, **80**
Italian parliament, **286**
IV needles, **252**
Ivins, Molly, **278**
Jack the Ripper, **23, 174**
Jackson, George L., **272**
Jackson, Lester, **244-45**
Jackson, Michael, **199**
Jackson, Sarah, **149**
Jackson, Sr., Jesse, **30**
Jagger, Bianca, **30, 219**
James, Jesse, **173**
James, Mary, **104**
Jarrah, Ziad, **20**
Jeffrey, Conrad, **95**
Jensen, D. Lowell, **99, 115**
Jesse James Farm and Museum, **173**
Jessica's Law, **15**

# An Eye for an Eye
*William T. Harper*

Jewell, Jerry, **105**
Jimenez, Porfirio, **148**
Joan of Arc, **46**
John Jay College of Criminal Justice, **49, 51, 54, 163**
Joshua, Valencia, **72-73**
judicial law-making, **301**
Judicial Order, **213**
Julius, Arthur James, **98**
Justice for All, **27-29, 161**
Justice, William Wayne, **71**
Juvenile Death Penalty Speech, **31**
Kaczynski, Ted, **115**
Kahan, Andy, **213, 248, 255, 288-89**
Kangaroo Trial, **319**
Kanka, Maureen, **222**
Kanka, Megan Nicole, **221-23, 317**
*Kansas v. Marsh*, **225**
KAR Car Products Inc., **133**
Kastelhun, Charles Michael, **112**
Kelly, George (Machine Gun), **173**
Kemp, Darryl, **89-90, 168**
Kennedy, John F., **263, 307**
Kent, Debbie, **86**
Kentucky Coalition to Abolish the Death Penalty, **28**
Kentucky Commonwealth Attorney, **233**
Kentucky State Penitentiary (Castle on the Cumberland), **112, 120, 203**
Kentucky Supreme Court, **129**
Keppel, Robert D., **88**
Kevorkian, Jack, **302**
Khmer Rouge, **23**
King County Major Crimes Unit, **88**
King Jr., Martin Luther, **289**
King, Larry, **45, 211**
Kipp, Harold W., **43**
Kirk, Phyllis, **280**
Kirk, Chris, **112**
Kitts, Mary Sue, **117-18**
Kitzhaber, John, **109-10**
Kitzman, Richard, **92**
Klein, Stephen, **164**
Klemm, William R., **249-250**
Knippers, Sonja, **73, 211, 264**
Koch, Edward, **78**
Komisarjevsky, Joshua A., **320**
Koniaris, Leonidas, **248-49**
Korean War, **282**
Kosilek, Cheryl, **131**
Kosilek, Michelle, **131**
Koukl, Greg, **292**
Kraft, Randy Stephen, **157**
Kuklinski, Richard, **23, 225**
Kurtis, Bill, **101**

# An Eye for an Eye
*William T. Harper*

*L'Osservatore Romano*, **281**
Lacy, Oliver, **121**
Lamourie, Tracy, **204**
Land, Shirley, **136**
*Larry King Live*, **45**
Larson, Ray, **154**
Lasseter, Don, **157**
Latzer, Barry, **49, 51-52, 54, 163**
Latzer/Cauthan study, **52, 143**
Lavergne, Gary, **69-71**
law of the land, the, **295-296**
Lawson, David, **187-88, 300**
Leach, Kimberly Ann, **86**
LeBlanc, David, **37-38, 47-48, 73, 118, 177-81, 197, 199-200, 211, 317**
LeBlanc, Lloyd, **48**
Lee, Donald, **59**
Lee, Robert E., **16**
Legal Homicide, **213**
Leon, Francisco, **140**
*Les Miserable*, **46**
Lesbian, Gay, Bisexual and Transgender associations, **106**
Lesniak, Raymond, **107**
*less than competent*, **151**
Let's roll! **20**
LeValley, Kim, **95-96**
Levy, Chandra, **198**
Levy, Lisa, **88**
Lewis, Ernie, **154, 156**
Lewis, Jerry, **280**

Liebengood, Megan, **33-34, 110**
Liebman, James, **49-54**
lies, damned lies, and statistics, **74**
*Life of Riley, The*, **102**
LifeCodes, **61-62**
Life-Without-Parole, **8, 14, 21-22, 32-35, 69, 72, 80, 82-88-96, 101-04, 106-13, 117-26, 128-31, 134, 142, 148, 152, 158, 201, 204, 206-07, 223, 233, 236, 245-246, 262, 282, 290, 299, 315-16, 318**
Lindsey, Errol, **121**
Literati, **30, 269**
*Live from Death Row*, **278**
Lockheed Aircraft Company, **309**
Lockheed L-188 Electra, **308-09**
London, Julie, **300**
*Lonesome Dove*, **173**
Long, Huey Pierce, **259**
Lopez, Steve, **277-78**
Lopez, Wanda, **53**
*Los Angeles Times*, **227**
**Lost Souls: Stop Killing Mentally Retarded and Mentally Ill, 31**
Louisiana Board of Pardons, **195**
Louisiana Department of Corrections, **104**
Lovitt, Robin, **127**

# An Eye for an Eye
*William T. Harper*

Lunsford, Jessica, **11-15, 185, 294, 297, 317**
Luttig, Michael, **59, 144**
M*A*S*H, **282**
Mace, Michelle, **149**
*machinery of death*, **44-45, 308**
Mafia inmates, **118**
Magee, Fibber, **32**
Magee, Mollie, **32**
Maher, Robin, **306**
Mailer, Norman, **30, 269-272, 274, 278, 280**
Malkin, Michelle, **273**
Manard, John, **93**
Mandela, Winnie, **30**
Mandrax, **218**
Mankins, Sharron, **216**
Manson, Charles, **25, 206, 225, 289**
Manson, Donna, **85**
Marijuana, **12, 193, 218, 236, 275, 315**
Marion federal penitentiary, **191**
*Marlboro Man*, **191, 225**
Marquette University, **55**
Marquis, Joshua K., **18, 160-61, 230-31, 315**
Marsellus, Howard, **104, 147**
Marshall, Robert O., **107**
Martin, Jerry Duane, **83**
Martin, John, **128**
Mason, Perry, **264**
Massachusetts Citizens Against the Death Penalty, **28**
Massachusetts Legislature, **311**
Massie, Robert, **282**
Mayeski, John, **216-17**
Mayor, Palermo, Italy, **40**
McAdams, John, **55**
McAdams, Willie Joe, **130**
McCartin, Donald A., **157**
*McCleskey v. Kemp,* **163, 317**
McConnell prison, **100**
McDougal, Susan, **198**
McDuff, Kenneth Allen, **26, 38, 69-73, 75-76, 80, 85, 89-90, 105, 114, 130, 173, 206-08, 247, 282, 295**
McGarry, Patricia, **212**
McGarry, Paul **195**
McIntosh, Tommy, **105**
McMurtry, Larry, **173**
McNair, Richard Lee, **42, 91-92**
McQueen, Harold, **155**
McVeigh, Timothy, **20, 76, 172, 282**
Mease, Darrell J., **286-87**
Mecklenburg Correctional Center, **105**
Medellin, Jose, **239-40**
Medellin, Venacio, **239-40**
Medicaid, **158**
Medicare, **158**
Medlin, Cary Ann, **267-69**
Megan's Law, **222**
*Mein Kampf II*, **22**
*Mein Kampf*, **223**

# An Eye for an Eye
*William T. Harper*

*Memphis Commercial Appeal*, **267**
Men's State Prison, Hardwick, Georgia, **158**
Meramec River, **242**
Michael Unit Prison, **113**
Miller, Arthur, **202**
Miller, Ernest, **120**
Miller, Glenn, **275**
Miller, Robert, **33-34**
Mills, John, **272**
Minnesota Department of Corrections, **210**
Missouri Correctional Center, **113**
mitigating factor, **139, 146, 172, 177**
Mocan, Naci, **77**
Mona Lisa, **275**
*Monkey Trial*, **172**
Montgomery, Lillian, **153**
Moore, Regina, **72-73**
Moratorium 2000, **28**
Morgan, Richard, **34**
Morris, Debbie, **175, 180, 196, 208**
Mother Teresa, **39, 216, 287**
motion for rehearing, **140**
Moussaoui, Zacarias, **115**
MSNBC, **215, 230**
Murder Victim's Families for Reconciliation, **29**
Murderabilia, **32**
Murphy, Lyle, **136**
Murphy, Margaret, **136**
Murrah Federal Building, **20**
Mussolini, Benito, **40**
NAACP Legal Defense and Education Fund, **317-318**
Nagle, Daniel, **101**
Nalley, Mitzi, **288**
Naslund, Denise, **86**
National Center for Policy Analysis, **96**
National Conference of State Legislatures, **158**
National District Attorneys Association, **18, 315**
National Football League, **43**
*National Geographic Channel Presents*, **119**
National Highway Traffic Safety Administration, **312**
National Public Radio – *Morning Edition*, **49-50, 116**
*National Review*, **271, 278**
*Native Son*, **287**
Naumoff, Boris G., **282**
Nazi Germany, **236**
Nebraska Supreme Court, **235**
*Neighbor v. Neighbor*, **307**
Neufeld, Peter, **45**
Nevada Attorney General, Office of, **50, 54**
*New American, The*, **96**

# An Eye for an Eye
*William T. Harper*

New Jersey Supreme Court, **223**
New Mexico Coalition to Repeal the Death Penalty, **28**
*New Orleans Times-Picayune*, **179**
***New Republic***, **212**
New Testament, **292**
New York Court of Appeals, **57**
New York firefighters and police officers, **21**
*New York Times*, **31, 212, 227, 230, 273, 278**
New York University, **24, 255**
New Yorkers Against the Death Penalty, **28**
Nichols, Brian, **42**
Nichols, Terry, **115**
Nobel Peace Prize, **77, 273**
Nobles, Jon Wayne, **288**
Norris, Roy, 157, **289**
North Dakota Farmers' Union Grain Elevator, **91**
Northrup, Melissa, **72-73**
Northwest Orient Airlines, **308**
O'Brien, Derrick Sean, **78, 239-40, 243**
O'Dell, Joseph, **35, 38-40, 43, 46, 55-65, 73, 167, 208-209, 262, 264, 266, 286, 299**
O'Malley, Martin, **252**
O'Neal, Robert Earl, **113**
O'Toole, Otis, **215**
*Officers Killed and Assaulted, 2004* report, **100**
Ogg, Kim, **161, 231**
Ogloff, James, **227**
Ohio State University, **252**
Ohio Supreme Court, **148**
Ohioans to Stop Executions, **28**
Oklahoma Department of Corrections, **189**
Oklahoma Medical Examiner, **250**
Old Testament, **292**
Oliverson, Denise, **86**
Olsson, Karen, **275-77**
Olten, Elizabeth, **245**
*Orange County* (California) *Register*, **94**
Orange County Men's Jail, **123**
Ott, Janice, **86**
out with the bathwater, **301, 305, 307-08, 311**
over-worked and under-funded, **162**
Palmer, Frank, **136**
Palmes, Timothy Charles, **98**
Paranzino. Michael, **218**
Parents of Murdered Children (POMC), **286**
Parker, Ron, **110**
Parks, Kathy, **86**
Paul, Weiss, Rifkind, Wharton & Garrison, **59**

# An Eye for an Eye
*William T. Harper*

Peabody Award, **274**
Pearson PLC, **278**
Peña, Elizabeth, **78, 213, 239, 243-44, 317**
Penn, Sean, **30, 180**
Pennsylvania Abolitionists United Against the Death Penalty, **28**
Percodan, **218**
*Perfect Justice: Death Row and the Appeals Process*, **157**
permanent cigarette lighters, **205**
Peterson, Conner, **190**
Peterson, Laci, **190**
Peterson, Scott, **121, 190, 198-199**
Petit, Hayley, **320**
Petit, Michaela, **320**
Petit, William, **320**
Petka, Edward, **34, 230**
*Phil Donahue Show*, **45**
Picasso, **290**
Pima County Superior Court, **138-39**
Pinocchio, **85**
Placidyls, **218**
Pluto, **305**
Pope Benedict XVI, **294**
Pope John Paul II, **39, 287, 294**
Pope, Tony, **217-18**
*Porgy and Bess*, **264**
Porter, Cole, **147**
post-conviction relief, **50, 96, 139-40, 149**
poster boy of capital punishment, **62, 70, 166**
Pot, Pol, **23**
Potter, Karen, **31**
Power-Ball lottery, **298**
Prejean, Dalton, **99-100**
Prejean, Sister Helen, **8, 11, 15-21, 27, 30, 35, 39-42, 44, 46-47, 57-58, 61, 64, 72, 75, 78, 90, 92-93, 99-100, 111, 147, 152, 159, 163, 171, 174-80, 182-83, 187, 190-98, 207, 209, 221, 213, 219, 223, 229, 247, 255, 258-59, 261-65, 273, 283, 286, 292-92, 294-96, 304, 317-18**
Presentation High School, **17, 247**
*Primetime Live*, **45**
Prince William Sound, **236**
Prison Industrial Complex, **130**
Prison Talk, **27**
Prohibition, **312**
Pruett, Robert Lynn, **100**
Pruitt, Allen, **97**
*Psycho*, **289**
public defenders, **155-56**
Pulitzer Prize, **230, 269, 274**
pursuit of happiness, **260**
Quinnipiac University poll, **108**
Rabelais, John, **292**
racial bias, **31, 163, 229**
Radelet, Lofquist, and

# An Eye for an Eye
*William T. Harper*

Bedau, **226**
Radelet, Michael L., **18, 226-28**
Rader, Dennis, **185, 300**
Rains, Claude, **280**
Ramirez, Richard, **288**
Rancourt, Susan, **86**
RAND Corporation, **163-164**
Rather, Dan, **210**
Ratzinger, Joseph, **294**
Ray, James Earl, **289**
Reagan, Ronald, **192, 255, 258-59**
Rector, Rickey Ray, **256-57**
*Red Light Bandit*, **280**
Redford, Robert, **182-83**
Reed, Colleen, **72-73**
Reed, Susan D., **166**
Reid, Paul Dennis, **149**
Reid, Richard, **115**
*Remember Pearl Harbor!* **44, 279**
*Remember the Alamo!* **44**
*Remember the Maine!* **44**
Resendez, Angel Maturino, **161**
*Reuters News Service*, **91, 108**
Reyes, Ramiro, **166**
Reynolds, Morgan, **96**
Riaz, Angel, **319**
*Rich and Famous, The*, **198, 272, 290**
Richards, Ann, **257-68**
Riley, Leandress, **188, 300**
Rivas, George, **186-87**
Roache, Charles, **76**
Robbins, Tim, **30, 277-78**
Robertson, Pat, **219**
Robertson, Shelley, **86**
Robison, Clay, **257**
Rodricks, Dan, **256**
Rodriguez, George, **235**
Romans 13:1-2, **291**
Romans 13:3, **292**
Romney, Mitt, **9, 79**
Roosevelt, Franklin D., **150, 303**
*Roper v. Simmons*, **241, 244, 284**
Rose, Walter, **95**
Roselawn Cemetery, **179**
Rosenthal, C. A., **143, 154, 162, 234-35, 254**
Rosenthal, Lee, **234-35**
Rowe, Virginia, **212**
*Ruiz v. Estelle*, **71**
Ruiz, David, **71**
Rushdie, Salman, **278**
Ryan, George, **34, 77, 103, 122, 161, 230-33**
Ryder, Winona, **199**
Ryen, Doug, **273**
Ryen, Jessica, **273**
Ryen, Josh, **273**
Ryen, Peggy, **273**
Sam Houston State University, **15-16**
San Quentin State Prison, **117, 119, 121, 142, 203, 272**
Sanchez, Anthony, **79**
Sandoval, Frank, **239**
Sandoval, Roman, **239**
Santiago, Ronald, **149**

# An Eye for an Eye
*William T. Harper*

Sarandon, Susan, **15, 30, 182-83, 202, 209, 270, 274, 277-78, 280, 289-90**
Saturday-Night Special, **210**
Saucedas, David, **93**
Scale of Evil, **24, 26, 28, 102, 313**
Scalia, Antonin, **16, 18-19, 44, 57, 78, 227, 259, 292, 295**
*Scarsdale Diet*, **201**
Scarver, Christopher, **121**
Schartner, Helen, **39, 60, 64-65, 73**
Scheck, Barry, **68, 165, 313**
Schenksville, PA, **20**
Scott, Robert C., **51**
Scudder, Kevin, **46, 115, 145, 254, 263, 290**
Sears, Anthony, **120**
Sears, Roebuck & Co., **215, 286**
Seattle Institute for Forensics, **88**
security housing unit (SHU), **116**
Selepak, Patrick, **126**
Serpico, Andy, **146**
Serpico, Bonnie, 146
Sewell, Jr., Robert A., **149**
Shakur, Assata, **123**
Shakur, Tupac, **178**
*shamefully inadequate,***151, 163**
shank, **34, 101, 120**
*share the wealth*, **259**
shark-tank, **119**
Sharpton, Al, **257**
Shawcross, Arthur, **289**
Sheets, Jeremy, **235**
Shelley, Mary Wollstonecraft, **270**
Shepherd, Michael, **33-34, 110**
Shinn, Buren, **187**
Shinn, Wayne, **187**
shiv, **113, 120**
*Shreveport Times*, **265**
Sidney Austin Brown & Wood, **305-06**
silent majority, **7, 31**
*Silent Night*, **251, 298**
Simmons, Christopher, **241-43**
Simpson, O. J., **58, 165, 169**
Sinatra, Frank, **280**
Sinclair, Jerry, **113**
Sing Sing Prison, **43**
Sinthasomphone, Konerak, **121**
Sitzman, Richard, **79**
*Slate*, **212**
sleeping lawyer, **32, 149-151, 253, 255-56, 260, 276, 300**
Slosson Intelligence Test, **265-66**
Smith, D. P., **169**
Smith, Debbie, **86**
Smith, Eddie, **120**
Smith, Edgar, **271-72, 274**
Smith, Jr., W. Jack, **144**

Smith, Melissa, **86**
Smith, Patricia, **212**
Smith, Preston, **51**
Smith, Robert S., **59, 62**
Smith, Sam, **105**
social justice, **208**
Social Security, **93, 103, 205**
Soghanalian, Sarkis, **199**
*Soledad Brother*, **272**
Soledad Prison, **114**
Somas, **218**
Sonnier, Eddie James, **35, 37-38, 47, 118, 172, 178-179, 185, 197, 199-200, 211, 214, 247**
Sonnier, Elmo Patrick, **35, 37-38, 47-48, 76, 78, 111, 118, 171-72, 174, 178-80, 193-94, 197, 199-200, 208, 211, 213-14, 225, 247, 261-262**
South Florida Committee Against the Death Penalty, **28**
Southern Center for Human Rights, **318**
Sowell, Thomas, **233**
Spandau Prison, **22, 126**
Speck, Richard, **23, 101-102, 185, 225, 247, 288, 313**
Spencer, James R., **58-59**
spit masks, **116**
Springsteen, Bruce, **30**
Squire, Clark, **123**
Stalin, Joseph, **22-23**
Stand to Reason, **292**
Stanford School of Medicine, **252**
*Stanford v. Kentucky,* 241
Starkweather, Charles, **76**
*State of Texas v. Ruben Cantu,* **166**,
State Public Defenders Fund, **309**
Stateville prison, **34**
statistics don't lie but statisticians do, **74**
stay of execution, **139-40, 265, 281, 314**
Steenburgen, Mary, **273**
Steinem, Gloria, **182**
Stevenson, Bryan, **255**
Stewart, Potter, **78**
Stewart, Steven D., **311**
*Sting*, **182**
Stinney, George, **266**
Stoick, Robert, **136**
Stokes, Edward Harvey, **123**
Stone, Michael, **24-25, 102, 313**
Stone, Oliver, **278**
Strap-down teams, **188-189, 293**
Straughter, Curtis, **120**
Streisand, Barbra, **269, 272**
Students Against the Death Penalty, **27, 212**
Sturgill, Calvin, **202**
subcommittee of the Judiciary Committee, **51, 54**

Suff, William, **289**
Sullivan, Edna Louise, **70, 73**
Summerlin, Warren, **314-315**
SuperMax, **92, 113, 117**
Supreme Allied Commander in Europe, **304**
Sutton, Willie, **106**
Svetgoff, Ronald, **135**
Swarns, Christina, **318-19**
Swarzschild, Patricia M., **59**
*T.C. Jester Park,* **239**
Tabak, Ronald J., **151, 52**
Taborsky, Joseph, **97**
Tafolla, Roland, **93**
Tanner, Allen, **160, 162, 276-277, 306**
Tao, **285**
Tarnower, Herman, **201**
Taylor, Elizabeth, **182-83**
Tennessee Bureau of Investigation, **267**
Tennessee Coalition to Abolish the Death Penalty, **28**
Texas Moratorium Network, **28**
Test, Stephen G., **59**
Texas A&M University, **24, 96, 249**
Texas Book Depository, **299**
Texas Court of Criminal Appeals, **112**
Texas Department of Corrections (TDC), **25, 82**
Texas Department of Criminal Justice (TDCJ), **90, 101, 113, 130-31, 189, 219-20, 250**
Texas Forensic Science Commission, **310**
Texas Task Force on Indigent Defense, **310**
The "Texecutioner," **263**
The Framers, **293**
*The Hurricane,* **217**
*the usual suspects,* **219, 280**
Theater of the Absurd, **40**
Theis, Jerome, **92**
*There he goes again,* **154**
*They Cut George Jackson Down,* **272**
Thomas, David, **120**
Thompson, Brenda, **72-73**
Thompson, Charles Victor, **128**
Thornton, Deborah, **218-219**
Thou Shalt Not Kill, **64, 292-93**
Thou Shalt Not Murder, **293**
three-drug "cocktail," **185, 248, 299-301, 303**
Throw Away the Key, **29, 34, 92-93, 218**
Tibbs, Delbert, 235-36
*Time* magazine, **45**

Timmendequas, Jesse, **221-23**
*Tippecanoe and Tyler Too*, **44**
*Today* show, **45**
Tolson, Mike, **128, 260-61, 263**
Toumi, Steven, **120**
Trattner, Sin Lam, **74**
Trattner, Stephen, **74**
*True Crime*, **217**
Truman, Harry S., **304**
Trumbull, Lonnie, **85**
Truth in Advertising, **229**
Tucker, Jim Guy, **105**
Tucker, Karla Fay, **218-219**
Tufts University, **18**
Turner, Allen, **162**
Turner, Matt, **121**
Turner, Ted, **182-83**
Turner, Willie Lloyd, **143-145**
Turow, Scott, **230**
Twin Towers, **20**
Tyner, Rudolph, **94**
***Tyson Foods*, 257**
ultra-liberal legislators, **85, 269**
United Airlines flight #93, **20**
United Nations Convention on the Rights of the Child, **31, 266**
United States Court of Appeals for the Fifth Circuit, **152**
United States Court of Appeals for the Fourth Circuit, **56-59, 63-63, 143**
United States Court of Appeals for the Ninth Circuit, **280**
United States Department of Justice, **115, 124**
United States House of Representatives, **51, 54**
United States State Department, **7**
United States Supreme Court, **18, 47, 57-78, 63, 118, 139-41, 184, 297**
Unity Laboratory in Applied Neurology, **43**
University of Colorado, **77**
University of Florida, **18**
University of Houston Law Center, **79**
University of Houston, **77, 125, 230, 236**
University of Miami Miller School of Medicine, **248**
University of Miami's law school, **317**
University of Nebraska, **212**
University of Oklahoma, **79**
University of Surrey, England, **43**
University of Utah, **52, 54**
unnamed author, **251**
Urs, Lori, **58, 60**

# An Eye for an Eye
*William T. Harper*

Vaccaro, Joseph Jesse, **41, 151-52, 170, 174, 176-78, 180l, 185-86, 194-96, 207, 209, 211**
Valenzuela, Walter Contreras, **148**
Valium, **218**
Valjean, Jean, **46**
van Schaik, Roger, **232**
Varnado, Michael L., **169-170, 175-78, 193-94, 196, 209**
Vatican, **281, 286, 294**
Velez, Rosa, **79**
Vengeance is mine, **293**
Vera, Luis, **79**
*Victims of Dead Man Walking*, **169**
Villarreal, Raul, **239**
Vinci, Leonardo de, **275**
Virginia Capital Representation Resource Center, **59**
Virginia Supreme Court, **58, 97**
*voir dire*, **143**
Wade, Henry, **307**
Wagner III, Louis H., **73, 180-81, 196, 198, 211**
Wagner, Donna, **196**
Waldorf-Astoria Hotel, **31**
Walls Unit, **25**
Walsh, Adam, **214-15**
Walsh, John, **214-15**
Walsh, Reve, **215**
War Between the States, **16**
Ward, Mark, **131**
Ward, Ron, **189**
*Warden*, **25**
Warner, Mark, **45, 127, 287**
Washington Coalition to Abolish the Death Penalty, **28**
*Washington Post*, **31, 212, 2227, 230**
*Washington Times*, **105, 233, 241**
Washington, Denzel, **217**
Washington, Wilhelmina, **288**
Watson, Steven, **59-60, 62**
Watts, Coral Eugene, **315**
We do it all the time, **18-20**
*We, On Death Row*, **286**
Webb, Jack, **39, 67**
Wechsler Adult Intelligence Scale-Revised Test, **265-66**
Weinberger, Jeremiah, **121**
Weiss, Mildred, **59, 282**
Welborn, Vickie, **265**
Welner, Michael, **24**
WHAT IF factor, **314**
White House, **257, 303**
Wilcox, Nancy, **86**
Willett, Jim, **25-26, 220**
Williams, Dobie Gillis, **35, 38, 47-48, 55, 73, 167, 174, 208, 264-66, 299**
Williams, Jr., Lewis, **188, 300**
Williams, Robert E., **212**

Williams, Ted, **277**
Willie, John Kelton, **186**
Willie, Robert Lee, **35, 38, 41, 76, 111, 121-22, 129, 151-52, 170-71, 173-78, 180-81, 185-86, 190-97, 207-09, 211, 214, 225, 247, 262, 297**
Willingham, Amber, **165**
Willingham, Cameron, **164-67**
Willingham, Kameron, **165**
Willingham, Karmon, **165**
Wilson, Pete, **216**
Wiltsey, Armida, **90, 168**
*win at all costs*, **151**
Wise, Robert, **133-36**
Wohlers, Joseph, **136**
World Socialist Web Site, 278
World Trade Center, **21, 46**
World War II, **30, 226, 279, 303-04**
Wournos, Aileen C., **76**
Wright, Richard, **287**
Wygesics, **218**
Yale University, **318**
Yarborough, Ray, **100**
Yarbrough, Susan, **217**
Yeazel, Keith, **148-49**
You know it when you see it, **24**
Young Republican, **87**
Young, Toby, **93-94**
Zangara, Giuseppe, **150**
Zielinski, Victoria, **271**
Zinnerman, Mark, **26**

# An Eye for an Eye
*William T. Harper*

## Notes

[[It is regretfully noted and apologies are made herewith because the author was remiss at the outset of writing this book that he did not properly insert date of access for many of the Internet citations used herein.]]

---

### Introduction Notes

[1] Stephan M. Minikes, U. S. State Department Ambassador, Organization for Security and Cooperation in Europe, at OSCE Permanent Council meeting, Vienna, Austria, June 6, 2002.
[2] www.gallup.com/1606/death-penalty.aspx - accessed August 14, 2012
[3] "Studies create new round in death penalty debates: Do executions deter other murderers?" Robert Tanner, Associated Press national writer, *Chicago Tribune*, June 10, 2007
[4] boston.com/news/globe/magazine/articles/2006/01/01/death_wish/

### Chapter One Notes

[5] www.nndb.com/people/903/000092627/ – accessed August 5, 2012
[6] Supreme Court Justice Antonin Scalia, personal letter to author, April 29, 2005
[7] http://svcn.com/archives/wgresident/01.26.00/cover-0004.html
[8] Helen Prejean, C. S. J., *Dead Man Walking* (New York, N. Y., Vintage Books), 1994, 21
[9] Ibid., 159
[10] Glenn Frankel, *Washington Post*, May 14, 2006, W08
[11] *Houston Chronicle*, August 7, 2005
[12] *Kansas v. Marsh*, certiorari to the supreme court of Kansas [June 26,

2006], Justice Scalia concurring

[13] Helen Prejean, C. S. J., *The Death of Innocents* (New York, N. Y., Random House), 2005, 10

[14] Ibid, *Dead Man Walking*, 20

[15] Ibid, *Kansas v. Marsh*

[16] Ibid, *Dead Man Walking*, 218

[17] Ibid, *The Death of Innocents*

[18] Ben M. Crouch, interview with author, February 18, 2005

[19] Ibid, *The Death of Innocents*, 201

[20] www.rense.com/general63/dep.htm

[21] Ibid

[22] http://www.hpdlabinvestigation.org/

[23] Jim Willett, *Warden* (Albany, Texas, Bright Sky Press), 2005,175

[24] 136 Ariz. 312, 666 P.2d 57

[25] David M. Horton and George R. Neilson, *Walking George: The Life of George John Beto and the Rise of the Modern Texas Prison System*, (Denton, Texas, University of North Texas Press) 2005, 121

[26] www.moratoriumcampaign.org/2005

[27] http://www.gallup.com/poll/1606/death-penalty.aspx - accessed August 5, 2012

[28] *Houston Press*, October 3, 2002

[29] *Dead Man Walking*, 197

[30] http://deathpenaltyinfo.org/article.php?did=1862

[31] *Prisons: Today and Tomorrow*, Joycelyn M. Pollock (Aspen Publishers, Gaithersburg, Md.), 1997, 4

[32] www.lexingtonprosecutor.com/Default.htm

## Chapter Two Notes

[33] The *State v. Sonnier* (La. 1979), (Direct Appeal)

[34] Ibid., *The Death of Innocents*, 57

[35] *CNN*, July 23, 1997

[36] Robert J. Humphreys, Commonwealth's Attorney, Virginia Beach, *The Virginian-Pilot*, July 28, 1995, 6

[37] Ibid, Humphreys

[38] Ibid, *The Death of Innocents*, 164

[39] Ibid, 106

# An Eye for an Eye
*William T. Harper*

---

[40] Ibid, 109
[41] Ibid., *Dead Man Walking*, 217-18
[42] Ibid, 217
[43] Ibid, 137-38
[44] Bureau of Justice Statistics, filename: p0301
[45] *Dead Man Walking*, 20
[46] "Death Row," 1997 edition, 14
[47] Ibid., *The Death of Innocents*, 215
[48] www.npr.org/news/specials/blackmun/
[49] Scalia's concurrence in *Callins v. Collins*
[50] Ibid., *Dead Man Walking* , 46
[51] Scalia, J., Concurring, *Kansas v. Marsh*, June 26, 2006
[52] Ibid
[53] *Houston Chronicle*, January 13, 2006, A4
[54] Maria Glod and Michael D. Shear, *Washington Post* Staff Writers, January 13, 2006; A01
[55] *Shreveport Times*, January 24, 2005, by Vicki Welborn
[56] Carole Shapiro, *University of San Francisco Law Review*, Volume 30, Number 4, 1996
[57] Dan Sewell, *Associated Press*, March 21, 1996
[58] Ibid., *Dead Man Walking*, 38
[59] Ibid., 93
[60] www.npr.org/templates/story/story.php?storyId=1113181
[61] www.dpinfo.com/Liebman.htm
[62] Ibid.
[63] "Errors with the Death Penalty," National Public Radio, October 30, 2000
[64] www.tdcj.state.tx.us/stat/drowfacts.htm
[65] http://lobby.la.psu.edu/049_Criminal_Justice_Reform/Congressional_Hearings/Testimony/H_Judiciary_Gekas_etal_062000.htm
[66] Richard Willing, USA TODAY, "Study draft decries execution appeals process," March 1, 2007
[67] Barry Latzer, correspondence with author, June 5, 2007
[68] "We're not executing the innocents," Paul G. Cassell, *Wall Street Journal*, June 16, 2000
[69] http://www.pbs.org/newshour/bb/law/jan-june12/deathpenalty_05-24.html?print – accessed August 15, 2012

[70] http://www.huffingtonpost.com/2012/05/15/carlos-de-luna-execution-_n_1507003.html
[71] Ibid., Willing
[72] Ibid., *The Death of Innocents*, xv
[73] Ibid., 58
[74] Ibid
[75] *O'Dell v. Netherland*, United States Court Of Appeals For The Fourth Circuit , September 10, 1996
[76] *The History Channel*, April 21, 1992
[77] http://pewforum.org/deathpenalty/resources/transcript3.php3
[78] *People v. LaValle*, 3 N.Y.3d 88, 817 N.E.2d 341, 783 N.Y.S.2d 485 (2004)
[79] Ibid
[80] Ibid., *The Death of Innocents*, 87
[81] Ibid, 55
[82] Ibid, 88
[83] *O'Dell v. Netherland*, 93 F.3d 1214 (1996)
[84] Ibid., *The Death of Innocents*, 189
[85] Ibid, *O'Dell v. Netherland*
[86] Ibid., *The Death of Innocents*, 166
[87] Ibid, *O'Dell v. Netherland*
[88] Ibid., *The Death of Innocents*, 68
[89] www.pbs.org/wgbh/pages/frontline/shows/case/cases/vatoodell98.html
[90] Ibid
[91] Ibid., *The Death of Innocents*, 79
[92] U. S. Court Of Appeals for the Fourth Circuit, Nos. 94-4013(L), (CA-92-480-R)
[93] Ibid
[94] Scalia, A., *Kansas v. Marsh*, June 26, 2006

**Chapter Three Notes**

[95] www.thecriminologist.com/new_criminologist/volume1/portrait_serial/portrait_serial.asp
[96] www.garylavergne.com/badboyprologue.htm

# An Eye for an Eye
*William T. Harper*

[97] Ibid, thecriminologist.com
[98] Ibid
[99] John R. Lott, Jr., More Guns, Less Crime: Understanding Crime and Gun Control Laws, Second Edition, © 1998, 2000
[100] www.themilwaukeechannel.com/newsarchive/5958945/detail.html
[101] Ibid., *Dead Man Walking*, 106
[102] Maureen Hayden, "Death Row" magazine, 1997, 21
[103] www.chicagotribune.com/news/local/illinois/chi-ap-il-eathpenalty-dete,1,2297677.story
[104] Ibid
[105] Ibid
[106] Adam Liptak, "A debate revives: Does the death penalty save lives?" *International Herald Tribune*, November 18, 2007
[107] "Study: Executions as a Deterrent," *Des Moines Tribune*, November 30, 1976
[108] Rosanna Ruiz, Allan Turner, *Houston Chronicle*, May 15, 2006
[109] Ibid., *Dead Man Walking*, 39
[110] www.wesleylowe.com/cp.html
[111] www.boston.com/news/globe/magazine/articles/2006/01/01/death_wish/
[112] *Benton* (Arkansas) *Courier*, February 18, 2006
[113] *Houston Chronicle*, November 12, 2005, E1
[114] http://archive.aclu.org/library/case_against_death.html
[115] http://bjs.ojp.usdoj.gov/content/pub/ascii/rpr94.txt - accessed August 16, 2012
[116] Bureau of Criminal Justice figures
[117] http://www.disastercenter.com/crime/uscrime.htm – accessed August 15, 2012
[118] Marquart & Sorensen, "A National Study of *Furman*-Commuted Inmates" *Loyola of Los Angeles Law Review*, Vol. 23, No. 1, pp. 5-28 (1989)
[119] www.clarkprosecutor.org/html/death/US/bundy106.htm
[120] Ibid
[121] www.crimelibrary.com/criminal_mind/profiling/keppel1/6.html

# An Eye for an Eye
*William T. Harper*

### Chapter Four Notes

[122] Ibid., *The Death of Innocents*, 100

[123] http://news.yahoo.com/s/nm/20071029/od_nm/jailbreak_dc;_ylt=AsBSoHzjo.IM42m5MchQOXis0NUE

[124] Richard A. Serrano, *Los Angeles Times*, June 6, 2006

[125] http://crime.about.com/od/wanted/p/richardmcnair.htm

[126] Michael Rezendes, "Predator priest seen as obvious prison target," *Boston Globe*, August 25, 2003

[127] http://news.yahoo.com/s/ap/20071029/ap_on_re_us/suspect_escapes;_ylt=Alns_lFWdp1Ac12xG4mbeJFH2ocA

[128] Margaret Stafford, *Houston Chronicle*, "The Crate Escape," February 17, 2006, A3

[129] David Margolick, *New York Times*, September 7, 1991

[130] "Death Penalty" magazine, 1997, Vol. 7, 226

[131] Robert James Bidinotto, *Freed to Kill*, (Washington, D.C., Safe Streets Coalition, 1960) 33

[132] www.amw.com/fugitives/case.cfm?id=24465

[133] www.disastercenter.com/crime/uscrime.htm

[134] www.thenewamerican.com/focus/cap_punishment/vo06no17_murders.htm

[135] http://www.deathpenaltyinfo.org/executions-year

[136] "Murders That Could Have Been Averted By Capital Punishment," The New American, Vol. 6, No. 17, August 30, 1990

[137] www.amazon.com/exec/obidos/ASIN/B000006QNB/truecrimes-20/104-3684993-3633565#product-details

[138] http://www.fbi.gov/about-us/cjis/ucr/leoka/leoka-2010/officers-feloniously-killed

[139] ftp://opinions.ca5.uscourts.gov/byDate/Dec2011/Dec27/10-70024.0.wpd.pdf – accessed August 22, 2012

[140] www.lexingtonprosecutor.com/Outrage.htm

[141] Ibid., , *The Death of Innocents*, 143

[142] Ibid, 170-71

[143] www.prorev.com/missingclinton.htm

# An Eye for an Eye
*William T. Harper*

---

[144] www.smartvoter.org/1999dec/ca/sf/vote/hallinan_t/bio.html
[145] Mike Tolson, *Houston Chronicle*, February 5, 2001
[146] http://www.reuters.com/article/2007/12/14/us-usa-deathpenalty-newjersey-idUSN1324400820071214
[147] Ibid
[148] Kent Scheidegger, Legal Director, Criminal Justice Legal Foundation, October 24, 2006
[149] http://www.oregonlive.com/pacific-northwest-news/index.ssf/2011/11/gov_john_kitzhaber_oregon_deat.html - accessed August 17, 2012
[150] www.officerronparker.com/history2.html
[151] www.burkfoster.com/PardonMeGovernor.htm
[152] Michael Collins, *Kentucky Post*, February 1, 2000
[153] MSNBC-TV, "Lockup," 2005
[154] Interview with author, September 27, 2006
[155] Allan Turner, *Houston Chronicle*, March 4, 2005, A1
[156] *Houston Chronicle*, August 31, 2006, B3
[157] *Missouri v. O'Neal*, 766 S.W. 2d 91 (Mo. Banc 1986)
[158] Catherine Tsai, Associated Press, *Houston Chronicle*, November 8, 2006, A7
[159] Joseph T. Hallinan, *Going Up the River* (Random House, New York City, N.Y., 2001), 37
[160] http://bjs.ojp.usdoj.gov/index.cfm?ty=pbdetail&iid=4293 – accessed August 17, 2012
[161] www.thenewamerican.com/focus/cap_punishment/vo06no17_murders.htm
[162] Bureau of Justice Statistics
[163] Jim Doyle, *San Francisco Chronicle*, January 12, 2006
[164] "Mob may have weighed hit on Warren Burger," *Houston Chronicle*, July 19, 2007, A13
[139] Ibid, *Dead Man Walking*, 16-17
[166] http://www.livedash.com/transcript/lockup-(inside_kentucky_state_penitentiary)/5304/MSNBC/Friday_October_15_2010/477565/ - accessed August 30, 2012
[167] Michael L. Varnado and D. P. Smith, *Victims of Dead Man Walking*, (Gretna, Louisiana, Pelican Publishing Co.) 2003, 138
[168] www.burkfoster.com/PardonMeGovernor.htm
[169] Ibid

# An Eye for an Eye
*William T. Harper*

---

[170] *San Diego Union Tribune*, "Child molester released from SoCal prison," April 14, 2004

[171] Rick Hepp, *Newark (N. J.) Star-Ledger*, May 02, 2005

[172] Ibid

[173] http://allhiphop.com/2005/05/02/u-s-government-declares-1-million-bounty-for-assata-shakur-tupacs-godmother/

[174] http://deathpenaltyinfo.org/article.php?did=1971

[175] David R. Dow, *Houston Chronicle*, November 12, 2006, pg. E1

[176] David N. Goodman, *Associated Press*, July 14, 2006

[177] The *Bryan/College Station Eagle*, November 26, 2005, C1

[178] Maria Glod, *Washington Post*, November 26, 2005

[179] Peggy O'Hare, *Houston Chronicle*, November 4, 2005

[180] Mike Tolson, *Houston Chronicle*, Feb. 7, 2001

[181] Ibid

[182] Ibid

[183] www.bestofneworleans.com/dispatch/2003-07-15/news_feat.htm

[184] http://www.lexingtonprosecutor.com/Outrage.htm – accessed August 23`

[185] http://shaking.stanford.edu/schedule/californiaPrisons.html

[186] Ibid, *The Death of Innocents*, 232

## Chapter Five Notes

[187] http://www.sfgate.com/news/article/Judge-grants-sex-change-for-Mass-murder-convict-3838432.php – accessed September 5, 2012

[188] Arizona v. Harding, 5587, October 12, 1983

[189] Gomez v. U. S. District Court 112 S. Ct. 1652

[190] www.azcentral.com/specials/special32/articles/06230622EXEharding-ON.html on 1/17/07

[191] *Tucson Citizen*, March 23, 1984

[192] Ibid

[193] Ibid

[194] *Harding v. Lewis*, 795 F. Supp. 953 (D. Ariz..1992)

[195] Bob Egelko, Peter Fimrite and Kevin Fagan, "Killer put to death at San Quentin," *San Francisco Chronicle*, January 19, 2005

[196] Ibid., Rosenthal

[197] Turner v. Jabe, United States Court of Appeals for the Fourth Circuit, No. 95-4005, May 24, 1995

[198] Ibid
[199] Ibid, *The Death of Innocents*, 79
[200] "US News & World Report," June 17, 1997
[201] William Yardley, *New York Times*, February 2, 2005
[202] www.lexingtonprosecutor.com/ Ibid
[203] Ibid
[204] Lisa Siegel, Connecticut Law Tribune, July 25, 2005    Ibid
[205] Ibid
[206] Peggy Wright, *Daily Record*, August 18, 2005
[207] http://www.jaapl.org/content/36/2/250.full - accessed August 18, 2012
[208] Ibid, Wright, correspondence with author, December 7, 2006
[209] *Houston Chronicle*, August 9, 2006, A7
[210] Michael Hall, "Why Can't Steven Phillips Get a DNA Test?" *Texas Monthly*, January 2006
[211] www.theleafchronicle.com/news/stories/20030427/localnews/194554.html
[212] Ibid, Rosenthal
[213] Ibid, *The Death of Innocents*, 17
[214] Ibid., 189
[215] Ibid., *The Death of Innocents*, 166
[216] Ibid., 155
[217] Ibid., 155-156
[218] *Hubbard v. Haley*, U. S. 11th Circuit Court of Appeals, Docket No. 94-02639-CV-N-W
[219] Ibid., Rosenthal
[220] www.Lexingtonprosecutor.com/
[221] www.crimelibrary.com/serial_killers/predators/bittaker_norris/10.html
[222] Shannon McCaffrey, "Aging Inmates Clogging Nation's Prisons," Associated Press, September 29, 2007
[223] *Dead Man Walking*, 130
[224] Allen Tanner, interview with author, April 18, 2005
[225] www.msnbc.msn.com/id/5578095#storyContinued
[226] Ibid, Rosenthal
[227] Ibid
[228] Bernard Goldberg, *100 People Who Are Screwing Up America*,

(New York, NY, HarperCollins*Publishers*), 2005, 279
[229] *The Death of Innocents*, 214
[230] Barry Latzer, correspondence with author, June 5, 2007
[231] www.deathpenaltyinfo.org/article.php?did=1848&scid=64
[232] David Atwood, "In Texas, it is broke, but Legislature won't fix it," *Houston Chronicle*, July 15, 2007, E5
[233] www.clarkprosecutor.org/html/death/US/willingham899.htm
[234] www.star-telegram.com/2012/08/04/4154746/effort-continues-to-examine-texas.html#storylink=cpy
[235] www.bexarcountydistrictattorney.org/body_pages/morenocantuinvestigation.pdf

## Chapter Six Notes

[236] http://www.ktvu.com/news/news/trial-begins-in-30-year-old-lafayette-rape-and-mur/nKSwT/ – accessed August 16, 2012
[237] Ibid
[238] Michael L. Varnado and D. P. Smith, *Victims of Dead Man Walking* (Gretna, Louisiana, Pelican Publishing Co.) 2003, 39.
[239] Ibid, 12
[240] Ibid., *The Death of Innocents*, 120
[241] Ibid, 153
[242] Ibid., 32
[243] Ibid., 5
[244] Ibid., 146
[245] www.pbs.org/wgbh/pages/frontier/angel/reporternote.html
[246] www.bestofneworleans.com/dispatch/2003-07-15/news_feat.html
[247] Ibid
[248] Ibid
[249] Alan Sayre, Associated Press, "25 years later, detective tell his story of famous case," July 12, 2003
[250] John Fahey, *The Times-Picayune*, December 27, 1984
[251] *Dead Man Walking*, 162
[252] Ibid, 119
[253] Ibid, www.bestofneworleans,com
[254] Ibid, *Dead Man Walking*, 141

# An Eye for an Eye
*William T. Harper*

---

[255] Ibid, Varnado, 73
[256] Ibid, *Dead Man Walking*, Prejean, 38
[257] Ibid, 108
[258] Associated Press, *The Times-Picayune*, April 7, 1984
[259] www.theevidence.org/episodes/episode14.php
[260] Ibid, *The Death of Innocents*, 267
[261] Cindy Horswell, *Houston Chronicle*, July 15, 2003, B3
[262] "Victim's brother rips Sarandon's death row visit," Cindy Horswell, *Houston Chronicle*, July 16, 2004, B9
[263] "People" magazine, August 26, 1996, Vol. 46, No. 9, p. 42
[264] Ibid
[265] "U. S. News and World Report," June 17, 1997
[266] Ibid, *Dead Man Walking*, 137
[267] Guy Coates, Associated Press, December 28, 1984
[268] www.cbsnews.com/stories/2000/12/25/national/main259624.shtml
[269] Ibid, *The Death of Innocents*, 235
[270] Ibid, 265
[271] Ibid, 235-6
[272] C-Span interview, January 16, 2005
[273] *Witness to an Execution*, October 20, 2000, "All Things Considered," Copyright © 2000 Sound Portraits Productions, All Rights Reserved
[274] Ibid., *Dead Man Walking*, 199
[275] Ibid
[276] Ibid, 200
[277] 201
[278] Ibid
[279] Ibid
[280] Ibid, 203-4
[281] Guy Coates, Associated Press, December 28, 1984
[282] Ibid, *Dead Man Walking*, 206
[283] Ibid, 207
[284] 136
[285] 208
[286] Ibid
[287] www.pbs.org/wgbh/pages/frontline/angel/interviews/eharvey.html
[288] Ibid, Varnado, 177
[289] Ibid, *Dead Man Walking*, 186

# An Eye for an Eye
*William T. Harper*

[290] Ibid
[291] Ibid, Varnado, 163
[292] Ibid, 21
[293] 26
[294] 196
[295] Ibid, *Dead Man Walking,*, 90
[296] Ibid, 92
[297] Ibid, 222
[298] 13
[299] 13
[300] 18
[301] 69
[302] http://news.yahoo.com/north-carolina-death-row-inmate-writes-letter-life-152637993--abc-news.html – accessed January 25, 2012
[303] http://corrections.ky.gov/Pages/NewsandEvents.aspx – accessed August 6, 2012
[304] "Lockup," MSNBC-TV, May 28, 2007
[305] Inmates escape to Internet by way of intermediaries," *The Bryan/College Station Eagle*, May 1, 2005, B5
[306] Joseph T. Hallinan, *Going Up the River* (Random House, New York City, New York, 2001), 163-4
[307] *Prisons: Today and Tomorrow*, Joycelyn M. Pollock (Aspen Publishers, Gaithersburg, Md.), 1997, 257
[308] Fins, Esq., Deborah , DEATH ROW U.S.A., Spring 2012, NAACP Legal Defense and Educational Fund, Inc.
[309] Ibid, *Dead Man Walking*, 138
[310] www.pbs.org/wgbh/pages/frontline/angel/interviews/eharvey.html
[311] Ibid, *The Death of Innocents*, 240
[312] Ibid, *Dead Man Walking*, 198
[313] Ibid
[314] Ibid, Varnado, 15
[315] Ibid, 14
[316] Andy Kahan, Crime Victims Advocate for the City of Houston, interview with author, May 24, 2005
[317] www.amw.com/victims_rights/

[318] http://www.msnbc.msn.com/id/28257294/ns/us_news-crime_and_courts/t/police-killing-adam-walsh-solved/ – accessed August 11, 2012
[319] "A mother, life destroyed, waits for justice to be done," *Washington Post*, April 18, 1992
[320] Ibid
[321] www.aim.org/publications/aim_report/2000/08a.html#7
[322] CNN, May 19, 2005, "Paroled murderer in Tennessee is charged with killing again."
[323] *Houston Chronicle*, December 14, 1997
[324] Kathy Walt, "Execution may haunt Texas," *Houston Chronicle*, December 14, 1997
[325] Ibid, *The Death of Innocents*, 245-6
[326] *Houston Chronicle*, 12/14/1997
[327] Jerry Cox, Texas Department of Corrections, interview with author, November 29, 2005
[328] Jim Willett, Texas Department of Corrections, interview with author, May 9, 2007

**Chapter Seven Notes**

[329] Russ Flanagan, *The Express-Times*, February 26, 2004
[330] Ibid., *The Death of Innocents*, , 200
[331] Ibid, 200
[332] Supreme Court of the United States, Kansas v. Marsh, June 26, 2006
[333] Jennifer C. Honeyman and James R.P. Ogloff, "Capital Punishment: Arguments for Life and Death," Canadian Journal of Behavioural Science, Volume 28: 1 January, 1996
[334] Ann Coulter , Jewish World Review June 27, 2000, "The last guys 'proved innocent'"
[335] Ibid., Honeyman and Ogloff
[336] http://justice.uaa.alaska.edu/death/history.html#unitedstates
[337] http://web.amnesty.org/library/index/engAMR511822004?open&of=eng-392
[338] *Houston Chronicle*, January 30, 2005, Zest, 20, review of *The Death of Innocents*

# An Eye for an Eye
*William T. Harper*

---

[339] Edward Petka, Illinois State Senator, correspondence with author, June 22, 2005
[340] www.msnbc.msn.com/id/5578095#storyContinued
[341] *Pittsburgh Tribune-Review*, October 13, 2003
[342] http://en.wikipedia.org/wiki/Kenneth_Allen_%28murderer%29
[343] Jeff Flock, *CNN*, "'Blanket commutation' empties Illinois death row," January 13, 2003
[344] www.lexingtonprosecutor.com/Outrage.htm
[345] Ibid, *Death of Innocents*, 61
[346] Dale Lezon, *Houston Chronicle*, August 25, 2006, B1
[347] *Houston Chronicle*, March 15, 2004, A-1
[348] *Kansas v. Marsh*, June 26, 2006, Justice Scalia concurring
[349] Ibid
[350] David R. Dow, *New York Times*, June 16, 2006

**Chapter Eight Notes**

[351] Rosanna Ruiz, Allan Turner, *Houston Chronicle*, May 14, 2006, B1
[352] *Roper v. Simmons*, Supreme Court of The United States, March 1, 2005
[353] Tony Blankley, "Black robes and betrayal," *Washington Times*, March 2, 2005
[354] Charles L. Scott, MD, "*Roper v. Simmons*: Can Juvenile Offenders be Executed?" Journal of the American Academy of Psychiatry and the Law Online
[355] Ibid., *Roper*
[356] *USN&WR*, March 28, 2005, 67
[357] Correspondence with author, March 14, 2012 – see also http://homicidesurvivors.com//2012/03/26/the-odd-victim-sympathies-of-liberal-justices---what-makes-activists-mad----and-what-doesnt/print.aspx
[358] http://www.msnbc.msn.com/id/22160493/
[359] Eric Berger, "Study: Inmates suffer during lethal injections," *Houston Chronicle*, April 14, 2005, B1
[360] Interview with author, 8/13/06
[361] Ibid, Berger
[362] Paul Elias, Associated Press, May 11, 2007
[363] *Witness to an Execution* premiered October 20, 2000, on *All Things*

# An Eye for an Eye
*William T. Harper*

---

     *Considered.* Copyright © 2000 Sound Portraits Productions. All Rights Reserved
[364] www.antiessays.com/free-essays/2146.html
[365] www.ojp.usdoj.gov/bjs/glance/tables/exetab.htm
[366] Ron Word, Associated Press, December 15, 2006
[367] Ibid
[368] Ibid
[369] John Wagner and Ovetta Wiggins, "O'Malley Seeks End To Md. Executions, *Washington Post*, February 22, 2007, B06
[370] Ibid., *The Death of Innocents*, , 106
[371] Ibid., 209
[372] Ibid., Rosenthal
[373] Ibid
[374] www.msnbc.msn.com/id/5578095#storyContinued
[375] Ibid, *Death of Innocents*, 209
[376] Dan Rodricks, "Death penalty support looks tough but does not good, *Baltimore Sun*, May 13, 2002
[377] http://members.fortunecity.com/beecee56/sharpton_q.htm
[378] http://www.skeptictank.org/treasure/MISC4/AANEWS.363
[379] Ibid., *Dead Man Walking*, 203-4
[380] Ibid, 7
[381] Mike Tolson, *Houston Chronicle*, February 5, 2001
[382] Ibid., *Dead Man Walking*, 11
[383] Ibid., 22
[384] Ibid., 31
[385] Ibid., 69
[386] Ibid., *The Death of Innocents*, 90
[387] Ibid, *Dead Man Walking,* 119
[388] Ibid., 100
[389] www.tysknews.com/News/criminal_invasion.htm
[390] Bid., *The Death of Innocents*, 29
[391] Ibid., 32-3
[392] Vickie Welborn, *Shreveport Times*, January 24, 2005
[393] Karen Potter, Juvenile Death Penalty Speech, November 18, 1999

**Chapter Nine Notes**

# An Eye for an Eye
*William T. Harper*

---

[394] Memphis, Tennessee *Commercial Appeal*, October 17, 1999, A16
[395] Bernard Goldberg, *100 People Who Are Screwing Up America*, Harper/Collins Publishers, New York, N.Y., 2005, pps 97-98
[396] "Time" magazine, September 27, 1968
[397] Ibid
[398] Lona Manning, The Great Prevaricator, "Crime" magazine, August 25, 2003
[399] www.usdoj.gov/oig/reports/BOP/a0325/app6.htm
[400] Michelle Malkin, *Human Events*, "Hollywood's Death Row Fetish," March 2, 2004
[401] Karen Olsson, Boston Globe, January 1, 2006 Sunday magazine
[402] Steve Lopez, *The Los Angeles Times*; Dec 21, 2001
[403] Jonah Goldberg, "National Review," June 10, 1999
[404] http://en.wikipedia.org/wiki/Live_from_Death_Row
[405] www.wsws.org/articles/1999/apr1999/mumi-a21.shtml
[406] "30 Years After Officer's Killing, Inmate Will Leave Death Row," *New York Times*, December 8, 2011, A22
[407] *San Diego Union-Tribune*, October 29, 2006
[408] *Chessman v. Dickson*, 275 F.2d 604, 607 (9th Cir. 1960).
[409] Mayer, Michael, S., *The Eisenhower Years*, Facts on File, Inc., 2009, 109
[410] "Time" magazine, February 29, 1960
[411] www.clarkprosecutor.org/html/death/US/massie703.htm
[412] Ibid., *The Death of Innocents*, 2005, 177
[413] www.wesleylowe.com/cp.html
[414] http://archive.salon.com/news/feature/2000/04/17/benetton/index1.html
[415] Ibid., *The Death of Innocents*, 159
[416] Cathy Lynn Grossman, *USA TODAY*, November 8, 2005
[417] "Time" magazine, October 20, 1941
[418] http://steveearle.net/index.php
[419] Ibid., Andy Kahan, Crime Victims Advocate for the City of Houston, Interview with author, August 13, 2006
[420] www.klaaskids.org/v6n2p5.htm
[421] Waltrina Stovall, "Victims' advocates blast macabre hobby," *Dallas Morning News*, September 14, 2000
[422] Cindy Horswell, *Houston Chronicle*, "Inmates selling art in spite of state's 'murderabilia' law," April 3, 2005

# An Eye for an Eye
*William T. Harper*

---

### Chapter Ten Notes

[423] Ibid., *Dead Man Walking*, 21
[424] Ibid
[425] Ibid., 77
[426] "U. S. News and World Report, "June 17, 1997
[427] http://pewforum.org/deathpenalty/resources/transcript3.php3
[428] Ibid., *The Death of Innocents*, 129
[429] Ibid., 130
[430] Ibid
[431] http://deathpenaltyinfo.org/article.php?scid=15&did=410
[432] Death Penalty Information Center, Executions in the U.S. 1608-1987: The Espy File
[433] B. J. Thornton, Letter to the Editor, *Houston Chronicle*, May 24, 2006, B8
[434] Daniel James Brown, *Under a Flaming Sky*, (Lyons Press, Guilford, Connecticut, 2006), 83-4
[435] http://archive.aclu.org/library/case_against_death.html
[436] http://www.scientificamerican.com/blog/post.cfm?id=deaths-from-avoidable-medical-error-2009-08-10 – accessed August 20, 2012
[437] http://www.abanet.org/deathpenalty/docs/american_lawyer.pdf
[438] National Public Radio News, October 29, 2007
[439] http://www.hpdlabinvestigation.org/reports/070613report.pdf - accessed August 20, 2012
[440] *Callins v. Collins*, February 22, 1994
[441] http://aviation-safety.net/database/type/type-stat.php?type=334
[442] Ellis, Rodney and Cory Session, "Finding ways to reduce wrongful convictions," *Houston Chronicle*, September 5, 2010, B10
[443] www.boston.com/news/globe/magazine/articles/2006/01/01/death_wish/
[444] Ibid
[445] www.wesleylowe.com/cp.html
[446] http://www.clarkprosecutor.org/html/death/death.htm

# An Eye for an Eye
*William T. Harper*

---

[447] http://www.cnn.com/2012/07/23/travel/us-traffic-fatalities/index.html - accessed August 20, 2012
[448] http://www-fars.nhtsa.dot.gov/Crashes/CrashesAlcohol.aspx - accessed August 20, 2012
[449] http://onin.com/fp/fphistory.html - accessed August 20, 2012
[450] Bradley Brooks, Associated Press, "Nation nears 1,000 mark for executions," Nov. 24, 2005
[451] www.npr.org/templates/story/story.php?storyId=1418865
[452] www.msnbc.msn.com/id/5578095#storyContinued

Made in the USA
Charleston, SC
13 September 2012